The Complete Book of
Saltwater
Fishing

Milt Rosko

Published by

krause publications

700 East State Street • Iola, WI 54990-0001
715/445-2214 • FAX: 715/445-4087   www.krause.com

Please call or write for our free catalog of publications. Our toll-free number to place an order or obtain a free catalog is 800-258-0929 or please use our regular business telephone 715-445-2214.

Library of Congress Catalog Number 2001088583
ISBN 0-87349-293-5

Books by the author

Secrets of Striped Bass Fishing

Fishing from Boats

Spingfishing, the System that does it all

Fishing the Big Four, Striper, Bluefish, Weakfish, Fluke

Dedicated to our granddaughters
Jacqueline, Jennifer, Kristine and Kelsey

ACKNOWLEDGMENTS

I suspect that with the passage of time a person develops a greater appreciation of the people and circumstances that have resulted in one's destiny. As I sit to acknowledge the people and circumstances that have aided me throughout a lifetime, I reach back many years.

Little did I realize that June Whitmeyer, the attractive young girl who sat alongside me in junior high, would one day become my wife. She is mother to Linda and Bob, our wonderful children, and their respective spouses Kelly and Joe, who are as dear to us as were they our own. She is also grandmother to our four granddaughters to whom this book is dedicated. Jacqueline, Jennifer, Kristine and Kelsey all caught their first fish while fishing with Grandma and Grandpa.

Moving back to school days for a moment there was a very young English teacher at West Side High School in Newark, New Jersey. Miss Rizzolo always had a smile and patience beyond words when it came to me. I authored many fishing stories as English compositions. She encouraged me with words I remember to this day. "Keep trying Milton. Eventually you'll get it right!"

An average student overall, I was a straight-A scholar in typing. Miss Carpenter strolled back and forth as we typed asdf jkl; for hours. Little did I realize that the skills I learned on those vintage Underwoods would serve me so well in the years to come. They were there in every aspect of my life, in the Marine Corps, in my love of journalism and 45-year professional career at Anheuser-Busch.

June never thought she'd become a cover photographer. As my right arm as we traveled about, she recorded on film thousands of images. Many appeared as covers on national publications, in articles and books. June was the typist of many of my manuscripts of prior books. She is most thankful that now, by just depressing a key, the computer's printer takes over and does the finished copy while she's cooking dinner!

As to the content of this treatise, I struggled as I tried to rightfully acknowledge those people who directly assisted in this work. The first person to come to mind was the late Frank Woolner, editor of *Salt Water Sportsman*, who in 1954 published my first article. I authored and typed it on a vintage Underwood in the USO located in the lobby of the Philadelphia YMCA. For it was there that I was billeted prior to release, after having served in the Marine Corps during the Korean War. Frank was my writing mentor, a fine gentleman, absolutely great fisherman and superb editor who aided me tremendously.

Throughout this book are numerous line drawings that depict a variety of tackle, knots and techniques far more clearly than could photographs. They are the work of Alan Sherman, a talented young artist from Manasquan, New Jersey. He painstakingly created the drawings after viewing my samples of terminal rigs, tackle, boats and penciled illustrations. I am indebted to Alan for his perseverance and am pleased that his quality art is herein being presented to a larger audience.

A special thanks to the great anglers, both women and men, who shared photos of memorable catches to be included as part of this work. We have shared many days together and recorded images on film beyond count.

Then, too, there were so many people, in so many places, that helped me develop the skills and techniques that I am in this book attempting to pass on to you, the reader. I feared that a list of names could never be complete, for so many I just knew in a casual way. To all I say a sincere thank you. You've made my days along the sea coast a great joy. As you read this book I'm certain you'll observe those tips, techniques and methods that you were responsible for and to you I am eternally thankful.

To June, she's made my life a continuous pleasure. We've enjoyed countless years as we traveled about together, with our family and, now in retirement, often just the two of us. This work would never have been possible without her encouragement, companionship, and importantly, her fine ability to capture on film the great experiences we've shared and are attempting to share here with you.

Milt Rosko

INTRODUCTION

Mention saltwater fishing and you'll find it means many things to many people. Briefly stated, this book is about how to catch fish in saltwater on the Atlantic, Gulf and Pacific Coasts. Included within the chapters are more than a dozen ways of seeking out and catching a wide variety of species. Each is a challenge. Some techniques require years of dedication to achieve the level of expertise needed to be consistently successful. The thread that holds all these varied types of saltwater fishing together is they're all part of what I like to call a "contemplative" pastime.

It's difficult to put into words just what contemplative means. It's not just catching fish. It's being on the water on a warm summer day and watching a mother mallard and her brood of 10 ducklings swim by. It's enjoying a breathtaking sunrise, where the sun, like a great orange ball, appears to slowly lift from the ocean. It's strolling a beach in the dark of night, with the heavens filled with a million stars, and experiencing a majestic meteor shower. It's observing tuna as they streak through a chum line 100 miles offshore, knowing they could travel 100 miles in just a day. Most importantly, it's being with family and friends, enjoying the great wealth that our outdoor heritage provides along the sea coast.

Unfortunately, in recent years some have attempted to introduce the word "competitive" into sportfishing. Competing means a rivalry, a contest between people, a match to catch the biggest fish, to catch the most fish, to win the most money. This is not saltwater fishing is all about, and it was not the reason for writing this book. If your interests run in the direction of competing, read no further. This book is not for you.

If, however, you're looking for a relaxing pastime, where you spend a lifetime learning, of enjoying the camaraderie of others, in a healthy outdoor environment where you're actively participating, then this book is for you.

Within the covers of this book I hope you'll learn how to enjoy the saltwater fishing experience, what equipment to use, the places to fish and the species that you'll find in North America's waters.

The excitement of planning a trip, getting the tackle and bait ready, packing a lunch—it all contributes to the experience. The climax is when the weather is pleasant, the fish cooperate and everyone experiences a day of which memories are made.

Fishing in saltwater to many is an evolutionary process, where a newcomer begins aboard a party or charter boat, or perhaps fishing from a coastal pier or jetty. As an interest is established, a desire to sample other types of fishing and catch different species grows.

Some people enjoy offshore trolling and pursue pelagic species for a lifetime. Others enjoy the serenity of drifting along coastal bays and estuaries, the smell of the marshes, the abundant waterfowl, and the plentiful bottom feeders that provide constant action and are a welcome treat on the dinner table. It's what you enjoy that's important.

Throughout this book each chapter covers a specific type of fishing, discussing tackle and techniques that make it fun to catch the targeted species. If you're new to saltwater fishing, you're invited to peruse the chapters and try each type of fishing. Once you've tried them all, you'll find what's right for you.

In recent years it has become apparent that the ocean's fishery resources can quickly be depleted if not properly managed. In some instances, bureaucracy and poor management of international, federal and state agencies has allowed some species to be exploited to the point of near-extinction. In other instances, prompt regulation has resulted in surprisingly fast recovery of species that were in a downward cycle.

It is incumbent that all saltwater fishermen adhere to existing regulations. Equally important is for all of us to take an active role in both conservation and preservation of the valuable resources that the seas have to offer. Your input will often make a difference at public hearings on pending regulations. Your participation ensures that future generations will have the opportunity to enjoy the wonderful fishing currently available off all three of our coasts.

In the closing chapter of this book the author details the care and cleaning of catches fresh from the sea. June Rosko includes a selection of her seafood recipes, all of which are truly delicious. While sportfishing in saltwater is in itself a totally enjoyable and contemplative pastime, it certainly is appropriate to enjoy a dinnertime treat of your catch. By all means enjoy the fish you catch, but be guided by reason. Where the regulations limit your catch, set a personal goal to retain only what you feel is reasonable. Doing so will guarantee the joys of saltwater fishing for generations to come.

The Complete Book of Saltwater Fishing

By Milt Rosko

GETTING STARTED

Within the world of saltwater fishing there is a variety of basic fishing equipment that is geared to a specific type of fishing. This usually centers around the rod and reel used in seeking a particular species and the technique being employed to catch it. Throughout this book the balanced rod and reel combinations that are most appropriate for a specific type of fishing are discussed in depth.

There are many additional items of tackle and equipment that saltwater fishermen employ. It would be redundant to discuss each type of line in each chapter. That would also be the case with hooks, swivels, sinkers, snaps and the various pieces of allied equipment such as nets and gaffs, rod belts and shoulder harnesses. For ease in understanding, these topics will be part of getting started.

It's important to take your time when selecting tackle. Balanced tackle also makes casting and lure presentation easier, and affords an opportunity to enjoy every moment of the challenge when landing a strong fish.

(Left) Selecting the proper fishing tackle for saltwater fishing often makes the difference between success and failure. These happy anglers used light conventional casting outfits to probe the depths off the state of Washington for these fine vermillion rockfish.

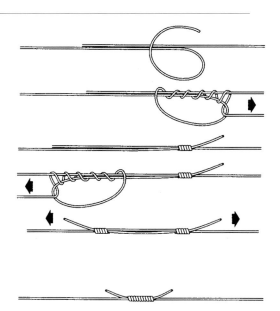

Overlap about 12 inches of the ends of two lines. Form a uni-knot circle with the tag end of one line. Wrap that line five times around the remaining line to form a uni-knot around it. Snug the knot by gently pulling both ends of the line, but not so tightly that it grips the standing line.

Form another uni-knot circle with the tag end of the remaining line and wrap that line five times to form a uni-knot around the remaining standing line. Firm up the second uni-knot as you did the first. Then pull each line slowly, and they will slide together until they jam. Finish by tightening the wraps around the standing lines by firmly pulling the tag ends of each uni-knot, and trim the tag ends with a nail clip.

Lines designed for a variety of purposes

There are many types of line used in saltwater fishing. Each is designed for a specific purpose. Unfortunately, there is no one line that is suited to every angling situation, and as such it becomes important to have an understanding of each type of line and its application.

Nylon monofilament line by far the most popular

Monofilament is available with a wide variety of features. Some is soft and supple, and ideal for casting. Other monofilament is somewhat stiffer, yet offers more abrasion resistance and proves advantageous when bottom fishing, or wherever obstructions may be encountered. Most monofilament tends to stretch quite a bit, which can prove a disadvantage when bottom fishing in several hundred feet of water. The stretch can also be helpful, however, for as a result the line is very forgiving, such as when a fish makes a sudden run for freedom at boatside. It's important to read the label and select the line designed to closely approximate the type of fishing you plan to do.

For years nylon monofilament lines were of reasonably fine diameter, compared to the braided nylon and Cuttyhunk linen lines that preceded them in popularity. For comparison purposes, a typical 20-pound test monofilament line has a diameter of 0.018, and this can vary slightly from brand to brand.

Microfilament line has fine diameter and no stretch

As technology advanced, the introduction of lines made of Spectra and Dyneema fibers resulted in fine diameters that were never thought possible. Today's anglers now can spool microfilament line in 20-pound test that has a diameter of only 0.009 inches, just half that of monofilament. The larger the test, the more dramatic the diameter reduction, with 100-pound test microfilament line having the same diameter as 20-pound test monofilament.

This has caused a problem in some types of fishing, such as chumming on party boats. An angler hooked to a big tuna or wahoo on microfilament line may have his line literally cut through the lines of others along the rail as his fish makes a line-peeling run. This problem, coupled with its fine diameter, makes it virtually impossible for mates on boats to untangle lines. As a result, microfilament lines are prohibited aboard some party boats. This practice may be an overreaction to a dynamic new product, and over time attitudes may change, recognizing, of course, that some people just accept change slowly.

Fluorocarbon will dominate in the future

For many years fluorocarbon was employed primarily as a leader material. It possesses a high refractive index, which in layman's terms means that it is practically invisible in the water. As with most new science, at the time fluorocarbon was introduced its cost was very prohibitive. Hence, it was used as a leader material only, and in conjunction with other types of line such as monofilament and Dacron.

As is often the case, with the passage of time, improved technology, increased demand and the resulting volume of sales, the cost of fluorocarbon decreased dramatically. As its cost dropped, anglers began to spool fluorocarbon as line, for its fish catching ability was far superior to nylon monofilament lines. Many anglers simply feel that it's better to use a nearly invisible line, and hence the popularity of fluorocarbon has increased substantially. It may never replace nylon monofilament line as a standard in saltwater usage, especially as a result of its high cost, but it certainly is the line of the future.

Dacron offers medium diameter and little stretch

Dacron line has been popular for years. It has a medium diameter and little stretch, making it especially popular among trollers, who find it offers little water resistance and is easily spooled on the reel. In heavier tests it is made in a flat line, so that it lays evenly on the reel and doesn't dig in, a consideration when using 130-pound test for giant bluefin tuna and marlin.

With the introduction of microfilament line, Dacron has lost some of its popularity. However, because of its ease in handling when offshore trolling, it continues to be popular in 30-, 50-, 80- and 130-pound test.

Monel a popular choice for deep trolling

Wire line is not recognized by the International Game Fish Association for record catches. Wire line does have numerous applications in saltwater fishing and is included here because of its popularity among anglers who prefer deep trolling and bottom fishing in extremely deep water.

Monel is the wire of choice of saltwater anglers, for it is relatively soft and lays well on the reel, although soft stainless steel wire is also used. For most applications wire in 30-, 40-, and 50-pound test is used and generally wound onto the reel over Dacron backing line of heavier strength. In most trolling situations 200 to

Wire line aids trollers in getting lures deep in the water. Solid stainless steel, monel and stainless cable are used, with 200 to 300 feet of it spooled on top of Dacron backing line. Wire line trolling is very effective for striped bass and bluefish in the Northeast, king mackerel and wahoo in Florida and along the Gulf Coast, and wahoo and yellowtail off California.

13

300 feet of wire is the maximum amount used. Anglers often overlay the monel with a half-inch section of fine telephone wire at 50-foot intervals, thus marking the line and enabling them to know precisely the amount of line being trolled.

Use of monel wire line for trolling requires great care. When the line is streamed astern, the reel's click mechanism is engaged, offering resistance and preventing the line from overrunning and fouling, which can result in a disastrous mess. Thumb pressure on the reel spool also helps prevent an overrun.

In certain deep-water fishing applications, such as fishing for tile fish in deep canyon waters and targeting snapper and grouper in the Gulf and rockfish in the Northwest, monel is occasionally used. The weight of the line, coupled with a heavy sinker, enables the angler to keep the line perpendicular to the bottom, which is difficult with monofilament or Dacron. With the advent of microfilament line, this technique has lost favor.

Dave Arbeitman (right) discusses a new hook pattern with noted offshore skipper Mike Petrole. Modern technology has resulted in more improvements to the basic fishhook in the last few years than in the prior 50 years. As a result many of the hooks in tackle boxes are obsolete. The newer models have better design and hooking qualities, are stronger and resist corrosion.

Stainless steel cable line also effective

Stainless steel cable line is easier to handle on the reel spool than solid monel or solid stainless steel. It's especially popular for inshore trolling applications. Its one drawback is that occasionally a single strand of the wire will break, and the resulting burr can play havoc with one's thumb while extending or retrieving the line. Anglers who employ cable line often wear a leather thumb guard, which offers protection from sharp burrs.

A wide array of hook styles necessary

Hooks used by saltwater fishermen come in a wide array of styles and sizes suitable for hooking and landing every species that swims, from 1-pound mackerel to bluefin tuna weighing more than 1,000 pounds. Ideally, one hook could be used to catch any species, but this is not the case. An angler must take care to select a style and size suited to the particular species being sought.

For more than half a century hooks used by saltwater sportfishermen changed very little. During that time there were fewer than a handful of companies that made fishhooks. Perhaps a dozen patterns with a tinned or bronze finish were standard and with few exceptions never changed.

Thanks to tremendous technological advances in hook manufacturing, spurred by several new manufacturers entering the market, the hooks available to the saltwater angler today make practically every hook manufactured just a few years ago obsolete.

The new hooks available to the angling public are better designed, stronger and have sharper points and finishes that enable them to resist the corrosive action of saltwater.

The line drawings of various hook styles included herein are representative of the more popular hooks used by saltwater fishermen. Remember that there are many other styles available. As fishing opportunities are expanded there may be times when a style not included here may help improve your score when using a specific bait or lure for a particular species. In the entire arena of fishing tackle, technology is moving along at much the same pace as computers, here with hook styles, but also with lines, rods, reels, line guides and myriad other gear. The alert angler should closely monitor ongoing developments and capitalize on those that enhance the enjoyment of the sport and improve your catch.

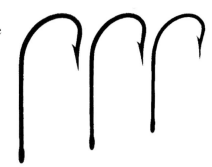

The O'Shaughnessy style is primarily used in the manufacture of lures such as spoons, metal squids, and lead-head jigs. Its design works well in hooking a fish that strikes a moving lure. Some anglers find them a good choice with natural baits as well.

Some styles for natural baits and some for lures

In years past hook styles were uniform and somewhat basic. An O'Shaughnessy style hook was much the same regardless of the manufacturer, although there were differences in manner of manufacture, quality and performance. An O'Shaughnessy hook was still an O'Shaughnessy, as was the case with a Claw, Carlisle, Chestertown, Limerick, Kirby, Salmon, Tuna and Sheepshead style, the latter three being named for the fish they were designed to catch. These same styles continue to be made by manufacturers today. What has happened is that the old styles just aren't as effective as the new styles, some of which differ drastically from the old. As such, it's awkward to discuss specific models, for with today's marketing concepts, every manufacturer has created new names to identify their hooks, so as to distinguish them from others.

Circle hooks were developed hundreds of years ago, and in recent years have grown in popularity. With them it is not necessary to strike a fish, and most fish are hooked in the corner of the mouth, which makes release easy.

Some of the basic styles that have the broadest application in saltwater are identified in this book. It is important that the angler make an effort to select the styles that are best suited to his particular type of fishing, for in the years ahead the old standards of uniform styles and finishes will be things of the past. Indeed, as this is being written it is fair to say that in excess of 90 percent of the hooks in most anglers' tackle boxes are obsolete. I recall as a youngster employing hooks snelled to tarred-line leaders, before the advent of monofilament leaders. Both the tarred line and hook styles of that era have disappeared from the angling scene. That required years to fade away. In the future the angler can expect new hook technology at regular intervals, and it will serve you well to keep abreast of it.

The greatest example of changing hook styles rests with the circle hook. This basic style dates back centuries. Only in the last decade has this hook style increased in popularity among sport fishermen. This came about primarily as a result of its design, which results in hooking fish in the corner of the mouth, as opposed to hooking them deeply. Not only do circle hooks improve the strike-to-hookup ratio, but enables quick release of fish that are to be returned to the water.

Circle hooks have also undergone an evolutionary change. Some now are available with offset points, some are barbless, many have exotic finishes impervious to saltwater, and some have computer-designed and sharpened points, ensuring quick and deep penetration. Each of these improvements means a great deal, and collectively they've revolutionized how anglers fish. Each chapter in this book deals with a specific type of fishing. In the chapter detailing America's favorite species, hook styles are also discussed. In combination with the illustrations provided herein, the angler is afforded the basics of hook selection. It's always wise to have any one of the many high quality diamond hook sharpeners available to ensure that your hook points are always sharp.

Remember that choice is critical, and don't hesitate to discard old styles. Also remember the old adage that the only place for a rusty hook is in the trash can. Being alert to that small tip will serve you well.

Leaders vary in application

Webster's defines "leader" as "a short line of transparent fiber, used to attach the end of a fishline to the lure." At the time those words were written there really wasn't a "transparent" fiber available, as most leaders were made of nylon monofilament, single-strand stainless steel wire or stainless steel cable. Today there is, however, a nearly transparent material: fluorocarbon. This space-age material with a low refractive index has revolutionized saltwater leader material. Through extensive comparison testing, fluorocarbon leaders consistently outperform monofilament, single-strand wire or cable. There's just no comparison. The fluorocarbon admittedly is the more expensive, but when one takes into account the total expenditures when sportfishing, the cost of the leader material is indeed minimal, and certainly worth it.

As noted earlier, some anglers have opted to employ fluorocarbon line. In the case of casters employing spinning or conventional tackle, it occasionally becomes unnecessary to use a leader at all, simply attaching their lure directly to the end of the line.

In many cases, however, anglers who fish saltwater prefer to employ a leader of heavier test than the line being used, as this facilitates landing the fish, and is especially helpful when dealing with fish that have teeth.

For a leader material that is nearly invisible in the water, fluorocarbon is the only choice.

When purchasing hooks snelled to a short length of leader material, it is wise to make certain they're snelled to fluorocarbon and not monofilament. Unless you're able to purchase hooks snelled with fluorocarbon leader material, it is definitely to your advantage to purchase leader coils of the preferred size fluorocarbon and take the time to make your own rigs.

If, however, you're targeting bluefish, barracuda, sharks or other species with sharp teeth, then stainless steel cable leaders that are fabricated using sleeves and crimps are the most effective. Single-strand stainless steel wire leaders that employ a haywire twist are also effective. As with other leader materials, balance the cable or solid wire to the line being used, as it serves no purpose to use leader material that is too heavy.

A rule of thumb, whether fishing inshore for small fish or offshore for big gamefish, the leader should be longer than the fish being sought, as frequently a fish will twist or become entangled in the leader. If the leader is too short, this may result in the lighter line being cut, frayed or broken during the fight.

Terminal rigging snaps and swivels

The saltwater angler will find there are dozens of swivels, snaps and connectors available. There are four, reading from left to right, that will accommodate almost any situation from fishing for small species inshore to big game on the offshore grounds. Always take care to use the smallest sizes and limit the amount you use to the bare essentials. Too much hardware at the terminal end of your tackle can adversely impact your catch.

Duo lock snap

The duo lock snap locks around itself and is very reliable. It may be used at the end of a leader, to conveniently attach a lure. A duo lock snap may also be attached to a three-way swivel and used as a sinker snap, which makes changing sinkers easy.

Barrel swivel

The barrel swivel is used for its swiveling action to conveniently join the terminal end of the line to a leader. It's also used as a connector for ease in attaching many bottom rigs.

Ball-bearing swivel with coastlock snap

The ball bearing swivel with coastlock snap is the finest quality swivel an angler can employ where the probability exists of a lure or bait causing line twist. It has positive swiveling action that is very reliable. The coastlock snap locks around itself and is also reliable and makes for ease in attaching and changing leaders.

Three-way swivel

The three way swivel has many saltwater applications, both in trolling and bottom fishing. It is most often used as a connection between line and leader, with a sinker attached to the swivel's third eye.

Duo lock snap **Barrel swivel** **Ball-bearing swivel with coastlock snap** **Three-way swivel**

Swivels play an important role

The swivels employed by saltwater anglers are designed to permit rotation when two objects are joined. Thus, a swivel joining a line and leader enables the connection to rotate, and should the lure twist, or a fish twist, the rotation of the swivel prevents the twist from being transmitted to the line. Without a swivel, a trolled spoon or other lure that has a tendency to spin would result in a badly twisted line in a matter of minutes.

There are several basic types of swivel that find favor among saltwater anglers. By keeping the four basic swivels in your tackle kit, you're prepared for most every angling contingency.

The ball bearing swivel is the single most popular swivel for offshore trolling. The bead chain swivel is also a very effective swivel and is especially popular for inshore trolling. Anglers who bottom fish often use a three-way swivel, which has three rotating eyes, permitting you to tie your line to one eye, attach your sinker to a second eye, and your leader and hook to the remaining eye. The two-eyed barrel swivel, in models where the wired eyes are secured within the barrel, or those where the wire eyes are exposed outside the barrel, is especially popular for joining line and leader. It finds favor among casters who employ it more as a convenience for joining line and leader, as opposed to its swiveling action.

With all swivels, care should be taken to match the swivel to the task at hand and the size of the line and leader being employed. Many swivels have their coast-lock or duo lock snaps attached to facilitate changing. Don't make the mistake of using too large a swivel, or swivel and snap combination, as it serves no useful purpose and may even detract from its effectiveness by adding too much bulk to the connection.

Each sinker type serves a purpose

Sinkers play an important role in a variety of saltwater fishing applications, in that they literally sink the line, either to a desired depth in the water column, or take a bait or lure directly to the bottom. They're available in a variety of shapes, each designed for a specific purpose. Just a half dozen different models will adequately handle the great majority of situations in which you require a sinker.

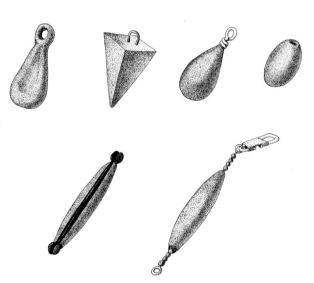

The pyramid sinker, and several variations of this style, are the favorite of surf fishermen, as their shape effectively holds bottom in even a very rough surf. The general range in weights of the pyramid style is from 1 to 6 ounces. To go beyond this weight would be simply impractical, as most rods could not handle a heavier sinker. They are also a good choice for bank, bridge and pier fishermen, who are fishing sandy bottom areas where current or rough water would tend to carry other types of sinkers away.

For general bottom fishing applications the bank style sink-ular. It slides effortlessly along the bottom while drifting, and is not apt to foul easily on bottom obstructions. Beginning with 1/2-ounce sizes for inshore fishing, anglers in the Northwest often use up to 20-ounce weights when probing for rockfish and lingcod, while Northeast canyon fishermen targeting tilefish also use the heavy weights.

included here will cover most every saltwater fishing application. Included in the top row are: The bank, pyramid, dipsey and egg sinker styles. The bottom row includes the rubber-cored sinker and the torpedo-shaped trolling sinker with bead-chain swivel and snap.

The dipsey style sinker is another that is popular with bottom fishermen. Unlike the bank style, where the sinker is molded with a hole in it for attaching a line or sinker loop, the dipsey style sinker has a small barrel swivel molded into its head. The sinker has an elongated egg-shape, with the swivel on top, and is a very neat, effective sinker, used in the same sizes as identified for the bank style.

The egg sinker has a hole running lengthwise through its center. It's especially popular along the Southeast coast and along the Gulf. With an egg sinker the line is run through the hole in the center and tied to a tiny barrel swivel, after which comes the leader and hook. When a fish picks up the bait and moves off with it, the line

17

slips through the sinker and the fish feels no resistance. This rig is used with both live and dead baits.

Egg sinkers are also used extensively while rigging baits such as split-tail mullet, mackerel, balao and flying fish. The weight is usually rigged beneath the head of the bait, and keeps it from skipping about excessively, especially during rough water trolling conditions.

Rubber core sinkers have a number of applications for saltwater anglers. As the name implies, the sinker has a rubber core. The sinker is long and thin and has a depression in the lead running its entire length. Within the depression is a core of rubber having an ear at each end. The line is placed in the depression atop the rubber core, and each ear is twisted, one clockwise, the other counter-clockwise. This twists the core around the line, holding it securely, yet not damaging the line. Semi-soft plastic is now used as the core, but the name rubber core remains the popular way to describe this fine sinker.

The rubber core sinker is really the state-of-the-art model of the traditional clinch-on sinker. The clinch-on has a similar design, except that there are two ears that are molded as part of the sinker, and are bent over to secure the sinker to the line. These are a poor choice, as the pressure of the lead against the line, especially when a burr is encountered, results in a weakening of the line and subsequent line break.

Trolling sinkers are designed to take a trolled lure into the depths, with sinker weight combined with boat speed determining what depth the sinker and lure will track. There are many models and shapes of trolling sinkers, but by far the most popular is the torpedo-shaped sinker, with a brass or stainless steel eye molded into each end of the sinker. Some also have a bead chain swivel with eyes molded directly into the sinker.

Some trolling sinkers have a coastlock type snap or duo lock snap attached to the eyes. The sinkers are most often attached at the terminal end of the line, to a ball-bearing swivel. The leader is attached to the sinker, and the lure or natural bait attached to the end of the leader.

Some anglers also employ the trolling sinker when chumming or drifting to take their baits to a desired depth.

The egg sinker is most often used for bottom fishing. It can be used for trolling, as shown here, by rigging mullet, balao, flying fish and mackerel skip baits. Rigged just beneath the jaw of the bait, the sinker causes the bait to track deeper and keeps it from skipping excessively in rough water.

A variation of a trolling sinker is the cannonball sinker often used by trollers seeking salmon in the Northwest. As its name implies, it is round and shaped like a cannonball, weighing 1, 2, or even 3 pounds. It is used in conjunction with a sinker release pin and swivel combination. The weight of the sinker takes it to the desired depth in the water column. The force of the strike causes the sinker release pin to activate, the cannonball sinker drops to the bottom, and the angler can fight the salmon unimpeded by the weight of a heavy sinker. The drawback of this sinker style is that every time you hook a fish you lose the sinker.

Downriggers are a great aid to boatmen, for they enable an angler to fish his lures at any depth. An electronic control center adjusts the depths at which the lures are fished.

Downriggers an important tool for probing depths

Downriggers have gained popularity in deep fishing, especially in the Northwest, but are also becoming popular in many areas along the seacoast. The downrigger trolling weight places your lure or bait at the desired depth in the water column, enabling your line and lure to detach from the weight so you can fight the fish unencumbered, yet easily retrieve the trolling weight via cable.

Downrigger design is another example of rapidly advancing technology that benefits sportfishermen. A basic downrigger is really little more than an oversize, wide-diameter reel on which stainless steel cable is spooled, onto the end of which is a retrievable weight designed to take your lure or bait into the depths. Advancements in design include a companion electronic display unit that is called a navigational command center, on which are displayed the operation of up to six individual downriggers. All downrigger functions, including raising and lowering, and bottom tracking are accomplished right from the fishfinder unit, with a large viewable screen, enabling the angler to know where his lures are at all times. The unit actually adjusts to the bottom conformation, raising and lowering the trolling weights automatically as the bottom depth changes. The unit also has the capability of imparting a jigging action to your lures as you troll along, causing them to dart ahead and falter, much like a wounded or struggling baitfish.

Still another revolutionary development is for the downriggers to set up a positive field of ions around your boat. This positive ion field attracts more fish, as opposed to some boat and tackle combinations that create a negative ion field which may detract fish.

The cockpit electronics also enable a troller to look off to the side as the boat trolls, instead of just straight down. This highlights fish at all depth levels, from the surface to the bottom, enabling you to position yourself directly over the fish on subsequent trolls.

Downriggers are a great tool for getting your lures where the fish are. As with most equipment and techniques, it takes time and patience to develop the skills to understand the gear and to effectively utilize it on the fishing grounds.

This young lady wisely wore a rod belt while fishing from a party boat off the Dry Tortugas. The rod belt distributes the strain and supports the rod butt while an angler is pumping a big fish from the depths, as was the case with the grouper she just landed. Ankle boots are also comfortable and keep feet dry, as decks are washed down regularly to keep them from becoming slippery.

Rod belts and harnesser prove helpful

When fishing inshore waters for small species of fish, the amount of pressure brought to bear on the angler while fighting the fish is minimal. With larger fish and tackle in the 30- through 130-pound class, it's essential that an angler employ either a fighting chair or a shoulder harness and rod belt to assist in landing the fish. Serious injury can occur when hooked up to a big fish and the rod butt is jammed into your stomach, making it important that an angler be properly equipped, especially when seeking heavyweights.

Most offshore sportfishing boats are equipped with a fighting chair in the cockpit. With an adjustable back, the chair can also easily be turned to keep the angler pointed in the direction of the fish. Most often a bucket harness is used in conjunction with the chair. The angler sits in the bucket harness, and it has straps and snaps which in turn are attached to the harness lugs on the reel. With the aid of a gimbal knock into which the rod butt is placed, an angler can sit comfortably, with feet extended and supported by a foot rest, and fight a big fish for hours.

For light inshore fishing from boat or beach, a rod belt made of leather or plastic, with a cup into which the rod butt is inserted works just fine. Many come equipped with a Velcro fastener that makes it easy to quickly put them on. Belts of this type are just great when fighting fish such as tarpon and bonefish, white sea bass, and yellowtail. Bottom fishermen targeting lingcod, rockfish, grouper, snapper and codfish often wear a lightweight belt too, as it helps hold the rod steady and relieves the pressure when pumping a big fish from the depths.

On the long range party boats that fish off southern California and those that work the canyons of the Northeast, the favored combination is to use both a shoulder or kidney harness with a wide rod belt that distributes the pressure across your entire stomach.

The shoulder harness has harness snaps that are attached to the harness lugs of big game reels, and this enables you to relax your arms periodically, something that would be otherwise impossible to do. The fighting belt's cup, into which the rod fits, has either a vertical or horizontal pin, into which the rod butt's gimbal fits. This holds the rod and reel in an upright position and even with a strong lunge of a heavy fish enables you to be in control at all times. This is especially important aboard any boat where there isn't a fighting chair and you can't sit down. With a properly fitted harness and rod belt an angler has complete freedom to move along the rail of a party boat, following a hooked fish with ease. The fact that you can periodically relax the tension on your arms and wrists is very helpful, especially during a prolonged battle.

Equipment needed to land or release fish

With the exception of very small fish, the majority of fish weighing from just a few pounds, on up to several hundred pounds, requires that they be either netted, gaffed or otherwise gripped to be landed. The most critical time in landing any fish is when it's close at hand, when a sudden burst of speed coupled with poor rod handling might result in a broken line. It's also a time when it's easy to bruise or otherwise injure yourself.

Some toothless fish may be landed by simply obtaining a firm grip on their lower jaw with your thumb and forefinger. With most, however, it's better to employ a landing net, gaff or gripper to safely land the fish.

Nets universally popular for catch and release

Without question the landing net is the most popular device used by both boatmen and land-based anglers to land their catch. Very simple in design, the landing net is a nylon mesh bag attached to a large metal loop, which in turn is fastened to a long handle. Anglers fishing from small boats employ nets with just a four foot long handle and net bag of a size to accommodate the species in residence. Aboard the party boats the nets often have 12-foot-long handles and a net bag capable of capturing and lifting aboard fish weighing 50 pounds or more.

The key in netting any fish is that the angler lead the fish to the open mouth of the net, which is partially submerged in the water. Done properly, the angler reels and guides the fish towards the net, while the person handling the net positions it, so ideally the fish swims right in, at which time the net is lifted and the fish promptly boated.

Care should be taken to avoid reeling the fish too close to the boat, and in the course of the excitement, lifting the fish's head clear of the water. This often presents a difficult target for the net handler, as the fish should be netted head first, as opposed to bringing the net around from behind. When the fish thrashes at the surface it often uses its leverage to either break the line or shake free of the hook. Care must be exercised for both angler and the person handling the net to coordinate their efforts.

Once in the net and aboard, the fish should be held in the net, as it is easier to control. Reach in and unhook it, and if it is going to be released, just return the net and fish to the water, turn the net, and the fish is easily released. If the fish is being kept for the table, deposit it from the net right into your ice chest.

The long-handled landing net is the most popular device used by saltwater anglers to land fish. Various regulations concerning seasons, size and bag limits, results in many fish having to be returned to the water unharmed. When safely aboard, the fish should be held within the net, unhooked, and if it is to be released, gently placed back in the water without handling it.

The Boga Grip is an effective gripping device used to land fish. The gripper is activated with easy thumb or finger pressure. Once the hook is removed, the gripper's jaws are opened and the fish is released, without it ever being handled. The unit also has a scale built into its handle.

Boga Grip an ideal tool to land, weigh and release

There are several gripping devices available that are designed to grasp a fish's lower jaw, thus immobilizing it, and enabling the angler to lift it aboard. When dealing with fish that may weigh from 15 to 30 pounds, a tremendous amount of pressure is brought to bear with such a device, and a poorly designed one may permit a fish to twist free unless extreme pressure is exerted to hold onto it.

Recognizing the problem inherent in the gripper-type release mechanism, Gary Alldrich of Eastaboga, Alabama set about and engineered what he's called the Boga Grip. Made entirely of stainless steel and space age plastic, the gripper is spring activated and can easily be handled by the angler playing a fish one hand and activating the Boga Grip with the other.

The gripper has two jaws that securely lock on the fish's lower jaw, and doesn't require any pressure whatsoever on the part of the angler. A strong lanyard holds the Boga Grip securely to your wrist, enabling you to remove the hook with ease. Just as easily, the fish can be held aloft for a moment and its weight determined.

There is a built-in scale in the handle that is so accurate that the International Game Fish Association recognizes it when establishing and certifying world record catches. The fish may then be held in the water, giving it time to recover and water to pass through its gills. When you feel it's time to set it free, you may do so with just a slight amount of thumb pressure which releases the claws that secured the fish. In an instant the fish is free, never having touched the deck or been touched by anyone.

Gaffs helpful with big game

A gaff is a strong hook, attached to a handle, used to impale a fish and aid in landing it. There are many styles of gaff designs used for various applications. The most popular gaff style used by boatmen consists of a 3-, 4- or 5-inch stainless steel hook attached to an aluminum handle. Small-boat anglers employ 2- or 3-foot long handles, while anglers fishing from offshore craft often employ handles 6- to 8-feet in length. It's not uncommon on party boats to employ 10-foot handles in order to reach the fish from the high bow decks.

Offshore anglers who target big pelagic sharks such as the mako and thresher often use a flying gaff, as do blue marlin fishermen and those targeting giant bluefin tuna. A flying gaff has a hook measuring 6, 8 or 10 inches, that is not permanently attached to the gaff handle. Instead, the hook is temporarily secured to the handle, and in turn is attached to a length of 1/2-inch rope, the end of which is secured to a stern cleat on the boat or the pedestal of the fighting chair. The handle of a flying gaff usually measures in the range of 8- to 10-feet. When a big fish is struck with the flying gaff, the hook is released from the handle, and the rope is then used to bring the fish alongside. There it is either brought over the gunwale, through a transom door or lifted aboard via a gin pole with block and tackle. With increased emphasis on catch-and-release sportfishing, this type of gaff is fast-fading from the scene.

A variation of a flying gaff is using a harpoon head instead of a gaff hook. As a fish is brought alongside the fish is struck with the harpoon, which releases from the handle, and then the fish is boated using the rope that is attached to the harpoon. As a general rule, sportsmen frown on its use.

A release gaff is a short-handled gaff, usually 6 to 12 inches long, with a 3- or 4-inch hook. A lanyard is attached to the handle and is placed around the wrist of the person gaffing. As a fish is brought alongside, the gaff hook is carefully placed in the lower jaw of the fish, such as a big tarpon, redfish, snook or permit, which temporarily immobilizes the fish. The fish is promptly unhooked while being held in the water at boatside. The fish continues to be held by the gaff in its jaw until it regains its strength. With the fish swimming upright and with water passing through its gills, the hook is backed out and the animal swims off unharmed.

Admittedly, many of the items discussed in this initial chapter are dry and factual. They are, however, extremely important as the succeeding chapters will show. The importance of balanced tackle, the right line, correct size and style hook, best sinker style and appropriate swivel and snap, all play an important role. They apply in some way to every type of saltwater fishing you're about to participate in. Importantly, the allied equipment discussed also adds to the enjoyment and provides you the tools to really enjoy your days spent along the sea coast, whether it be at sea or wading the thousands of miles of America's coastline.

(right) Bob Rosko just gaffed this yellowfin tuna for Kelly, his wife. It struck a green machine while they were trolling aboard the "Linda June" at Hudson Canyon, along the edge of the continental shelf. Gaffs are very effective tools for bringing big fish aboard that are to be kept. Small release gaffs are used on fish that are to be released.

CHARTER, PARTY, RENTAL AND PRIVATE BOATS

Saltwater fishermen and newcomers to the sport who wish to fish from boats have four basic options from which to choose: Chartering a boat, fishing aboard a party boat, renting a boat they'll pilot or investing in a private boat of their own.

Many saltwater fishermen develop their skills over a period of time. A fine way to develop those skills, especially if boating is your forte, is to begin aboard a charter or guide boat. There you and your party of from one to six anglers has the complete use of the boat and services of the captain or guide for the duration of the charter. This is especially suited to newcomers, for the captain and crew take care of your every need.

This is all you'll need for a fun-filled day on a party boat, whether you fish out of Atlantic, Pacific or Gulf Coast ports. A balanced party-boat outfit, complete with the latest depth-counter reel, will handle most species. The tackle box includes: Plain hooks, snelled hooks, swivels, sinkers, chromed jigs, leadhead jigs, bait tails, floats, pliers, sun block, a wooden dowel, knives and dehooker.

(Left) Vin Sparano's beautiful charter boat "Man O'War" sails from Islamorada, Florida, and is what you should look for in a six-person charter boat along the sea coast. Its owner takes pride in challenging anyone to find a rusty hook on the boat. It is equipped with a variety of custom fishing tackle suitable for offshore big-game fishing and chumming on inshore reefs.

As your skills develop through hands-on experience aboard a charter craft, and observation and retention of the techniques employed, it often becomes appropriate to move on to a party, or open boat. Aboard the party packets anglers board on a first come, first served basis, where no reservation is usually required. There's a great deal of camaraderie aboard these boats, where perhaps 12 to 100 or more anglers enjoy a day of fishing. It's a learning experience where you may rent an appropriate outfit for the fish being sought. You'll receive assistance from mates and deckhands, but you do the actual fishing, from rigging up, baiting your hook and bringing the fish to boatside.

Once a comfort level has been achieved on the party packets, many anglers get that itch to get out on a boat and do everything on their own, coming and going at their leisure, and seeking the species of their choice. Renting a boat for a half-day or full day, or even an entire week's vacation, becomes a fine option.

Unfortunately, rental boats usually aren't available at small coastal ports, although they are available at most major fishing locales. The boats may range from small aluminum skiffs and wooden rowboats powered by outboards, to 24-footers with inboard power plants.

After experiencing sportfishing from charter and guide boats, party packets and rental boats, the next big step is private boat ownership. This is decision time, for you take on a big responsibility, and a substantial investment. It requires thought and planning, but when properly approached, can provide you with many years of enjoyment.

Some fishermen find that they're content to enjoy the fellowship and fun of the party packets. Others choose to fish with their favorite guide or charter captain, often once a week or once a month, often for years on end. Many rent a boat of their choice at their leisure and ply local waters and register fine catches. Some go on to private boat ownership and develop a lifelong love affair with their boats. Importantly, there is no right or wrong choice. What is important is that you select the option that makes you comfortable, that helps you enjoy the contemplative pastime that saltwater sportfishing is all about. You'll know when you've found it, because words will not be able to describe the enjoyment you and your family and friends will experience.

Included in the discussion of the various options are helpful hints to help you determine just what is the right choice for you.

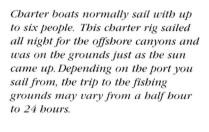

Charter boats normally sail with up to six people. This charter rig sailed all night for the offshore canyons and was on the grounds just as the sun came up. Depending on the port you sail from, the trip to the fishing grounds may vary from a half hour to 24 hours.

Charter, guide boats a great learning experience

Charter boats are generally in the 24- to 45-foot class, with comfortable accommodations for the captain and mate, plus from one to six anglers. They're seaworthy, roomy boats designed for the comfort of the passenger. The majority of charter boats are privately owned by a captain who has made it a lifelong profession, dedicated to guiding his passengers to a good catch, which makes for a pleasant day's enjoyment on the water. Most charter captains were fishermen first and gained experience as mates aboard charter and party boats before deciding to break out on their own.

The six-pack charter boats, so named because their captains have a Coast Guard license enabling them to sail with up to six passengers, are found on all three of our coasts, whether you're seeking salmon and halibut in the Northwest, redfish or yellowfin tuna along the Gulf or striped bass and white marlin along the middle Atlantic.

Much the same is true of the guide boat captains, who are also licensed by the Coast Guard, but who usually have smaller boats, in the 20- to 26-foot range, designed to comfortably accommodate from one to three anglers. The guide boats give a more personalized service than the bigger charter boats, and they enable what is commonly referred to as the total fishing experience, which is possible as a result of fewer anglers actually being aboard and fishing.

Charter boats often supply tackle that tends to be on the heavy side. Most captains are happy to accommodate anglers who wish to bring their own tackle, such as the light conventional casting tackle employed by this angler to land a magnificent king salmon from the waters off Washington.

Where possible, visit the docks before you charter

Perhaps the best advice to a newcomer is to visit the locale you plan to fish and to walk the docks of the local marina, inspecting the charter boat fleet and observing what takes place on the docks.

Observe the charter party as it returns from a day on the fishing grounds. If the fishing has been good and the anglers treated properly and had an enjoyable day, it is readily evident. Observe as they disembark and say their goodbyes to the captain and crew, and observe whether their catch has been properly cleaned, packaged, and iced for their trip home. These little details tell you a lot, without you ever asking a question.

If you observe a boat that looks appealing, as does its captain and crew, by all means ask permission to board and discuss the prospects of chartering. Most often you'll be welcomed aboard, and graciously shown the boat, its accommodations, fishing tackle, and equipment.

This is your time to learn, so don't hesitate in asking questions. Determine the cost of the charter. Often, weekend rates are the most costly, with reduced rates during the week and for half-day or evening charters. Ask about the departure and return times, the species being fished for, and the captain's suggestion as to what you and your party should bring along for your comfort.

Charter boats are especially good for children not used to boating. You can work with the skipper to determine a convenient sailing time, as nothing spoils a day's outing more than waking children at an unreasonable hour and then expecting them to enjoy a day on the water after having inadequate rest. Many skippers cater to trips with children and will often recommend fishing inshore or in the protected reaches of bays and sounds in order to avoid the potential of rough seas, and yet be close to dockside should there be a need to return early due to the wishes of the charter party or as a result of rain or wind and accompanying uncomfortable sea conditions.

For children and newcomers to fishing, a charter boat captain will often target species that are plentiful and easy to catch and don't require exertion or extraordinary skills to land. Along the Atlantic coast, mackerel provide exciting fishing during spring and fall, as do summer flounder during the warm-weather months. Sand bass, Pacific bonito, and Pacific barracuda fishing around the kelp beds are ideal activities for a family outing during the summer months. Along the Gulf Coast, sea trout, bluefish and redfish can be depended upon to provide a good catch and pleasant experience.

Unfortunately, some parents who want to introduce their youngsters to fishing make the mistake of chartering a boat and telling the captain they'd like to fish for a "big one" so the youngsters can have something to boast about when they get home. On occasion the captain will oblige, often to the detriment of the child. Take care to heed the counsel of the captain and be guided accordingly, for it's far more enjoyable to begin with the plentiful, smaller, inshore species and work up as experience is gained.

When checking out your charter options, determine if the boat is the kind of boat that you and your friends or family would like to be aboard. If the captain has neglected the boat with an unkempt head, dirty galley, rod guides held on with electrical tape and rusty hooks and lures littered about, it might be best to move on. A charter trip should be a total fishing experience, with all of the pieces contributing to the day's enjoyment.

In addition to determining the cost of the charter, it's wise to ask specifically if that cost includes the opportunity to keeping all of the fish caught by your party. In some cases, particularly where valuable market fish such as tuna, broadbill swordfish, mako sharks and other species may be caught, some captains maintain that the catch remains the property of the boat. It's best that these issues are resolved before sailing.

The subject of releasing fish is another item that merits discussion, for there are many anglers today who simply enjoy the relaxation of catching fish, but do not wish to kill them. This, too, should be resolved before finalizing a charter.

"When checking out your charter options, your charter options, determine if the boat is the kind of boat that you and your friends or family would like to be aboard."

If you've developed as an angler and decided to purchase your own tackle, it's important that you discuss with the skipper beforehand your desire to use your own gear, rather than the gear provided by the boat. Many captains will graciously accede to your wishes, although some are so ingrained with just putting fish on the dock with heavy gear that they may be reluctant to do so. Keep in mind that it's the good catch on the dock that attracts others and results in good exposure for the captain and his boat. If you choose to bring and use your own gear, make certain that it's suitable to the method of fishing and species being targeted.

Once you've chartered a boat, ask the captain what you should bring along. He may suggest specific clothing, particularly if inclement weather may be encountered. He may also suggest seasick medication in the event members of your party may never have experienced a day offshore on the water. The captain will usually supply ice or a refrigerator for the lunches and beverages that you are expected to bring, (including food for the captain and mate, in most instances). Towards this end, some charter boats wisely prohibit alcoholic beverages. If you like a cold beer while on the water, opt for non-alcoholic brew.

It always pays to bring a pair of sunglasses, sun block lotion, aspirin or Tylenol, and even a pack of antacid. These little items can sometimes save the day out on the water.

Most anglers new to charter fishing are not out to establish world-record catches, the certification of which involves certain specific requirements of the International Game Fish Association. It's important to note that these requirements prohibit anyone other than the angler handling the rod and reel—the mate hooking a fish and handing off the outfit is prohibited—and also specify the length of double line permitted, maximum leader size and also the number of hooks on a lure. If you're just out to learn and don't mind the mate handling the tackle and fish, just enjoy yourself. If, however, you're serious about living within the parameters as established by IGFA, then make this known to the captain and mate.

The trip to the fishing grounds is often a good opportunity to talk with the mate about the day's fishing. Remember that your party will be in the cockpit, working with the mate throughout the day with the captain usually at the helm. If trolling is to be employed, with only two or three lines being fished, it may prove advantageous to decide which angler aboard will have the first opportunity to fight and land a fish, to avoid confusion when a strike is received. Many charter groups use a rotation system so that everyone gets a fair chance at making a catch.

If chumming and bottom fishing are the techniques, then each angler aboard is provided with an outfit and instructed how to use it. This does require some active participating, such as paying out and retrieving line while chumming, or actively working the rod tip and retrieving while jigging. In the case of bottom fishing, the mate will instruct you in the basic techniques you will need to know for the day.

Guide boats for one or two anglers are very popular throughout the Florida Keys. Here the boat is anchored and shrimp chum is dispensed on the flats to attract bonefish, permit and tarpon.

You're totally involved when fishing on guide boats

On the smaller guide boats, where usually only one or two anglers are on board, the fishing is more intimate and the angler is more heavily involved. This is particularly true with guide boats in the Florida Keys. These are specialized craft designed for fishing the very shallow water of the flats. The boat is often poled by the guide while the anglers stand and look for feeding or cruising species such as bonefish, permit, and tarpon. Once the fish are sighted, it becomes the angler's opportunity to cast his bait or lure to the fish. This admittedly takes skill, and a newcomer that tries this type of fishing for the first time may become frustrated. Guides will often accommodate a newcomer if so asked, but it's the angler's choice, and if you're the person chartering, don't be discouraged if you miss the target, as there will be other opportunities.

Along the Carolina and Virginia Barrier Beaches, guides fish from small boats with their anglers casting to surface-cruising redfish. In Georgia, casts are often made to feeding tarpon. Oregon and Washington anglers often fish aboard guide boats while targeting silver and king salmon where they enter the Northwest's mighty river systems. Each of these types of fishing requires more angler participation and involvement. They can also be extremely rewarding.

When chartering either a guide boat or charter boat, don't hesitate to communicate with the guide or captain throughout the day. It's their job to accommodate your wishes, within reason, and if the fishing you originally wanted to do results in very poor action, perhaps the guide or captain might be able to suggest an alternate type of fishing that might liven up an otherwise uneventful day. Chartering is often done months and sometimes a full year in advance, and there are times when a run of a specific species of fish doesn't materialize. When things don't go according to plan, it's often best for all concerned to opt for another choice.

The general rule of thumb with respect to tipping is not to tip the owner, but to tip the mate of a charter boat based on the service provided throughout the day. Mates work hard and most often are rewarded with a tip valued at 10 percent of the charter rate. If it's obvious you've been neglected through the day, a tip may not be appropriate at all, while extraordinary service may result in more, with you and your guests being the final decision makers.

There are often occasions when a tip is certainly appropriate aboard a guide or charter boat. Sometimes it may have been a slow day, and you're asked if you'd like to stay out an extra hour or two at no additional charge to catch a change of tide where the fish may be more cooperative. Often such action turns an uneventful day into an extraordinary one, and it becomes appropriate to acknowledge this extra effort with a gratuity.

Party boats such as this catamaran are big and spacious, providing comfort for anglers on extended trips. Most party boats have a galley aboard. Long-range boats that stay at sea for a day or more have bunks for sleeping. The party boats have varied schedules and fish both inshore and offshore grounds for a wide variety of species.

Party boats offer enjoyment for all

The term "party boat" includes a variety of sportfishing vessels that are known by various local names, including: Drift boats, long-range boats, head boats and day boats. Unlike charter boats, where the boat is chartered by a group of anglers, the party boat is there to accommodate the individual angler who wishes to step aboard and go fishing (hence the term "head boat" used in some locales, as fare is based on a per-head basis as you board).

Party boats range in size from vessels carrying as few as a half dozen anglers to huge vessels a 100 feet or more in length, complete with bunks, galleys and accommodations for trips of a week or more. They sail out of most every coastal port on the Atlantic, Pacific and Gulf coasts.

The Coast Guard licenses the captains of these vessels and the owners must adhere to strict regulations designed to ensure the safety of passengers.

Each vessel must undergo a meticulous inspection to be certified as safe. Captains of the vessels must pass a comprehensive written exam before receiving their license to carry passengers for hire.

Camaraderie and diversity combine

For many anglers, fishing aboard a party boat is among the most enjoyable of fishing experiences. The camaraderie of those who board these vessels adds to the excitement of the trip, for you have a group of people brought together with a common interest. Most have never met before, but during the course of the trip relationships develop, fishing stories are exchanged and a bond develops. People so enjoy this fishing that couples have been married on party boats and it's not unusual for just-married couples to spend their honeymoon on board, enjoying the fresh air, sunshine, good fishing, and importantly, the affordability.

The length of these party packets can vary greatly. The normal day trip usually leaves dockside at 7 or 8 a.m. and lasts eight or nine hours. There are, however, half-day boats, three-quarter-day boats, and twilight trips. In many areas, a second shift takes over the craft on its return for the night schedule. There are half-night, three-quarter and all-night trips.

Along some sections of coast there are trips that last several days. Examples include week-long excursions off Mexico's Baja Peninsula, two- and three-day trips to the Dry Tortugas off Florida, deep-water wreck fishing off Nantucket for two days or more, and sailing to the underwater canyons along the edge of the continental shelf off Long Island and New Jersey. Some boats include a bunk as part of the regular fare, while on others a bunk is optional for a limited fee.

Wide variety of species available

Anglers may elect to select a party boat to seek a specific species of fish via a specific method of fishing. Almost all of the boats have signs prominently displayed at the docks identifying the species that will be sought and the method of fishing.

The basic types of fishing include: Bottom fishing; with the boat either anchored over wrecks, reefs or irregular, broken bottom; or drifting over smooth bottom. Some boats specialize in chumming, and this may be done at anchor or while drifting. Trolling is often done, too, but this limits the number of anglers who can stream their lines from the stern. Trolling is often used to locate schools of fish, after which chum is used to hold the school close to the boat and attract the fish to hook baits. Jigging is another popular method while fishing at anchor or while drifting.

There are many variations to the above. In the Northwest, downriggers are used while trolling for salmon with each angler assigned a specific station. On the Pacific coast while deep-water trolling, with breakaway sinkers to get the baits deep, anglers often rotate positions with their tackle to ensure each has a chance of his baits working as the grounds are covered.

Because conditions change so frequently, party boat crews must be able to adapt quickly So while you may anticipate bottom fishing all day, if the skipper locates a school of surface feeding fish, he may ask anglers to switch techniques and take advantage of the developing fishing opportunity.

Bluefish are very popular with party-boat anglers along the middle and north Atlantic Coast. Jeff Melito caught this big blue while using a diamond jig aboard the party boat "Gambler" while at the famed Klondike Banks off New Jersey. Bluefish are also hooked when attracted to the boat with ground menhaden chum, as anglers drift chunks of butterfish bait back in the slick.

Be familiar with fishing regulations

Each state has jurisdiction over fishing in its coastal waters, while the federal government regulations cover offshore ocean fishing. It is wise to check with the party boat captain to determine whether or not you need a license. In most jurisdictions you do not need a separate license while aboard a party boat because the boat is licensed. However, some jurisdictions require a license that may be obtained on a one-day, three-day, monthly, or yearly basis.

There are both state and federal regulations in effect in most jurisdictions that deal with specific seasons in which fish may be taken, minimum and maximum sizes, and the quantity, or daily bag limit, that may be retained. Some jurisdictions have possession limits, too. It is prudent to always follow the instructions of the captain or deckhand in this regard. The deckhands are usually very knowledgeable and carefully measure regulated fish, ensuring that undersize fish, or those in excess of the limit, are returned to the water.

The long-finned albacore is a favorite of long-range party-boat anglers on all three U.S. coasts. Most party boats troll with up to 16 lines, and when fish are hooked the boat shuts down and chumming begins. This albacore was landed off California. A numbered plastic tag was stapled to its gill plate before the fish was placed in a community ice box to ensure freshness until return to port.

Party boats perfect for beginners

Party boat fishing is a great way to get started in sportfishing. The newcomer is usually welcome by the veteran anglers, who are quick to share their techniques and help in any way they can. The captain and his mates also go to great lengths to help the beginner, well realizing that they may gain a regular customer as a result. For the regular customers, this type of fishing becomes almost an addiction, with anglers often sailing on a specific day each week all year round, taking advantage of the changing seasons and changing species and types of fishing.

Whether you're a veteran or a newcomer to party boat fishing, it's wise to do some homework before boarding a packet. As a first step you might watch the local fishing reports in coastal newspapers. Fishing reporters are on the scene, talking with captains daily, and they usually relay reliable fishing information from which you can make a determination as to the length of the trip, species sought and costs.

This party packet is returning from the waters of the Gulf of Mexico with a fine catch of bottom feeders that were landed while the boat drifted across an offshore reef. The fish were iced in a community box while offshore, and hung at each angler's station when the boat returned.

Visit the docks before sailing

Perhaps the best approach if you're new to this fishing, or visiting an area for the first time, is to head down to the docks and visit as the boats come in. Talk with the people who are disembarking. Ask how the fishing and weather was, and whether or not they were satisfied with their captain and crew. You want to board a packet where the captain and mates work together as a team and will move from spot to spot until they score. If a disembarking passenger tells you the captain anchored on a reef and spent the day in one spot, asleep in the pilothouse, while the mate handled the decks, you'd be best served looking elsewhere.

You'll find party boats that are dirty, but you find charter boats and guide boats that are dirty, too. When at the docks don't hesitate to ask the captain if you can board, and then discreetly inspect the boat. In this way you'll know what's in store for you before you sail. Look at the restrooms. If the toilets are grimy it's generally a reflection on the crew. Likewise in the galley. If it's a greasy grill or dirty microwave that appears to not have been cleaned in ages, move on to another boat.

Tackle is another consideration. Look at the tackle, in the event you'll be required to rent an outfit. Is it what you'll enjoy using? If the reel only has a half spool of line, a guide is missing on a rod, and the metal parts of the reel are corroded, it shows lack of concern on the part of the crew.

You can find a boat that's right for you by walking the docks, talking to people and just plain observing.

Party and charter boats sail daily from Fisherman's Wharf in San Francisco. Offshore of the Golden Gate Bridge they troll for king salmon and silver salmon, and bottom fish for a variety of rockfish. Many boats also fish the waters adjacent to the bridge for striped bass.

Rail position is important at times

While initially it may sound unimportant, rail position in certain types of party boat fishing can make a difference in your luck. In many types of reef and wreck fishing, the boat is anchored over a sand bottom and the current holds the boat in position either close to, or over, the choice bottom. In this kind of a situation the people who line the stern have the choice spots, for as the fish are chummed the first baited hooks they respond to are those of anglers positioned at the stern.

As a rule of thumb, it's difficult to beat the stern position for any kind of fishing, and it's not unusual to see party boat regulars arrive extra early, even hours before boarding time, so they can place their outfit in a choice stern location.

When drift fishing the captain usually will position the boat so anglers on one side will have their lines stream away from the boat, and the other side's lines will drift under the boat. Every half hour or so the skipper will make a move over new bottom, and alternate the position of the boat, so the anglers whose lines drifted under the boat will stream away from it and vice versa for the other side.

The best position on boats that drift is the bow, where only two or three anglers can fish. In this way they can take advantage of their lines streaming away on either drift, and it enables them to cast out and away from the bow, which results in more bottom being covered.

When the party boats are crowded, each angler has a spot at the rail, usually marked by a painted stripe on the rail or piece of cord. Some boats have rod holders at each position.

When the boat isn't crowded you can move about more readily. At such times it's often wise to move away from areas where the anglers tend to cluster near the stern, and to situate yourself alone. Such a move can result in more strikes and less chances for a tangle.

Carry a pair of outfits

As anglers become proficient on the party boats, some will expand their horizon from the species normally targeted and seek bigger game. A case in point, many packets chum for yellowtail snapper throughout their southern range. These average 2 to 4 lbs. and are fished for with small hooks and light tackle. Frequenting the same grounds as the yellowtail are big grouper and snapper, some weighing 50 lbs. and more, which are targeted by anglers who bring heavy tackle and use big baits. Many anglers will bring a pair of outfits aboard, one heavy and one light, and catch some smaller gamesters before moving on to the heavyweights.

Along the mid-Atlantic coast the catch of species such as summer flounder is limited with respect to size and bag limits, and once anglers have filled their limit they'll often switch over to diamond jigging or squidding for bluefish, striped bass, Atlantic bonito, and Spanish mackerel.

Pacific coast anglers fishing off the kelp beds often experience mixed-bag action. Pacific bonito, white sea bass, and kelp bass are usually the target of baits drifted near the surface, while bottom rigs down on the sand bring strikes from Pacific halibut, rockfish and other bottom feeders. The key on all three coasts is to be prepared, and to quickly respond as situations develop.

Of particular interest to the beginner is the fact that you're not required to supply anything on party boats. Rental rods and reels are provided, with a nominal fee in addition to the regular fare. If you should lose the rig you may purchase another from the deckhand, who is always circulating around the rail, rigging tackle, baiting hooks, gaffing or netting fish or otherwise being helpful.

In the Florida Keys the party boats generally charge a fixed fare, and if you lose a hook or bottom rig while fishing the reef the mate simply replaces it as a part of the basic fare. The additional nominal amount the fare is increased as a result of not charging for hooks, line or sinkers is welcomed as a convenience to the passengers and results in less work for the mates.

Big fish pools are fun

Almost all party boats have a pool, to which anglers contribute a nominal amount, ranging from a couple of dollars to ten dollars or more. The pool money ultimately goes to the angler catching the largest fish of the day. There are rules which identify which species of fish are eligible for the pool money, and it's great fun as momentum swings from one angler to the other as the size of the biggest fish increases through the day. Often the pool money is divided into two or three places, especially if the boat is crowded. It's not unusual to be rewarded with several hundred dollars for the biggest fish of the day, a double-barreled bonus, for you've got a big one for the dinner table. There are, however, those rare occasions when not a single fish is caught during the trip. Then the pool money is awarded via a drawing, so even on the poorest fishing day, some lucky angler disembarks with a bonus. It's customary that the pool winners share a portion of the pool via a tip for the deckhands or mate.

Big fish pools are popular on party boats. The anglers on board contribute several dollars into the pool. If the boat is crowded there are often two or three pools. The angler who catches the largest fish disembarks with the pool money. The pools generate camaraderie during the day, as the leader with the biggest fish often changes several times.

37

Learn from the veterans

Much can be learned from veteran party boat anglers, as they have this type of fishing down to a science. Because fishing time on the grounds is often limited, the veteran is extremely well organized with his tackle, so not a moment is wasted. Many of the veterans develop a personal party boat checklist to ensure that they have everything with them that is necessary for a successful day on the packets:

Party boat check list

√ Proper clothing, including rain gear and hat
√ Ice chest, with ice, for fish, and a compartment for food and beverages
√ Plastic bags in which to place cleaned fish on ice
√ Deck shoes or slip-on boots to keep dry sea-sick pills, antacid pills and aspirin or pain relief pills
√ Sunglasses
√ Foldable toothbrush and toothpaste
√ Sun block (25 or higher)
√ Sleeping bag for overnighters

Little things like a toothbrush to freshen your mouth after a night in a bunk, or an antacid tablet for indigestion, or especially sun-tan lotion to prevent a burn, often make a big difference on a fishing trip.

While the regulars carry all of the above gear with them out of habit, you'll also find they bring at least one completely rigged rod and reel, and many veterans bring a spare outfit as insurance.

As with the sundry items noted above, the veterans bring a tackle box loaded with the essentials:

Party boat tackle box

√ A roomy, plastic, waterproof box, with all items easily accessible
√ Sharp filleting knife
√ Serrated knife for steaking and cutting bone
√ Diamond knife sharpener
√ Stainless steel dehooker
√ Vice grip cutting pliers in sheath
√ Eight-inch piece of broomstick for wrapping line around to pull free from bottom snags
√ Sinkers for the type of fishing expected
√ Terminal rigs for the type of fishing expected
√ Jigs, spoons, feathers and other lures and rigged leaders

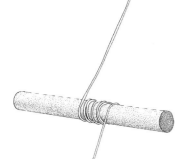

No matter how careful you are there will be times when your line becomes snagged. Rather than risk injury to fingers and your tackle as you attempt to pull free from the snag, just carry an 8-inch-long piece of broomstick with you. Make five or six turns of the line around the dowel and while holding each end, give a hard pull and you will easily pull free or break the line.

Having boarded with this array of equipment and tackle, most experienced fishermen discuss with the deckhands the exact method to be used on arrival at the fishing grounds, and the techniques that have proved most effective. They in turn rig accordingly as the boat travels to the fishing grounds. As indicated earlier, there is a limited amount of time on the fishing grounds, and the veteran anglers fully utilize it by being totally prepared. They often wear their cutting pliers and bait knife in a sheath on their belt.

Many anglers wear a carpenters tool apron, in which they place a couple of extra sinkers and complete terminal rigs, so they can quickly re-tie and get back in the water should they lose a rig. This prevents wasting time rummaging through a tackle box, or worse still, having to make up a rig, or have to purchase one from a busy mate.

Included in the tool apron is the eight-inch piece of broomstick, which is a godsend when it's necessary to break off a snagged bottom rig. It prevents breaking costly tackle as you try to break off, but more importantly keeps you from cutting your hands or arms with monofilament, microfilament or thermofused lines. Once the fishing grounds are reached the captain will either announce over the loudspeaker or by sounding the horn that fishing can begin. At each fishing location along the rail the deckhands will have placed a container of bait. If live bait is used it is readily available at the circulating tanks. Once baited up and fishing, it's a good practice to be alert of the actions of other anglers. Watch the first fellows to score and don't hesitate to copy their techniques.

Boat crews care for fish properly

When bottom fishing or drift fishing, where the species sought are small in size, it's customary for anglers to reel their catch to boatside, lower their rod tip and gently swing the fish aboard. The deckhand will quickly unhook your fish, replace your bait, and place your fish on ice or in your bag. On some boats the mate places your catch on a stringer and then puts the fish on ice in a community box.

Along some sections of coast, particularly in Florida and along the Gulf Coast, where the weather is often hot and fish could easily spoil, the deckhands place fish in a community box filled with crushed ice. Each fish is marked via a specific marking that is assigned to each angler on board. As an example, the first angler to catch a fish is assigned "one cut on the bottom," which means the deck-hand makes a single knife cut on the bottom of the fish near the head. The next angler to score is assigned "two cuts on the bottom." After four cuts are assigned, the next spot is the top of the head, with one to four cuts assigned. Next the top of the tail is cut, then the bottom, and a single X on the side of the left side of the head, then the right, then a double X, and so on.

The system works extremely well, as the angler doesn't have to handle the fish. The fish is unhooked, marked and placed on ice immediately by the deckhand, who is often assisted by the captain when the fishing is hectic. Upon returning to dockside, the anglers disembark and form a semi-circle with their opened ice chests. The mate removes each fish from the community box, calls out "top tail," and places the fish in the top tail angler's ice chest. "Two cuts on the bottom," "bottom tail," "double X on the left," and the chant goes on. In just a few minutes hundreds of fish from the community box are distributed. The fish always arrive back in port in excellent condition with this system.

On some boats each angler is assigned a number for the fish he catches. The mates staple a tag with your number on the gill plate of each fish you catch before depositing it in the community box of shaved ice or cooler.

Immediately after distributing the fish to the people who caught them, the deckhands repair to the cleaning table where they fillet and package your fish if you wish them to do so. For their efforts they are rewarded with a tip for this extra service, depending of course on the size and number of fish cleaned.

In tourist areas many deckhands have foam coolers available and will clean your fish, pack them in double-plastic bags, then bury them in bagged ice in the cooler and seal it with duct tape. The double bagging of the fillets keeps them from becoming water-soaked, and the double bagging of the ice prevents the water from leaking as it melts. Packed in this way the fish easily keep several days, arriving home in prime condition.

Restaurants accommodate anglers

In many tourist locales the restaurants encourage you to bring your catch in. They will graciously use their local recipes to prepare it, which is a great way to conclude a pleasant day's fishing on a party boat.

On long-range boats or party boats with excursions that last several days, the fish are often tagged with a tail tag, then placed either on ice or refrigerated until you return to dockside.

Be patient when fighting big fish

In some types of fishing, such as when working the Pacific kelp beds, or when

"It's much easier for a fish to be gaffed or netted when it is a foot or so beneath the surface, and not thrashing on the surface, or with its head lifted from the water."

chumming around the shrimp boats in the Gulf or seeking bluefish when chumming in the Atlantic, the fish that are hooked are so large and strong that you just can't stand at the rail and bring the fish to you. At such times it's necessary to follow the fish up and down the rail. Most party boat anglers are extremely courteous and when they hear the time-honored "fish on, coming through" they'll clear the rail, raise or lower their line, to permit you to follow your fish. With a big fish the deckhand will frequently accompany the angler to make certain no tangles occur.

As a big fish is brought alongside, it's especially important the angler be alert to any last-minute runs. The deckhands are at the ready with a long-handle net or gaffs—sometimes two are necessary for big yellowfin tuna—and as soon as the fish is within range they either net or gaff it. At this time it's critical that the angler just reel the fish close enough for the deckhands to handle. Sometimes in the excitement, anglers make the mistake of trying to lift the fish. A big fish thrashing at boatside can often result in a line break. Stay calm, reel the fish within range, and let the deckhands show their skill. It's much easier for a fish to be gaffed or netted when it is a foot or so beneath the surface, and not thrashing on the surface, or with its head lifted from the water. As the fish is brought aboard, place your reel in free spool or open the bail on a spinning reel so the mate can move away from the rail and other anglers as he unhooks your fish.

Skills come with experience

Party-boat regulars often become extremely proficient and their skills are on a par with the best of guides, mates and charter skippers. This doesn't just happen. It's a dedication to the sport, learning the fundamentals and then honing the techniques to perfection. It's not at all unusual to see veteran anglers aboard the packets consistently catching more and bigger fish than other anglers. This should never be construed as luck, although occasionally it may be. More often it is an understanding of the species sought, its feeding habits, the weather conditions, speed of drift, current, water clarity and a host of other factors.

It's often the little things that count. On a summer morning with a lazy drift all of the anglers on board may be catching summer flounders while using a 4-ounce sinker to hold bottom. As afternoon winds develop velocity, the boat drifts faster and at times it may take a full 16 ounces of sinker weight to keep a rig on the bottom. Those anglers who respond by changing weights continue to score, while those who maintain their 4-ounce sinkers actually have their baits drifting at mid-level, well above the active bottom feeders.

Always keep a fresh bait on your hook. Keep the hooks sharp. Use light-weight or fluorocarbon leaders that are less visible to fish. Tie the correct knots and, above all, be alert. These are just a few little suggestions that collectively can make a big difference.

Costs vary

It's difficult to identify the exact cost you should pay for a party packet. Generally, the closer to shore that you fish, and the shorter duration, the lower the cost. Many of the half-day packets that bottom fish close to port charge less. Costs are a bit more if chum is used. The three-quarter-day boats move up in proportion to the hours fished, while the full-day fare is the most costly. For night trips the same applies, depending on duration and distance to the grounds.

As you move into specialized fishing, such as the 24-hour trips to far offshore wrecks and reefs, and trips to the Northeast canyons, Dry Tortugas and the Coronados, the fare schedule moves up substantially. For two-day trips, such as those targeting tuna and other pelagic species in the Northeast canyons, the fares are also costly, as the boats often travel 100 miles seaward to locate fish. In some cases bunks are included, but it's always best to check this out before boarding. Likewise with tackle rental, as there is a charge on some boats for the heavier gear required for big game, although some provide it as part of the basic fare.

On really long-range trips, such as those leaving San Diego, Newport Beach and other California ports to fish off Mexico, it's all a matter of the boat and its accommodations, whether or not meals and bunks are included, and the length of the stay. While initially the fare may seem costly, it's really quite economical when you consider that the same trip on a charter boat would cost much more. Considering the camaraderie, potential for great gamefish, and the prospects of bringing home great table fare, these long-range trips are certainly worthy of consideration.

Spots are guarded

With increased fishing pressure on all three coasts, party boat skippers must continually work hard to find fish for their patrons. Often, this means finding spots not fished by others. Frequently, these spots, such as wrecks, reefs and rocks and ridges, are reported from commercial fishermen who get their nets fouled in the bottom obstructions. Party boat skippers will reward finders of such locations with sizable cash payments, for this expands their fishing opportunities and results in more enjoyment for their anglers. The captains are very secretive about the spots, as they are indeed investments.

In recent years there has been piracy of some spots. People have used electronic equipment, such as handheld global positioning system (GPS) units, and recorded the locations when they were on the fishing grounds, much to the consternation of the captains. As a result, some captains will not permit portable GPS units or other electronic monitoring gear to be carried aboard by passengers.

While no captain lays claim to any spot, as the oceans are available to anyone to enjoy, they feel very strongly when people try to take advantage of them. This is particularly true of captains who use their off-season time or slow days to run many miles seaward as they methodically monitor their electronics to search for bottom conformations and wrecks that may hold a bonanza catch.

"The captains are very secretive about the spots, as they are indeed investments."

Gratuities appropriate for good crew

Aboard many party boats the crew members are paid on a per-diem basis. Their wages are fair and they depend in part on gratuities from passengers for services rendered. The question is often posed as to when should you tip. Use the same judgment you might render when at a restaurant. If the service is great, the food served piping hot, the table cleared promptly and any requests promptly accommodated, then your meal is thoroughly enjoyed and a 10 to 15 percent tip is in order.

If, however, you board a packet in the morning and the deckhand is sitting there reading a newspaper instead of helping you with your gear and throughout the day he's not helpful in removing the hook from a deeply hooked fish, or isn't interested in cleaning your catch, then it's certainly appropriate not to tip. Also, be leery of the deckhand who is more interested in catching fish for the market, instead of being concerned with your welfare.

If, on the other hand, he greets you with a smile, gets you set at a spot, keeps your bait container filled, is immediately at hand to net or gaff your fish, and gets them into the cooler or on ice, and back at dockside does a professional job of cleaning your catch, then certainly a little extra consideration is in order.

Party boat anglers catch everything from giant bluefin tuna and the marlins, to 1-pound bottom feeders. They catch them trolling, drifting, chumming, bottom fishing, jigging and casting and employ a wide variety of techniques within these disciplines. You are well served by reviewing these techniques periodically, for to master them all is a lifetime challenge.

Rental boats great for more experienced anglers

There are many anglers who enjoy fishing from boats, but who find charter fishing expensive, and party boats crowded. They also can't afford the investment or time required to own their own boat. For them, rental boats are the perfect option, and many saltwater anglers travel about the coasts using rental boats and enjoying superb fishing. Some do this through many years of fishing, content to do their own thing, and getting great satisfaction as a result.

Rental boats aren't available everywhere. If you search for them, however, you're usually able to find them in areas where the fishing is good. Some of the rentals do the bulk of their business with tourists interested in just taking a boat ride, but others cater specifically to fishermen.

The key is familiarizing yourself with an area and knowing just where the rental liveries are located and, as with chartering, discussing with the livery operator the rental rates, duration of the trip, whether fuel is extra, and if insurance is provided or is an extra cost.

Once anglers get into renting, they pretty much follow a ritual whereby they become familiar with the rental stations wherever they plan to visit and fish and, as with chartering, they often call ahead to reserve a boat and motor. Some liveries have boats where you're afforded the opportunity to use your own outboard motor, while others provide both boat and motor. Almost all rental liveries will take advance reservations, enabling an angler to bill his personal credit card and ensure that a boat will be ready to go when he arrives at dockside.

Renting a boat requires a bit more involvement on the part of the angler. First, you need to know basic navigation and be familiar with the area you plan to fish. You'll also need your own equipment, terminal tackle, and bait. Once you get used to it the whole procedure is rather easy. The difference aboard charter, party boats and your own craft is that usually everything is already on board. With a rental boat you've got to bring everything. Many rental boat devotees use a written checklist with each item needed for a day's fishing so that nothing is left to chance. It is maddening to be on the fishing grounds and realize you don't have a supply of jigs on hand, or sinkers that are of insufficient weight.

Unlike charter and party boats that sail both day and night, rental-boat hours are usually daylight only, with a specific time that you must return to dockside. Failure to return to dockside on time, which is a safety consideration, as many of the rental boats aren't equipped for night navigation, can result in an overtime charge. It may also result in being ticketed by marine police, the Coast Guard or conservation officers for not having proper navigational lights. So return on time.

Rental boats are available along many sections of sea coast, where anglers are able to fish the protected waters of bays and rivers for a wide variety of saltwater species. Here, Greg Hall and Al Ristori prepare to embark on a day of flounder fishing from an outboard-powered rental rowboat.

Private boat ownership is a big step

Most saltwater fisherman have fished from the types of boats just described. Most often it's been part of a learning process. Sometimes along the way an attraction to boats develops. It may be that you just want to do everything on your own. Other times it begins by taking in a boat show, where hundreds of boats from tiny prams to 70-foot long sportfishing craft are on display. Buying a boat begins to sound like a great idea, but what boat to buy?

It's a big undertaking, for the boat often represents a substantial financial investment, and it requires expanding your navigational skills. There must also be a commitment, for time and energy are essential in maintaining a boat throughout the year.

Anglers who fish from private small boats often keep them at marinas located in metropolitan areas. The scene here is the East River, with Manhattan and the Empire State Building as a backdrop. The river supports a large population of striped bass and bluefish. It is not uncommon to see many private boats, charter boats, and party boats enjoying the fine fishing.

Trailer boats are a good beginning

Anglers often move from charter and guide boats, to party and rental boats, before ultimately deciding on a boat of their own. This, too, is often an evolutionary process, and most boatmen will readily admit that they began small, and gradually moved up, often to begin moving back down in size as they got older.

Most boatmen begin with craft in the 20- to 26-foot range as a starter boat. Boats of this size are easily trailered, which makes them very practical. First of all, they can be kept alongside the house, where you can do routine care and maintenance without having the expense of dockage at a coastal marina. With this size boat, you're also not limited to sailing from one location all of the time.

Care should be taken to determine exactly what you want in a boat, and not to be taken in by the salesmen you're bound to run into at boat shows. Often those economical center consoles sound like just the boat, only to result in disappointment as you're rained upon, blown upon, baked in the sun and frozen in the cold. Nor is there comfort for the family without a cabin nor bathroom facilities. All of these things should be taken into account before you make a decision.

My first starter boat was a 24-foot Wellcraft deep-V Airslot hull with sponsons, making it an extremely seaworthy and stable craft. It was the first boat to carry the name "Linda June" for daughter, Linda, and wife, June. It had twin 120-horsepower Mercruiser sterndrives, and a 120-gallon fuel tank, with a speed of over 25 knots that got you to and from the fishing grounds with ease. Twin engines, either sterndrives, inboards or outboards, make for a comfort level on saltwater. Often, you're traveling long distances, and if one engine has problems, you still have an engine to get home with.

A boat of this size, when equipped with either a hard top or Bimini top and side curtains, makes it comfortable with up to four people on an extended trip, or six anglers for inshore fishing. The V-bunks and head in the cabin offered comfort and protection, which are essential for a family boat. The walkaround feature of the boat also made it a comfortable boat to fish from.

The 20- to 26-foot catamaran hulls introduced in recent years are excellent starter boats and making an ideal configuration for either protected water angling in bays and rivers, or extending seaward for offshore ventures.

The author and his family spent many years fishing from rental rowboats. Here the author unhooks a nice summer flounder while son Bob, age 5, looks on. You'll find many rowboat rental liveries along the sea coast, and with a 9.5-horsepower outboard to take you to the grounds, you can post many fine catches of tasty bottom feeders.

A day boat should provide comfort and range

The second "Linda June," which arrived as the Rosko family grew, was an ideal day boat. It could be used for far offshore canyon runs of 100 miles or more, yet proved practical for inshore fishing as well. It was a 33-foot long Bertram sport-fisherman, powered by 3208 Caterpillar diesels that reached a top end of 30 knots. She carried 300 gallons of diesel and had great range. The boat had amenities that made for comfort on the water regardless of the season, including a generator, air conditioning and heat, sleeping accommodations for four, a dinette, refrigerator, oven and range, full head with shower, and hot and cold running water.

A boat in the 26- through 40-foot range can comfortably handle six people. Even on overnight trips to the canyons they offer the amenities that make for creature comfort. The beamy, deep-V or semi-V hulls and the new, bigger, catamaran hulls are excellent choices that enable anglers to cruise many miles from their home port.

Luxury sportfisherman a floating home

The most recent boat to carry the "Linda June" name was a Post 43, with all of the amenities of a home, including a galley, refrigerator and ice maker, a pair of colored televisions, microwave, electric range and oven, sleeping for six, heat and air conditioning. Powered by 671 turbocharged Detroit Diesels, the boat moved along at a respectable top end of 30 knots, and carried 550 gallons of fuel and 120 gallons of fresh water.

A boat this size is unwieldy for fishing in bays and rivers, and an auxiliary craft makes for family fun when you don't care to use the big boat. For us, a 17.5-foot Seaswirl bow rider powered with a 115-horsepower Johnson outboard motor, affectionately called the "Baby Linda June," handles most protected water fishing situations nicely, and can comfortably fish four. Its windshield and Bimini offer protection from sun, wind, and spray.

Even while owning these boats over the last 25 years, it was not unusual for our family to fish aboard party, charter, and guides boats at different locales. It is all part of the complete fishing experience, where relaxation and enjoyment are the key.

Many boatmen now have either laptop computers or personal computers aboard their boats. When the computers are interfaced with other electronics, a boatman can observe NOAA charts that clearly identify his vessel with a satellite photograph also shown for added perspective.

Safety must always be primary concern

With all of these boats, properly equipping them was of paramount importance. Safety should be the first concern. Today, the electronics available to boat owners are more reasonable in price than at any time. Modern technology has resulted in miniaturization and capabilities that weren't even dreamed possible just a few years ago.

Handheld VHF radios are economical and enable people to communicate within a limited range from even the smallest craft. Many boatmen have a fixed-station VHF on board, which when rigged with the proper antenna can be useful up to about 25 miles. Handheld radios often serve as a backup. If you plan to fish beyond 25 miles it's a good idea to purchase a single-side band radio that enables you to communicate worldwide.

Along many areas of our seacoast, cell phones can be effective for varying distances at sea. Each area is different and it's necessary to investigate before you decide to use a cell phone as your primary means of communication.

For many years Loran, long-range aid to navigation, was the standard for navigating long distances over open water and finding even a small wreck 100 miles out at sea. While Loran continues to be used by many boatmen and serves them well, new GPS, Global Positioning System units that employ satellites offer navigational possibilities that could, if you wish, program your boat to leave your dock, maneuver through inshore waters and channels, and head out coastal inlets to a selected spot many miles at sea without the driver ever touching the helm.

GPS units coupled with autopilot and programmable plotters and computerized chart systems, such as Maptech, display National Oceanic and Atmospheric Administration charts and satellite photos side by side, with your boat shown as it navigates through a specific waterway. The technology is also of great value in locating specific fishing areas, wrecks, ridges and canyons.

Radar may be interfaced with plotters so that, even in the thickest fog, with vessels and obstructions surrounding you, it is possible to navigate. Radar units are now available and used by many anglers with boats in the 20-foot class, giving them a safety device never before available.

Fishfinders aid in finding fish and may be interfaced with other electronics units, such as sea temperature and speed gauges, to allow a boat to go trolling and eventually return to the spot where fish were originally located. They are now almost standard issue for the well-equipped boat fisherman.

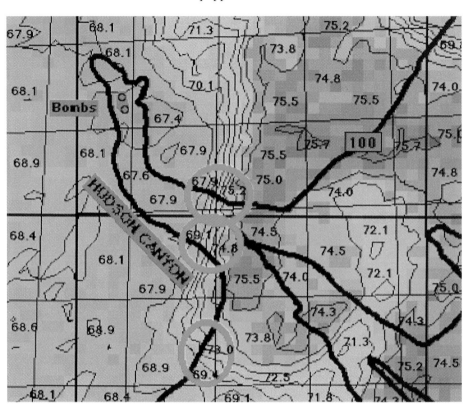

Offshore Satellite Services provides detailed ocean temperature fishing charts such as this to sportfishermen heading for the offshore grounds. The charts clearly identify major temperature breaks, such as those circled, where baitfish and gamefish congregate. These charts are downloaded from polar orbiting satellites, calibrated, and transmitted to onboard computers of sportfishing vessels. The boats can then sail directly to choice locations.

Satellites provide surface water temperatures

Surface sea water temperature also plays an important role in offshore fishing. Where there is a pronounced temperature break there are often huge schools of forage, with the food source finding a temperature to its liking, and being pushed along the edge of the temperature break to avoid the cold adjoining water.

Satellites are able to read surface temperatures as accurately as if there were a thermometer right in the water. This enables offshore fishermen to zero in on potentially good fishing locations, without the trial and error of covering miles of ocean.

Back in 1984 Len Belcaro founded Offshore Satellite Services, which captured temperature data from NOAA polar orbiting satellites and began to provide offshore fishermen with Ocean Temperature Fishing Charts.

The data now provided to party, charter, and private boat owners has the highest resolution obtainable to ensure the most detailed temperature-specific contouring possible. A calibration procedure is implemented on every satellite image for position accuracy. This assures captains that if a potential hot spot is indicated along a temperature break on the charts, it is indeed in that position, for often a vessel may travel 100 miles or more to reach it.

Computer technology enables captains to download color-enhanced temperature charts from a Web site at their leisure and receive updated data with each satellite pass.

Miniaturization of electronics a great advance for small boats

All of the preceding electronic units fit and can be comfortably grouped and integrated on boats as small as the first "Linda June." Add computer capability and cell-phone communications, and the small boat angler of today has great technology available.

My single most important suggestion to a newcomer to boating is this: Take the time and plan a total electronics package for your boat. Many units are integrated, with a single unit performing the functions of what had heretofore been three, four, or more units. Planning is critical, however, so that all of the electronics equipment is compatible and works in concert. Many of the major manufacturers today offer simulators at boat shows that display their equipment in an on-the-boat setting. You will be well served to take the time to study and experiment on the simulators before making any purchasing decision.

Complete equipment package enhances opportunities

Although the electronics play an important role, there are certain pieces of fishing equipment, other than the basic tackle, that will improve your angling opportunities.

Outriggers are an essential tool, whether probing inshore waters along the kelp beds, or trolling many miles at sea in the offshore canyons. Tailored to the size of a particular boat, the outriggers enable you to present a spread of lures or baits in a manner that will result in more strikes than if those same lures or baits were trolled directly astern.

Downriggers are a piece of equipment that enables you to get your lures and baits to depths not otherwise possible. All this is possible using relatively light tackle that enables you to enjoy the excitement of fighting a big salmon or bluefish unencumbered by wire line or heavy trolling rigs.

A fighting chair, or pair of fighting chairs, is another piece of equipment that will add to your angling pleasure and the functionality of the boat. Not only does the chair provide a good vantage point to watch over a spread of baits while trolling, but it makes for a comfortable platform from which to fight a fish—a special consideration for women and youngsters, especially when using light tackle.

Tuna towers are appropriate on many of the larger craft. They enable a person to station themself high above the water and see a broad view of the ocean all around the boat. This enables the helmsman in the tower to spot rips and eddies, surface-feeding fish, schools of bait, weed lines and color breaks that might not be viewed from water level or a flying bridge helm station.

Live wells are still another popular piece of equipment. A circulating pump keeps a supply of sea water running through the well and keeps fish alive for use as chum or bait when the fishing grounds are reached.

OFFSHORE FISHING

The saltwater angler who longs to head for the horizon will find offshore fishing a fulfilling adventure. Offshore fishing in a broad sense begins along the edge of the 30-fathom line along our coasts, where many pelagic species congregate. For the most part, however, offshore fishing involves travelling, often 100 miles or more, to the waters of the continental shelf, or the canyons etched into the bottom, that are the favored haunts of the world's pelagic gamefish.

With the tackle and equipment pictured here you're ready for almost any offshore fish, with the exception of giant blue marlin, bluefin tuna and sharks. The basic outfit consists of a 30- to 50-pound class stand-up rod and reel, with 50-pound-test monofilament line. The shoulder harness and fighting belt give support when fighting fish, and the Boga Grip makes releasing easy. The Lurebox includes an assortment of 40 offshore trolling lures in five trays.

To reach most of the haunts of pelagic gamefish means embarking on a trip lasting several hours. Water temperatures, currents, and world climatic conditions play key roles in the movements of the fish, and occasionally big gamefish can be found close to shore. More often that not, though, anglers must be willing to set sail.

Off the coast of California, the long-range boats often sail to the far-off waters of Mexico to find concentrations of gamefish. Gulf anglers travel great distances to leave the green-colored inshore waters and find the distinct demarcation where the water takes on the cobalt blue coloration, and its accompanying warm temperatures so favored by pelagic species. On the Atlantic Coast, anglers sailing from New England, Long Island, and Jersey ports sail to the canyons 75 to 100 miles offshore. Those who sail from Oregon and Hatteras Inlets in North Carolina have shorter trips as the Gulf Stream here comes within 20 miles of shore, carrying with it huge quantities of forage and the game pelagic species seeking it. Off the Florida coast anglers fishing out of Stuart need only sail 7 to 10 miles to find their quarry. The same is also true throughout the Keys, but only on the Atlantic side. Fishing the Gulf side often entails a 75-mile or greater trip to find the right combination of water coloration and temperature.

(Left) Bluefin tuna are extremely strong and fast. This school bluefin brought aboard by Jim Cary was hooked on a whole whiting fished on 50-pound-class tackle by the author 45 miles southeast of Montauk Point, Long Island.

It is said eternal vigilance is the price you must pay to hook a marlin. June Rosko sits patiently on the covering board as she watches the skipping baits. Often a marlin will spend up to 15 minutes in the baits, excitedly moving from bait to bait.

Many formidable species await offshore anglers

The primary targets of offshore fishermen are the tunas and billfish, although many other species are frequently encountered, some by design and others by accident.

The broadbill swordfish roams the waters of the world and is thought by many to be the ultimate conquest of the serious offshore angler. Growing to more than 1,000 pounds, it presents a great challenge. Its population is limited and enticing it to strike requires a perfect presentation and keen skill on the part of the angler. When hooked, the species usually lives up to its "gladiator" nickname.

The blue marlin is found off all three of our coasts and Hawaii and represents a formidable challenge to boatmen. The white marlin, its smaller cousin, is the light-tackle darling of the Atlantic and Gulf coast anglers who visit offshore waters. Striped marlin frequent the waters of southern California and provide sterling sport. The spearfish is still another exciting billfish. It often comes as a surprise because it is scarcest of all billfish and a trophy few ever have an opportunity to catch.

The Atlantic sailfish is caught in both the Atlantic and Gulf, while the Pacific sailfish is found in the ocean carrying its name. They are perhaps the most plentiful of billfish, and afford boatmen with exciting sport, particularly on light tackle. When attracted to trolled lures or baits they "light up," taking on beautiful coloration as they zero in on their quarry. This characteristic is typical of all billfish, which provide anglers with plenty of excitement as they move into a spread of lures or baits.

The tuna clan includes many varieties: Atlantic bluefin, bigeye, yellowfin, albacore and little tunny. The Atlantic bluefin tuna is thought by many to be the most powerful fish caught along the Atlantic and Gulf coasts. Occasionally reaching a weight of more than 1,000 pounds, the bluefin is a strong, determined adversary, often requiring several hours in a fighting chair to bring to boat, while using heavy tackle. Somewhat smaller, but equally strong, are the bluefin tuna of the Pacific, bigeye and yellowfin tuna, each of which occasionally reach 300 pounds and which are caught off all three coasts. The albacore, often called long-finned albacore because of its extremely long pectoral fin, grow to just shy of 100 pounds, and are also found off all three U.S. coasts.

The little tunny, as its name implies, is the smallest of the tunas. Many feel that pound for pound it is the strongest, fastest tuna in the sea. Growing to upwards of 20 pounds, it is ideally suited to light tackle fishing, including trolling, chumming and casting.

The wahoo is still another great gladiator found on the offshore grounds. Growing to more than 100 pounds, the wahoo has distinctive markings not unlike that of the marlins, yet possesses a unique jaw. Unlike most fish that have their lower jaw hinged, the wahoo's upper jaw is hinged, and its mouth is lined with razor sharp teeth.

Judged by many to be the prettiest of the offshore species, the dolphin is a scrappy adversary that is often caught incidentally by anglers trolling or chumming for tuna and marlin. It grows to 75 pounds, but the offshore angler usually encounters those in the 15- to 40-pound range, which are considered a gourmet treat. A spectacular jumper, the dolphin frequents weed lines and floating debris, feeding on small fish that seek the sanctuary of floating objects. The dolphin fish should not be confused with the mammal of the same name, also known as the porpoise.

Offshore anglers encounter several other species that regularly assault baits and lures intended for bigger game. They include the oceanic bonito, found in all the waters of the world; the Atlantic bonito, found in both the Atlantic and Gulf waters; and the Pacific bonito. The king mackerel also crashes baits, and is noted for its spectacular aerial attacks.

Sharks are also encountered in the offshore waters, often traveling with the schools of pelagic species, on which many sharks feed. On occasion sharks will strike lures trolled for marlin and tuna, but most often they are caught via chumming.

The mako shark in many respects looks and acts much like the broadbill swordfish, sans bill. Noted for its spectacular leaps and breathtaking speed, it will test an angler's skill to the utmost. The hammerhead shark is also regularly encountered on the offshore grounds and is an extremely strong adversary. Far-offshore fisherman may also encounter the thresher shark, noted for its extremely long tail, and the tiger shark, an awesome member of the shark clan that is vicious when coaxed into a chum line.

Billfish are the premier catch of offshore anglers. Noted for their aerial tactics, billfish jump repeatedly when hooked and test an angler's skill to the limit. This sailfish's exciting tail walking is typical of what you experience on offshore rounds.

Boats target pelagic species far from shore

While the techniques required to regularly catch inshore species in waters close to shore may often be learned on a catch-as-catch-can basis, it's really difficult to take the same approach when seeking big-game species.

An element of safety enters the equation when offshore trolling. Not only do you need an extremely seaworthy boat, but all the skills of seamanship come into play, as do the skills required to rig tackle, baits and lures, and present them properly. It is also crucial that, when a big game fish is hooked, anglers know how to handle it properly to boat or release it safely. All of these skills are acquired over a period of time, and an angler should be cautious before proceeding on his own without a good foundation.

Charter boats ideal as a learning experience

Charter boats are without question the perfect venue for newcomers to the offshore fishing experience. Charter boats are run by seasoned, highly skilled captains who are licensed by the U. S. Coast Guard and face strict safety requirements. An angler fishing aboard a charter boat obtains the immediate benefit of the huge investment in not only the boat, but the years of on-the-water fishing experience of the captain and crew and myriad fishing tackle and equipment necessary to pursue big-game species. Thus, for a fixed charter fee, an angler can learn and fish in a relaxed atmosphere and return with skills and knowledge that may have taken the captain and crew years to develop.

Many accomplished anglers have used this approach and saved thousands of dollars and days of frustration before ultimately heading seaward aboard their own craft.

Party boats ideal for many offshore trips

Having developed their skills on charter boats, many anglers often book passage on long-range party boats that specialize in big-game offshore fishing. Most party boats of this type fish the offshore grounds for several days, or even a week, at a time, using both trolling and chumming techniques. Many party boat owners have their crew hold seminars on the long, often slow, trip to the offshore grounds. The angler is given hands-on tutoring in how to tie knots, twist wire, set drags and other myriad details that will help them have a successful trip.

Private boat ownership is final step

Once you've managed to developed the skills of offshore fishing, either through fishing aboard a charter or party boat, or perhaps having sailed often with a friend, the ultimate experience is to step aboard a boat of your own. But even the smallest of offshore boats require a big commitment. Not only do you need the financial resources, but you've got to have the time to fully utilize the investment. Often anglers make hasty decisions about boat ownership, and suddenly they've got a great boat, wonderfully equipped, and just haven't got the time to fish.

Success on the offshore grounds requires active participation. As with any participant sport, whether it be golf, bowling, or tennis, in big-game fishing you've got to put in the time. Countless hours are required to develop the skills, rhythm, and comfort level that ultimately combine to produce exciting catches.

Most offshore boats designed to spend several days at sea are floating homes, with all of the comforts of home and then some. They range in size from about 20 feet up to 60- and even 70-footers, complete with diesel power and full electronics packages. It's not unusual for dedicated anglers to invest anywhere from $500,000 to $2 million or more on their boats and equipment.

There are areas where anglers fishing from 24- to 33-foot craft can feel reasonably safe. This is particularly the case with the new, high-performance twin outboard or stern-drive engines, which are designed expressly for offshore game fishing. Great numbers of the smaller boats are utilized to seek big game fish in such places as the Carolina Outer Banks, the east coast of Florida, and the Florida Keys

For far offshore runs to the canyons and the edge of the continental shelf, a boat such as the "Linda June" makes for a comfortable trip. The craft carries sufficient fuel for trips of more than 200 miles at sea and has all the comforts of home for trips lasting several days. Boats of this type have a top-end speed of about 30 knots.

on the Atlantic side.

From time to time individuals permit emotions to prevail over common sense, with disastrous consequences. Of all the types of fishing discussed in these pages, offshore sport fishing presents perhaps the greatest potential for danger. Even with big boats, accidents can and do happen. With small boats, heavy seas can be frightening at best. Let reason prevail and safety be your paramount concern when heading seaward.

Tackle should fit species

Offshore fishing tackle falls into three general categories:

Heavy tackle is employed when seeking the giant bluefin tuna, broadbill swordfish, blue marlin and the truly great sharks. This consists of 130-pound- and 80-pound-class tackle. The 130- and 80-pound outfits are matched as a total unit. The 130-pound-class reel holding approximately 950 yards of line with a breaking test of 130-pounds. The 80-pound reel holds approximately 950 yards of 80-pound-test monofilament or Dacron line.

These outfits usually require sitting in a big game fighting chair with a bucket harness snapped to the reel's harness lugs. This enables the angler to use their back and legs and not just their arms during battles that can last several hours.

Medium tackle consists primarily of 50- and 30-pound-class outfits, with the reels holding 850 yards of 50-pound-test line and 900 yards of 30-pound test, respectively. This is the workhorse tackle of the offshore angler, capable of handling a wide variety of species. Some anglers use it in lieu of heavy tackle, but this can test angler and boat crew to the limit, especially when encountering gamefish in excess of 500 pounds. Medium tackle is ideally suited to bigeye and yellowfin tuna up to 300 pounds. It's fine for white and striped marlin, medium-weight sharks, bluefin tuna up to 300 pounds and big wahoo and dolphin.

Medium-weight tackle is usually used while standing up, although some anglers find it more comfortable to fight their quarry from a fighting chair. Most anglers wear a gimbal fighting belt and a shoulder harness for stand-up fights. This unit distributes the pressure across your back while holding the rod securely in the belt and enabling you to relax arm pressure while fighting a fish for prolonged periods.

Light tackle includes 20- and 12-pound outfits with reels holding 750 and 850 yards of 12-pound-test monofilament or Dacron line, respectively. These outfits are ideally suited to both Atlantic and Pacific sailfish. They also work well for school bluefin tuna up to 50 pounds, yellowfin tuna and albacore of the same weight. The outfits also serve yeoman duty when school dolphin, king mackerel, bonito, and little tunny are plentiful. Because the fish are smaller and usually require less time to land, anglers most often use a lightweight gimbal belt in lieu of a harness. The belt's gimbal holds the rod securely and in an upright position and helps prevent stomach bruising.

There are several major manufacturers and many customer builders of basic tackle outfits. Understandably, the mass-produced reels and rods are cheaper than the custom models. Either way, offshore big-game tackle must perform to perfection, for the slightest flaw, such as a broken roller tip or irregular drag, may result in the loss of a great game fish that you have been waiting hours or even days to hook. The bigger the fish, the more important the tackle.

Throw-lever reels universally favored

Over the last half century big-game reels have evolved into precision instruments designed to subdue the strongest fish in the sea. The high-end reels today are built around machined, one-piece, aluminum frames and spools that are anodized and corrosion resistant. Tempered stainless steel gear systems perform flawlessly. Many of the reels have a two-speed system that lets anglers change gears while fighting a fish. The push of a button enables you to retrieve at a fast rate of speed, and another push shifts down for maximum power.

The throw-lever drag system enables you to conveniently disengage the reel spool and, with a forward push of the lever, to set it to a previously determined tension, or drag pressure. This tension ranges from minimal, called "strike" drag, to maximum, or "full" drag where the setting is just below the maximum for the line being used. Veteran anglers often use hand-held spring scales to check the drags, making adjustments so that all reels used in a trolling pattern have the exact same setting.

Little things like a loud, audible, click are important on a big game reel. The click must send a signal over the loud noise of the engines when a strike is received while trolling. State-of-the-art reels have handles designed to minimize fatigue and maximize leverage when fighting a big fish for several hours. The reel should be equipped with a heavy-duty clamp to hold it securely to the rod. Stainless steel harness lugs, which hold the snaps of a fighting harness or a shoulder harness in the case of the stand-up models, are important too.

Graphite, fiberglass and composites are best rod materials

Rods designed for use with 130- and 80-pound-class reels are truly amazing pieces of craftsmanship. The high-end rods are built around a blank constructed of high-content graphite composite, giving them fast recovery when pumping a fish, and importantly, the lifting power to budge hundreds of pounds from the ocean's depths.

The rods measure from 7 feet 4 inches to 7 feet 8 inches in length. The rod tip is equipped with a roller tip top and five roller guides, that evenly distribute the strain across the length of the rod.

The butt section of the rod is made of machined aluminum and attaches to the tip with a ferrule that locks into place, making a secure fit that won't move, twist or vibrate when fighting a fish.

Where the butt and tip meet, the tip section is equipped with a long, cushioned, comfortable foregrip. This eases strain on the hands when pumping fish for prolonged periods.

Most of the heavy tackle rods are built with curved bent butts. This design enables an angler in the fighting chair to effectively and effortless use a bucket harness to exert maximum lifting pressure when fighting a fish.

Medium-weight rods rated for 50- and 30-pound-class tackle are used primarily for trolling and the majority are built with straight butts.

For those anglers who prefer to fight their quarry standing up, there is a classification of "stand-up" rod, balanced to 50- 30- and 20-pound-class tackle. These rods are shorter than those used for trolling and measure 5 1/2 feet in length. They have shorter butts that position the reel lower than for rods used from a fighting chair. Stand-up rods may be used for trolling and chumming and enable an angler who is standing and fighting with a rod belt to exert tremendous pressure on a fish. The most advanced models are about half as heavy as regular trolling rods and are made with one-piece construction techniques with lightweight cushioned foregrips and butts.

The 20-pound and 12-pound light-tackle category employs both the conventional trolling models and the stand-up models. Design-wise they are comparable to medium-tackle rods, with their tips and components proportionally lighter.

Dacron and monofilament lines dominate offshore scene

Dacron and monofilament lines are favored by offshore anglers. Recently developed microfilament lines made of Spectra fiber with much finer diameter have also grown in popularity in some locales.

Choice of a line is an important consideration. In order to qualify for recognition as a world-record catch, the line must test within the parameters as identified by the International Game Fish Association. The categories include 130-, 80-, 50-, 30-, 20- and 12-pound test. A line may test anywhere up to, but not over, its designated line-breaking test for a world record to be certified. Economy lines occasionally test over in controlled tests, and thus have on numerous occasions disqualified a catch for world record status. Top-end lines by reputable manufacturers often carry a designation that they conform to IGFA standards.

Dacron generally stretches less than most monofilament lines. This helps in setting a hook, as there is minimal elasticity. However, this can work as a disadvantage, for Dacron is less forgiving.

Many anglers fill their reels with Dacron, but splice in several hundred feet of monofilament at the terminal end of the line. This allows for a margin of error, as a result of increased forgiveness in the line, when struggling to get a fish up to the boat.

Because the thin diameter of Dacron line may occasionally cause it to dig through the line on a reel and cause a line break, there are companies that have developed "flat Dacron." This variety of line is especially popular in 130-pound class, where drag pressure of 40 to 50 pounds is often employed.

"The microfilament lines can be extremely effective, but they take time and patience to master."

California yellowtail have a profile that enables them to move through the water with lightning speed. Many are caught offshore by anglers trolling lures. They often invade the kelp beds where they're coaxed into aggressive feeding with live anchovies as chum.

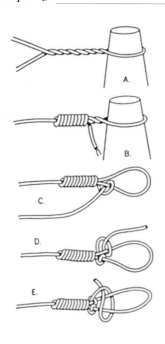

Bimini twist

The Bimini twist is excellent for doubling the terminal end of the line without weakening it appreciably.

A. Allow yourself as much line as you wish to double back, and place the looped end around some fixed object such as a cleat or reel handle. Take around six turns to the line, keeping tension on the line and the turns tight.

B. While holding the coils tight with your hand, wrap the free line over the first twists. Keep the coils close together and use as many as you need until you come up to the "V" of the loop. In making a long double line, you would have to pull the "V" up toward the end where the line was being twisted.

C. While still holding the twisted line tight with your thumb and forefinger, take a half hitch around one side of the loop and pull it up tight.

D. Next take a half hitch around the other side of the loop and pull it up tight.

E. Finish off the Bimini twist by taking a half hitch around the base of the loop and clip off any excess line.

Uni-knot

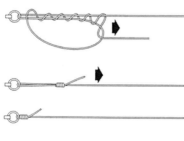

The uni-knot is a versatile, strong knot that is used primarily to attach the line to leader or hook, or a leader to a swivel or snap.

Begin by running at least 6 inches of line through the eye of the hook or swivel, and fold to make two parallel lines. Bring the tag end of the line back in a circle toward the hook or swivel.

Make six turns with the tag end around the double line and through the circle. Hold the double line at the point where it passes through the eye and pull the tag end to snug up the turns.

To create a loop connection, adjust the loop size by sliding the knot up or down the standing line. Then pull the tag end with pliers to tighten.

To create a snugged knot, pull the standing line to slide the knot up against the eye. Then continue pulling until the knot is tight.

Trim the tag end flush with the closest coil on the knot.

Surgeon's knot

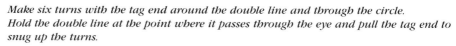
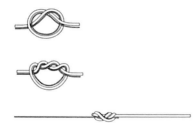

The surgeon's knot is an extremely easy knot to tie and perhaps most useful when tying two lines or pieces of leader material that are of different diameter.

Lay the line and leader alongside each other, overlapping 6 to 8 inches.

Treating the two like a single line, tie an overhand knot, pulling the entire leader through the loop.

Leaving the loop of the overhand knot open, pull the tag ends of both the line and leader through again.

Hold both lines and both ends to pull the knot tight. Clip the tag ends with a nail clipper so they can flow through the rod guides with ease.

Haywire twist

The key in making the haywire twist with a piece of stainless steel leader wire is beginning with a well formed loop held between the thumb and index finger. Next you take the thumb and index finger of your other hand and evenly twist the wire around itself at least three or four times. The next step is to make three or four turns with the short end of the wire neatly around the standing part of the leader wire. Complete the haywire twist by making a small handle in the tag end of the line by bending it 90 degrees, and then use the handle to bend the wire back and forth until it snaps off cleanly. Always break the wire clean and never cut it off with pliers. A sharp burr results no matter how close you cut with pliers, which could rip your hands and fingers.

Microfilament lines of Spectra fiber have extremely fine diameter and practically no stretch. This enables you to load a much greater quantity of line on a reel than with ordinary Dacron or monofilament. These lines have increased in popularity, particularly among the southern California party boat fleet, where huge 300-pound yellowfin tuna are regularly encountered on stand-up tackle.

There are ports, however, where Spectra fiber lines are prohibited aboard party boats, for their fine diameter will literally cut through Dacron and monofilament lines if two anglers get tangled up. The angler with Dacron or mono immediately becomes a loser. The extremely fine diameter of the microfilament lines can also lead to horrible tangles, which in turn lead to frayed tempers. Check the rules before you board, so as to avoid a conflict.

The microfilament lines can be extremely effective, but they take time and patience to master.

Terminal tackle an important consideration

As a general rule, the terminal ends of lines used in offshore fishing are doubled. While this practice existed for years and was the only way to give that bit of extra strength at the terminal end, offshore fishermen have recently begun to use "wind-on" leaders made of a heavier test. Thus, we now have two options.

Line may be doubled using a Bimini knot at the terminal end, or a uni-knot or double surgeon's knot, all of which have excellent knot strength and retain a very high percentage of the original line test.

After the line has been doubled, an offshore swivel knot is employed to attach a combination ball-bearing swivel and coastlock snap to the double line. The coastlock snap makes changing lures attached to a leader an easy task.

If you're using Dacron line for a wind-on leader, you must splice a length of monofilament line approximately double the test of the Dacron into the core or center of the Dacron. When inserted into the narrow confines, no matter how much pressure you bring to bear, the monofilament line cannot be pulled out. At the terminal end of the heavier monofilament leader, a uni-knot or a crimped sleeve is used to attach a ball bearing swivel and coastlock snap. There are some anglers, however, who forego the swivel and snap combination and attach their lure or bait directly to the end of the leader.

Of course, if you use monofilament line, you cannot splice mono into mono. In that case, anglers use a short length of Dacron, going from your primary monofilament line to Dacron, then to the heavier mono as previously described.

The advantage of the wind-on leader is that it enables the angler to reel the fish in close and eliminate the dangerous practice of handling a long length of leader with a large, wild fish attached to it. The dangers involved in handling big fish at boatside are well documented, and lives have been lost when cockpit personnel have become entangled in leaders and dragged overboard. While wind-on leaders don't completely eliminate any potential danger, they go a long way towards minimizing it, and in time will no doubt completely replace the double-line combination.

The International Game Fish Association has rules that govern the various combinations of line, double line and leader for the purpose of world records. With increased usage of the combination wind-on leaders, these regulations may be modified from time to time. Thus, it is wise to obtain the latest copies of the rules and regulations to ensure compliance if you are entertaining thoughts of chasing a world record.

Lures vs. natural baits

The offshore fraternity is divided over whether a properly rigged natural bait or replica lure is the most effective way to hook the wide range of pelagic species found on the offshore grounds. This debate is likely to continue, as both natural baits and lures both bring strikes and regularly account for many fine catches. The key is to master the techniques in rigging and presenting so that your quarry is attracted to a spread of your offerings and ultimately chooses to strike one.

"It is wise to obtain the latest copies of the rules and regulations to ensure compliance if you are entertaining thoughts of chasing a world record."

These are three of the most popular natural baits employed by offshore trollers. The mullet, balao and mackerel are painstakingly rigged so they track straight when tossed about in the churning wake of an offshore sportfisherman. Many trollers toughen their baits in a brine solution. Fresh, properly treated baits are the key to success.

A large selection of natural baits available

The offshore angler has a large selection of natural baits at his disposal. Some may be caught right on the offshore grounds, while others may be cut directly from fish already landed. At major offshore fishing centers vacuum-bagged natural baits, such as mullet, mackerel, balao, flying fish, sardines and squid, are available in a variety of sizes, either rigged or unrigged. With the rigged baits it's simply a matter of opening a package and placing the completely rigged leader, hook and bait into the water. No mess, no fuss, and the vacuum-bagged baits have no freezer burn and are in perfect condition and hold up extremely well for trolling. Some offshore anglers prefer to obtain fresh baits such as squid, eels, mullet and other baits directly from the netters, and then brine them for a day in a heavy brine solution of half kosher salt and half freshwater. This hardens the baits and they hold up better than a bait that hasn't been conditioned. They are then rigged on the fishing grounds.

Leaders for natural baits can be made of single-strand stainless steel wire, braided stainless steel cable, monofilament and fluorocarbon, the latter having a refraction index that makes it nearly invisible in the water.

When fishing in waters where species with teeth are prevalent, such as wahoo, king mackerel and members of the shark family, most anglers prefer to use either stainless steel wire or cable leaders, both of which are hard for fish to bite through.

When using 130-pound-class tackle it's customary to use leaders testing out at 200 to 300 pounds. With the 30- or 50-pound-class tackle, leaders in the 100- to 150-pound range are more than adequate.

Single-strand stainless steel wire is among the most popular leader materials. It is relatively easy to handle once you've mastered the basic haywire twist for making loops and attaching hooks and lures. The haywire twist takes a bit of practice. The end of the wire is looped and held securely between the thumb and forefinger. With the other hand the wire is turned away from you, while simultaneously turning the wire towards you with your holding hand. This twists each strand around itself. This is repeated six to eight times and results in a very neat spread of twisted wire. To complete the haywire twist, the tag end of the wire is then neatly wrapped around the standing part of the leader for another 4 or 5 tight turns. Then the remaining tag end is bent at a 90-degree angle to form a handle. This tag-end handle is then bent back and forth until it neatly breaks close to the standing part of the leader, resulting in a neat, smooth loop. The loop end is then attached to the coastlock snap at the terminal end of your line, and another loop is formed at the terminal end of the leader to your hook or lure.

With stainless steel cable leader, sleeves are employed with a crimping tool to make loops that are attached to the coastlock snap, then the hook or hooks.

With monofilament and fluorocarbon line, crimped sleeves may also be used, although most anglers employ a double surgeon's knot, improved clinch knot or uni-knot, and make direct ties to their hooks or lures.

The majority of sailfish are hooked by trolling strip baits or live goggleyes or blue runners. The spectacular jumper being fought by the author was hooked from an outboard-powered center console boat just a couple of miles from shore. As with most hooked sailfish, it was quickly released at boatside.

Strip bait universally popular

A strip of bait cut from a fresh fish makes an attractive trolling bait for all pelagic species. Strips may be cut from the belly of a little tuna, skipjack bonito, dolphin or any member of the tuna family. The size of the bait is tailored to the targeted species. When marlin are being sought it's not unusual to use a strip 12 to 15 inches long and 3 inches thick. If dolphin, albacore, king mackerel, yellowfin and bluefin tuna are in the area you're fishing, a strip measuring 8 x 2 inches should be about right.

The head of the strip bait should be tapered, as should the tail. Some anglers split the tail section to make it flutter during trolling.

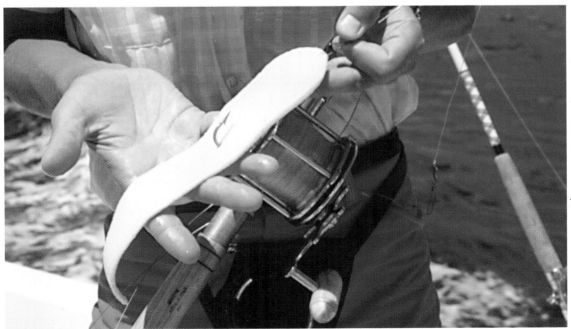

Strip baits are used by offshore trollers on the Atlantic, Pacific and Gulf Coasts. This strip bait is made of pork rind, cut to size and purchased with one bait to a jar. The pork is very tough and may be trolled all day without deteriorating.

Commercially packaged pork rind strips also are extremely effective and many offshore anglers keep a supply on board to tide them over when fresh baits aren't readily available. The pork rind strips are extremely tough and durable and may be trolled for an entire day and never deteriorate.

Strip baits are usually rigged on stainless steel leader wire. This is accomplished by passing approximately 6 inches of wire through the eye of the hook, then carefully making four or five turns of the wire, without overlapping it, around the shank of the hook. Finish the wraps so that the tag end of the wire is facing upright in relation to the eye of the hook and the hook's point.

Now make a 45-degree bend in the tag end of the wire approximately 1/2 inch from the shank of the hook, pointing the wire towards the leader ahead of the eye of the hook. Finally, where the tag end of the wire crosses the standing part of the leader, make a half turn onto the wire, giving it a safety-pin effect. Leave about a half inch of the tag end of the wire and cut off the remainder with pliers.

To complete rigging the strip bait, lay the rig flat and use an awl to make a small hole in the head of the bait. Open the safety-pin end of the wire and slip it through the hole in the head of the strip bait and then close it, which will securely hold the head of the strip to the wire. Finally, with the strip laying flat along the hook, use your knife point to cut a very small slit in the strip at the curve of the hook. Then slip the hook point through the cut in the strip bait and it's ready to troll. The leader of a strip bait rigged in this manner may be attached directly to a coastlock snap and trolled on the surface, where it slithers along enticingly. You may also add a trolling sinker to the coastlock snap, and then your leader and strip bait. This will cause the bait to work just beneath the surface in the boat's wake.

Baitfish are easy to rig

There are literally dozens of ways in which baitfish may be rigged. Each rigger adds his particular touch to the process. A newcomer would be wise to observe mates rigging baits on charter boats, or to purchase vacuum-bagged rigged baits, and then to copy the manner in which they're rigged.

You want to rig a baitfish on a hook so that it may be trolled without spinning. This is best accomplished by first attaching your hook directly to the end of your leader material. The hook is then placed into the baitfish's mouth, worked through the stomach cavity, and the point brought out in the belly of the fish, taking care that the hook's positioning doesn't cause the bait to curl. It should lay flat. A rigging needle and dental floss or waxed rigging twine is then run through the baitfish's lower jaw, through the eye of the hook, which is now located in the fish's mouth, and out the top of the head. The floss or twine is run through several times and then wrapped around the head of the baitfish three or four times and tied off securely. This results in a trim, smooth bait, with the hook held securely within. A fresh bait that has been cured in a salt brine to toughen it may be trolled for several hours without washing out. It must be noted that fresh bait is extremely important, for a bait that is soft will wash out and fall apart quickly.

Some anglers prefer to rig their baits by first placing the hook eye through a small slit cut in the fish's belly, and working the eye up into the mouth. Then an awl is inserted into the lower jaw, run through the hook eye and brought out the upper jaw. The awl is removed, and a piece of stainless steel leader wire is run through the hole in the lower jaw, through the hook eye and out the hole in the upper jaw. It is then looped back on the standing part of the leader and finished off with a haywire twist.

A variation of this rig involves putting an egg-shaped sinker onto the leader before it is inserted into the baitfish, with the final haywire twist holding the sinker securely under the jaw. This added weight helps keep the bait in the water and prevents it from skipping about excessively, which is important when rough seas are encountered. The rigging is completed by sewing the lips of the baitfish tightly shut with dental floss and securely tying off the gills with a few turns of dental floss.

Even this manner of rigging has a variation, as some riggers add a second hook by using a needle-eye primary hook and inserting it through the eye of a sec-

"There are many variations to rigging natural baits. Each rigger develops his own style."

ond hook that has been worked through the anal vent of the baitfish. This positions the primary hook just behind the head of the baitfish, and the second hook towards the tail. This method of rigging is especially popular in areas where wahoo and king mackerel are plentiful, as both of these species have a notorious habit of striking a bait in the midsection, often completely cutting off a single-hook bait just behind the hook. With the second hook, or "stinger" hook, the fish are invariably hooked.

With large baits, which tend to be stiff and less pliable than smaller ones, some trollers remove the backbone of the bait. This is accomplished with a deboner, a tool made expressly for this purpose. The deboner is simply a long, metal tube approximating the diameter of the backbone, with one edge sharpened so it will cut through the backbone. The deboner is inserted in the mouth of a baitfish and slid to the base of the spine, at which point it is turned and cuts around the spine. It is then carefully pushed while turning it around the spine, cutting as it goes, until you insert it to the desired length of backbone you wish to remove. Then, by bending the rear section of the bait somewhat, you continue to push and turn the deboner, cutting through the backbone. At this point the entire section of backbone remains within the deboner, and may simply be pulled back out of the fish. The backbone is then removed from the deboner with a wood dowel. Deboned baits are very flexible and can be rigged much the same as a solid bait. The difference being that, when trolled, the deboned bait will have more side-to-side movement.

Some anglers prefer to split the tails of their bait. With some baits, mullet in particular, this is easily accomplished by inserting an extremely sharp knife forward of the tail, and slicing rearward. Here too, when trolled, the bait has a more enticing action than a solid bait.

Another popular practice is to place a plastic skirt onto the leader and slip it down over the head of the bait after it has been rigged. The plastic skirt, and even feather trolling heads slipped ahead of the bait, work very effectively, and are available in most every color in the rainbow.

There are many variations to rigging natural baits. Each rigger develops his own style. Stick with a combination that works for you..

Trolling feathers or plastic-skirted trolling lures are often very effective when fished on the slope of the first or second wave of the wake. Many anglers use a combination such as this, with the trolling sinker aiding in keeping the lure just beneath the surface, and the ball-bearing swivel and coastlock snap allowing for an easy change of lures.

Some species attack a bait and neatly bite it in half just behind the head hook. This is true with wahoo, king mackerel and barracuda. To avoid a bite-off, many trollers employ a pair of hooks.

Countless lures available

There was a time when blue water trollers used only natural baits. As anglers began experimenting they found that lures could be fashioned to resemble natural baits and that when craftily designed and properly presented they would attract as many, and in some instances more, strikes than the natural bait they were designed to replicate. Some of the first lures were made of metal, such as the spoons, while others were made of bone. Ordinary feathers tied to chromed heads fitted with colorful eyes were made in the Orient years ago, and to this day the feathered jigs and their plastic-tailed counterparts continue to be included in the arsenal of nearly every offshore devotee.

The 50-pound-class tackle, fighting chair and high-speed trolling lures displayed here are a combination that is effective on all three U.S. coasts. The blue and white bird pictured to the left does not have a hook in it, and is attached to the end of the line about 8 feet ahead of the primary lure. It runs erratically on the surface, making a disturbance that attracts many gamefish.

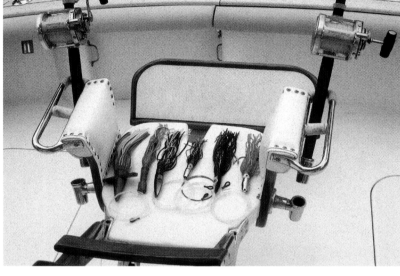

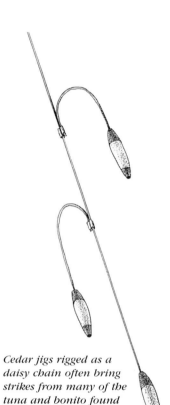

Cedar jigs rigged as a daisy chain often bring strikes from many of the tuna and bonito found inshore of the 30-fathom line. Note that two of the cedar jigs are crimped backward with heavy monofilament and when trolled they slip and slide like excited baitfish.

Forged tuna hooks

Forged tuna-style hooks are most often employed on offshore trolling lures targeting big marlin, sailfish, tuna, wahoo and dolphin. They are a heavy, forged hook, available in stainless steel, or with a tinned finish, and are strong enough to withstand the tremendous pressure of fish weighing several hundred pounds striking a lure with a heavily set drag.

The original lures, popularly called artificials, were most often trolled at the same speeds as natural baits, usually 3 or 4 knots. Through experimentation, anglers realized that lures were far more durable than natural baits. Trollers began advancing their throttles to 6, 8, 10 knots and faster, and found that most of the pelagics would aggressively attack lures trolled at double or even triple the speeds normally used for natural baits. This caused a revolution of sorts on the offshore scene, and high-speed trolling exploded in popularity. The reason was clear: When a troller moved three times faster, he covered three times the area, and most often caught many times the number of fish that were produced at the slower speed.

With high-speed trolling came the advent of trolling lures of every shape, size, and description. Many lures were designed to snake through the water and offer little resistance when trolled at high speeds. Other artificials were designed with flat or concave heads that pushed water or "smoked" to create a lot of commotion, much like a startled baitfish seeking to avoid a hungry gamefish. Lures grew to mammoth proportions, with some measuring 18 to 24 inches long, the actual size of the forage on which many of the big marlin and tuna feed. They were made with hard plastic heads, soft plastic skirts, or molded of soft plastic as a single unit. Eyes used by taxidermists were molded into the heads to make them more realistic, and in some cases actual fish heads were molded into the clear plastic head of a lure.

The color selection is mind boggling. Hot pink and fluorescent orange became the rage and often catch fish when colors that actually represented those of local forage species failed to draw any attention. To say there are currently thousands of offshore trolling lures on the market would be an understatement, and more varieties are made each day. Some, admittedly, are better at catching fishermen than fish.

The newcomer would be wise to seek the counsel of local anglers before making a huge investment in offshore high-speed trolling lures. In general, the choice comes down to selecting a variety of sizes to replicate the bait on which the targeted species are feeding. It's also wise to include the basic popular colors, with green, blue, yellow, red and white all historically providing good results.

In terms of practical advice for all pelagic species, the "green machine" lure has stood the test of time since the advent of high-speed trolling. Most are 8 to 12 inches long and are made with a transparent or green plastic, torpedo-shaped, trolling head with big eyes and trailing green plastic skirt. They have caught perhaps more fish than all of the exotic lures combined. A selection should most certainly be included in your tackle kit.

Birds a popular addition to single lures

Most of the aforementioned artificials are fished individually from a single line. Through experimentation, however, anglers found they could receive more strikes by adding a second lure 5 or 6 feet ahead of the primary lure. Termed "birds," these hookless lures create a lot of commotion and are attached to the coastlock snap at the terminal end of your line, followed by a leader and then the primary lure, usually a smooth running torpedo-headed model. The theory is that the birds act as an attractor, getting fish to zero in on the commotion and then ultimately turn their attention to the trailing lure. The birds have now become an entity unto themselves, and are available in a wide array of sizes, shapes and colors, designed to bring fish from the depths to the surface to investigate the commotion.

The bigeye tuna is a formidable adversary. Caught off all three U.S. Coasts. This beauty weighed more than 200 pounds and was landed aboard Pete Barrett's charter boat "Linda B" out of Manasquan Inlet, New Jersey.

Wahoo grow to 140 pounds, making them a tough adversary. The 68-pound beauty just lifted to the scales was caught on 30-pound-class tackle from the author's "Linda June" off Oregon Inlet, North Carolina. Wahoo is a gourmet treat as a bonus.

Daisy chain rigs add another dimension

Trollers also found that a spread of five or six lures rigged in tandem at 1- to 3-foot intervals, with no hooks in them, and run from outriggers, would also bring fish up to investigate, particularly marlin and sailfish. The only problem was that often the game fish would attack the teaser lines, and before the teasers could be pulled from the water the marlin or sailfish would either crash the teasers or completely lose interest.

This eventually led to the development of daisy chain, which uses several lures in tandem, with a hook rigged on the trailing lure. Most boats fish at least one or two of the daisy chain rigs, which slither through the wake. The teasers are usually made of the same lure, such as five green machines, trolling feathers, plastic squids, shell squids, cedar jigs, or the like.

Spreader bar rigs bring big change

If one lure caught fish, and if a bird ahead of a lure caught more fish, and a daisy chain of lures produced still more excitement, it was a natural evolution to take this to the next step—the spreader bar .

Spreader bars were originally used on the giant bluefin tuna grounds of the Canadian Maritime Provinces many years ago. Tuna trollers would use whole Atlantic mackerel, and tie them daisy-chain fashion to a single line ahead of a mackerel rigged with a hook. This worked well, as tuna would charge in and actually rip the mackerel from the rig, ultimately grabbing the hook bait. An enterprising troller added a stiff metal wire at the head of the spread of mackerel, which enabled him to string several more mackerel from the bar, at each end, resulting in a spread of fish sloshing about as they were trolled along. This created the illusion of a small school of frightened mackerel being herded to the surface. The tuna responded, and so the spreader bar, in its primitive stage, was born.

Today's spreader bar rigs are built of light, stiff, high-tech materials, and range from 3 to 5 feet in length. Pioneers like Dave Arbeitman and Grant Toman of the Reel Seat in Brielle, New Jersey, devoted years to experimenting with exotic materials. Their efforts help bring about rigs that entice strikes from almost all pelagic species.

The primary daisy chain lures, usually shell squid or plastic squid, are run through the center of the bar, with the primary lure and its hook at the trailing edge. Off the bar itself are two lures fished on either side of the primary spread, causing a winged effect and what appears to be five baits swimming abreast of each other, with the remaining lures trailing. Some anglers even rig just a single lure outboard, and a pair of lures one behind the other inboard, giving a delta-wing effect to the pattern. When set behind the boat and slowly trolled, the bar when, ideally positioned, is not dragging, but just working at or above the surface, with the spread of lures swimming along.

The spreader bar rig has taken coastal fishing storm in recent years. Many feel that by having it in their spread of lures fish are attracted to the surface by what appears to be a small school of nervous baitfish. The other baits appear to be separated from the school, and hungry gamefish excitedly attack. That's the theory, anyway. It's often a toss-up as to whether the spreader bar or other lures receive the strike.

The spreader bar rigs are made in many sizes to accommodate all of the species and replicate all of the forage species found on the offshore grounds. The 3- and 4-inch plastic shell squids resemble small squid and bring strikes from bonito, dolphin, little tunny and school bluefin tuna. Intermediate sizes target the bigeye and yellowfin tuna, albacore and wahoo, while spreaders rigged with foot-long lures bring strikes from giant bluefin tuna, striped marlin, white marlin and blue marlin.

Newcomers can learn a lot about these setups from the professional captains, especially the long-range party boat skippers. Aboard the packets it's become standard to include a spreader bar rig in the selection of lures trolled astern. Some of the big boats actually troll with as many as 16 lines abreast. A spread of eight to 10 tightly working lures can bring an entire school of tuna and albacore to the surface.

This often results in adjacent lures being bombarded with eight, 10, or more fish being hooked in rapid succession.

The only disadvantage to using spreader bars is they are cumbersome and, when a fish is hooked, there is a great deal of pressure brought to bear on both the fish and the tackle being used.

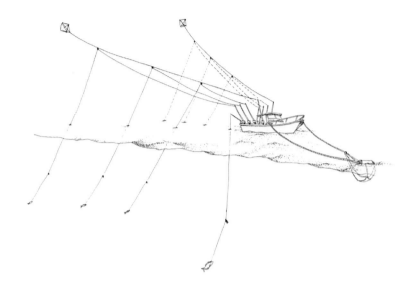

Kite fishing is an ideal way to present live baits while trolling or drifting across a choice location. Two or three baits may be fished from a single kite line, with a pair of kites easily fished from a small boat. Many kite fishermen employ a sea anchor to control their drift.

Kites can be helpful trolling aides

Although trolling dead natural baits and artificials are still the most popular fishing techniques among offshore anglers, in recent years many blue-water fishermen have added kite fishing with live baits to their arsenal.

Kites have been used by fishermen for many years, both boatmen and land-based, to carry baits over a greater area. When the kite is introduced with a live fish as bait, it brings an entirely new dimension to seeking pelagic game fish. For neither lures or dead baits have the appeal of a live fish. With a live fish on the hook far from the boat with the aid of a kite, an angler's chances of scoring are enhanced considerably. Live bait fish naturally emits distress signals which are picked up by gamefish searching for a meal.

Kites made for angling are more sophisticated than those you'd normally see flying in the park. But they work the same, carried high into the sky by upswelling air current and wind. A kite may be flown alongside, behind, or ahead of a boat. If a weed line is spotted, the boat can be positioned upwind, so the kite is flown just along the perimeter and above the weeds, with a live baitfish excitedly swimming just beneath the surface and just off from the weeds, while the boat may be a couple hundred feet away.

Actually, the kite acts much the same as an outrigger, from which live baits may be trolled as well. The line is run to a quick-release outrigger clip attached to the kite line. By adjusting the amount of line you let out from your reel you determine just where the live baitfish will be. Too little line and the baitfish will be suspended in the air, too much and the fish will swim into the depths. The idea is to ease the bait out as the kite is flown, and then to suspend the bait so that it is furiously swimming just a foot or so beneath, or right on the surface.

By carefully watching the baitfish swim about you will notice that it becomes extremely excited as a gamefish stalks it. Often sailfish and other species will swim within a dozen feet of the bait and look it over before crashing the bait and snapping the line free of the outrigger clip attached to the kite line.

Fishing live baits suspended from a drifting boat is another technique that can be very successful. Two or three lines are often suspended from a single kite's outrigger clips, enabling a boatman to fish two kites with as many as six lines.

Because wind and current affect the drifting pattern of a boat, many anglers employ a sea anchor while live bait drift fishing with kites. The sea anchor, really little more than a parachute that balloons out under water and slows the rate of drift, enables the boat to move along a choice location at a leisurely pace.

Kite fishing is an exciting technique that often pays handsome dividends. It does require skill to learn how to fly the kite. It also requires a lot of time to obtain live baits, which are usually obtained on the inshore grounds or purchased from live bait purveyors. Along the Florida coast, goggleyes are a favorite bait for sailfish anglers, while striped marlin fishermen who sail from San Diego often find great success using sardines.

Trollers will frequently employ small lures to catch mackerel or bonito, both of which make fine live baits. These are often held in plastic tubes with flowing water to keep them alive while on board, as they normally succumb in an ordinary live well. Smaller baits, such as jack crevalle, blue runners, grunts, pinfish, mullet, and other small forage stay alive in an ordinary live well with circulating water.

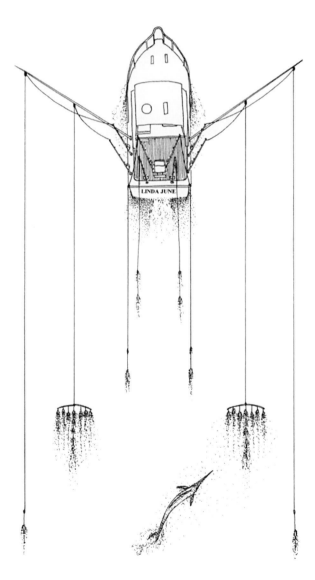

There is a wide divergence of opinion as to the ideal offshore trolling pattern. The author has enjoyed great success with an eight outfit spread as illustrated here. The lures fished directly from the stern are fished on the slope of the first or second wave, some rigged with birds. Next come the spreader bars from the outriggers, followed by the far out lines. On many occasions the spread is adjusted by bringing the spreader bars fished from the inboard outrigger lines up ahead of the lures fished from the stern. Adjust until you achieve the scoring combination.

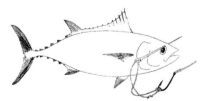

Offshore trollers often use live baits with great success. Little tunny, Pacific and Atlantic bonito, and any of the many mackerel, goggleyes and jacks are very effective baits. Use a rigging needle to thread a loop of rigging cord through the eye sockets of the baitfish. Tightly loop and twist both ends of the cord, securing the bait. Rigged in this manner, a bait stays alive and swimming for a long period of trolling or drifting.

Trolling is not just towing baits

There's a lot more to trolling than putting lures or baits behind the boat and riding around the ocean. Veteran trollers take great pains to study the area they plan to fish before venturing forth.

Thanks to modern technology, ocean temperature charts are available which utilizes satellites to prepare charts that clearly identify surface water temperatures, breaks in temperatures and offshore eddies. Where such changes occur there is often a congregation of forage and the accompanying pelagic species.

Bottom conformation also plays an important role on the offshore grounds. Where the deep water of canyons or the edge of the continental shelf meet the shallow flats, there is often an upwelling of current, where bait tends to congregate. While temperatures may appear ideal, water color may not be to the liking of gamefish. It's usually best to try to locate both the temperature and cobalt blue water that is often so productive.

Once you have a comfort level about the area you plan to fish, it's important to take the time to prepare tackle at dockside. Most anglers who fish from their own boats will troll anywhere from six to eight outfits. It's important that these outfits be rigged as near identical as possible, with the same drag settings, preferably set with the aid of a hand scale. Double lines should be retied and wind-on leaders checked. It is not wise to make several offshore trips without retying. Fatigued line and knots can lead to break-offs.

Anglers often neglect their trolling lures. Lures that are trolled for eight or 10 hours at a time, twisting and flopping around in the wake, often fray their leaders. After a couple of trips it's possible for 100-pound-test leader material to be abraided to the point where it will break with as little as 20 pounds of pressure. There are even occasions when a lure just breaks off from the leader. The breaks and abrasion most often occurs just beneath the head of the lure, where a rough burr that can hardly be seen causes the abrasion.

Once the fishing grounds have been reached, the boat's outriggers should be lowered and the engine idled back to trolling speed. With natural baits this may be in the range of 4 or 5 knots, while with lures and especially high speed lures, the throttles may be moved ahead to 8 knots or more.

Many lures in pattern enhance number of strikes

The more lures you fish from your boat, the greater your chances of scoring. That does not mean that fishing six or eight lures will result in twice the number of strikes as three or four. With double the number of lures or baits you'll often receive three times as many strikes. That is because big spreads generally attract many more fish. This is especially true with tuna and dolphin, both of which often travel in schools.

Boats 24 feet or larger, equipped with outriggers, can fish six to eight lines with ease. The normal pattern is to fish a pair of lines from each outrigger. The outboard lines are fished from outrigger clips run up to the tips of the outriggers and streamed astern 125 to 175 feet. The next pair of lines are fished from outrigger clips spaced approximately two-thirds the distance up the outrigger. These are called the inboard lines. These are streamed astern 75 to 100 feet.

The remaining lines are fished as flat lines. Two are usually fished from rod holders located in the transom's covering board, while two others are fished from rod holders located in the fighting chair. Two of the flat lines are fished straight astern, usually on the face of the second wave from the stern. The remaining two lines are fished from the fighting chair and run to outrigger clips attached to each corner of the transom, and run back on the face of the first wave of the wake.

This basic spread maintains an orderly spread of the lures. It also displays them in a variety of ways, from way back and outboard, where there is little disturbance from the boat's wake, to inboard and close to the transom, where the churning wake tumbles them about. There's nothing in this pattern that must be adhered to. Each boat presents a different wake pattern, and each angler eventually develops a pattern of his spread that produces.

When tuna are plentiful, it's often best to fish as many lures in the wake as possible. With billfish, baits trolled well back generally produce more strikes.

There are a number of lures that may be employed in this typical spread. With many offshore trollers the spreader bar rig has become a staple to be included in every spread of lures. An ideal position for a pair of spreader bars is off the inboard outrigger lines. This runs the line down from a good height, and enables you to position the spreader bar so that it works on the surface and doesn't drag beneath as it might if fished from a flat line.

Often a spoon with a 6-ounce trolling sinker, rigged between line and leader, and a deep-running wahoo plug is fished from the outrigger clips at the transom. Both lures run well below the surface in the churning white water of the wake, and most often draw strikes from tuna, wahoo and dolphin.

The remaining pair of flat lines are rigged with softhead-type plastic baits, or Kona heads that create a fuss.

While some anglers mix natural baits with lures in a pattern, the advantage of lures is that you can troll them at a faster speed. Should you include baits in the spread, you'll have to idle back, or have the baits wash out quickly.

Anglers who fish baits exclusively often put two or three different types in the spread. Small balao and squid are ideal for sailfish and white and striped marlin. When blue marlin are the target, it's wise to use baits that weigh 2 to 4 pounds or more, such as cero mackerel, Spanish mackerel, oceanic bonito and 18-inch-long squid.

Once you've established your spread and lure patterns, pay careful attention to how everything is working. If you're trolling into a head wind that may be slowing you down, the baits may not have the life they should, so just pushing the throttles ahead a notch may enhance their action. When heading down sea the baits may be flying out of the water and an easing of the throttles may be appropriate.

Veteran blue-water trollers never fall into the pattern of just cruising in one direction, at one speed, for miles on end. There's almost always wind or current affecting the manner in which your lures are working. Because of this it's important to troll all points of the compass. Often you'll find that a certain set, across the seas, into them, or gliding with them, results in strikes, while all other sets result in a blank.

If action is slow, don't hesitate to move the throttles ahead, or pull back. Sometimes it only takes a little adjustment. The speed that worked yesterday doesn't necessarily work today.

When your lures are set properly, turning is no problem, and by regularly putting turns into your trolling set, you have every lure or bait in your pattern reacting differently. The inboard lures on a turn will slow and often sink beneath the surface, while the outboard lures will double or triple their speed and skitter along the surface. Swinging the wheel in the other direction then causes the slowly swimming baits that may have settled beneath the surface to come charging to the surface and skipping across the wake, while the former outboard baits now settle. Often this hurried, varied action of the lures will excite tuna and marlin into wrecklessly crashing baits.

Ocean mounts and ridges hold bait and pelagic species

The peaks of underseas mountains, ridges, or even hills are prime locations for forage fish. Such high spots are found off all three U.S. coasts and warrant the attention of trollers, for wherever baitfish congregate, there are gamefish. There may be times when your fishfinder will record huge schools of baitfish right down on the bottom of a ridge, at the crest of a mount, or along its slopes, with no signs of big fish.

Often it becomes frustrating to be at what you perceive to be the right location, with an abundance of bait and good water temperatures, but no target species. Here's where patience comes into play. Tuna, marlin, wahoo, dolphin and other pelagic species aren't like bottom feeders that set up residence and stay put in a given area. All are known to travel 50 to 100 miles or more in a day. Pelagic species are much like birds on land, flying from place to place as they make the rounds of areas they know will produce a satisfying meal.

It isn't necessary to spend all of your time at one location, but in plotting your trolling strategy for the day, don't hesitate to revisit an area several times. Luck can change quickly in areas that were seemingly hopeless.

Offshore weedlines composed of floating sargassum offer sanctuary for a wide variety of forage species. Often gamefish will prowl along the edge of the weedlines, which continue for miles at times, lurking in the shadows as they wait for a meal. Floating objects such as tree branches, pilings, pallets and buckets also attract fish. Trolling the perimeter often produces strikes.

Look for weed lines, flotsam and jetsam

Always be alert for anything that is floating on the surface. There are times when you'll see a tree trunk, or in some cases an entire tree, drifting along many miles out to see. Perhaps it's only a wooden pallet, or it may be a partially submerged cargo container that broke free from a container ship in a storm. Invariably, floating objects as small as a 5-gallon pail, will hold baitfish in their shadow. The small fish are attracted to what little protection the flotsam may offer. Big fish know this and they too in turn are attracted, often spending time leisurely finning in the shadows beneath the object.

Carefully scan the water beneath floating debris as you approach it. Often you'll see the bait and sometimes dolphin and marlin, too. Your approaching lures may bring fast strikes.

Weather buoys and the marker buoys that are used by lobstermen and pot fishermen can bring similar opportunities. Always give them a troll-by and don't hesitate to return to them later in the day.

Weed lines can offer hectic action

Where there is a meeting of opposing forces, such as the wind and offshore currents, fishermen may find patches of seaweeds that can stretch for miles. Bits of driftwood, bottles, cans and anything else that floats is often tangled up in the weeds. The weed patches are frequently too thick to troll through, and it's best to stay along the perimeter.

Many trollers keep a medium-weight spinning outfit rigged and ready for such weed line encounters. If huge schools of dolphin are located under the weeds, many trollers pull in their lines and switch over to the casting tackle, sending leadhead jigs or just small pieces of bait towards the weeds. Dolphin can be excited into a feeding frenzy by tossing out small pieces of fish as chum. Once you get the dolphin vying for the chum, they'll wallop a lure or bait cast their way.

Porpoises and whales a good sign

Where you find concentrations of porpoises and whales, you'll often find many of the pelagic species targeted by offshore fishermen. The mammals and fish prefer much the same temperatures. Because whales and porpoises must surface periodically to breath, they're easy to spot. When you spot the playful antics of these huge mammals, by all means concentrate some trolling effort in the area, for gamefish are likely to be nearby.

Scan the horizon for surface activity and birds

It's been said that a single frigate bird will often disclose a group of feeding fish. Sometimes it's more than one bird, and at times the air can be filled with thousands of gulls and terns, feeding on helpless forage species being attacked from below by hungry tuna and billfish. It's important to always be alert to any bird activity, especially that of Mother Carey's chickens, those tiny black birds that almost seem to walk on water, dancing along feeding on remnants of what gamefish had been devouring below.

Some offshore trollers monitor their radars when there is a flat, calm ocean, and can pick up small groups of gulls flying low to the water, or congregations of gulls that are resting on the water. This often discloses that fish have been feeding in the area, and they may feed again.

Loran and GPS both have the capability to store and recall the numbers of any specific location. It's a good idea to save location information on promising areas so you can return and give them a second or even third shot during a trip.

Oil rigs attract bait and gamefish

The many oil-drilling platforms located throughout the Gulf of Mexico are prime locations for trollers. The rigs are huge and offer sanctuary and feeding grounds for many bottom feeders and forage species, both of which are fair game for hungry gamefish.

The huge pilings that hold the rigs securely to the sea floor result in rips and eddies being formed as the current pushes against them. Great varieties of species that live in the upper strata of the water column congregate in these rips and eddies. Jack crevalle, blue runners, rainbow runners, amberjack, mackerel, dolphin and other small fish often congregate in large schools. Wahoo, big dolphin and amberjack, tuna and marlin spend much of their time hanging close to the rigs, for they know a meal is always readily available, and offshore trollers can readily capitalize on this lazy habit by concentrating their trolling efforts around the rigs.

Anglers should be careful around oil rigs, however. There are occasionally crew boats arriving and departing, and the currents are often extremely swift, so make safety paramount.

No two days alike

Offshore fishing for the most part is dominated by the trolling techniques discussed in this chapter. There are also many occasions when chumming presents great opportunities to catch pelagic gamefish, especially tuna, dolphin and wahoo. Chumming techniques are discussed in greater detail in Chapter 7.

Offshore fishing is a lifelong challenge to many boatmen. Whether you fish from a private, charter or party boat, you'll find that no two days or nights offshore are the same. The weather, water temperatures, movement of bait, sea conditions, and migrational patterns of pelagic species all combine to play a role in this exciting pastime.

It's demanding, yet relaxing, and certainly rewarding. When that fish of a lifetime comes up in the spread, vaults from the sea and crashes down on a bait, there's an adrenaline rush that follows that is not for the weak of heart.

It's what offshore fishing is all about.

INSHORE FISHING

The saltwater angler who enjoys fishing from a boat has a wealth of opportunities at his disposal. Inshore waters may be fished from small, aluminum, car-top boats, outboard-powered rental rowboats and skiffs, the wide array of medium-size runabouts, center consoles, and walkaround cuddy cabin models. You'll regularly see cruisers and sportsfishermen plying these waters too. Not to be forgotten are the party boats, which sail daily to fish inshore waters for a wide variety of species.

Inshore waters are popular because, as the name implies, they are close to shore. There is limited travel time necessary to reach the fishing grounds, and should you encounter stormy weather, or wish to return to port for other reasons, the trip home is short.

The "Linda June" Betram 33 was perfect for all types of inshore fishing and had all the amenities for a family trip.

LINDA JUNE
MANTOLOKING, N.J.

(Left) Barnegat Light looms in the background as anglers fish the quiet waters of Barnegat Bay, N.J., shortly after sunrise. The protected waters of bays, rivers and estuaries hold a wide variety of gamefish and bottom feeders that are caught using a variety of techniques.

Many species available

Inshore waters hold a wide variety of popular gamefish and bottom feeders. Coastal estuaries, generally identified as the area where the tide line meets the river current, are the spawning grounds, and in turn the nursery grounds, for many species. The estuarial waters are where the freshwaters of the rivers join the salt-water of the ocean. These areas also accommodate many freshwater species that find it comfortable living in brackish water of nominal salinity.

Light tackle preferred

Inshore fishing is ideally suited to light tackle. The waters are protected and the species usually small, although there are many heavyweights such as striped bass, bluefish, snook, tarpon, redfish and salmon.

Tackle should always be geared to the species sought. For the devotee of conventional tackle, a light or medium casting or popping rod, 5 1/2 to 6 feet in length, and a multiplying, levelwind casting reel loaded with 150 yards of 10- to 15-pound-test line is ideal. It will serve you well on all three coasts, whether you fish from a party packet, rental boat or anything in between. It's well suited to casting artificials, drifting natural baits, chumming and bottom fishing.

A one-handed spinning outfit and a conventional casting outfit, often called a popping outfit, are ideal for any inshore fishing situation. A tackle kit should include: loose hooks, snelled hooks, sinkers, plastic splasher floats, hot-pink or orange snap floats, leadhead jigs, plastic bait tails, plugs and metal jigs. A towel, pliers, sunblock, knife and dehooker complete the kit.

Fixed spool popular

Spinning tackle has its devotees on inshore waters and here, too, light equipment often provides maximum enjoyment. Rods built of fiberglass or graphite, ranging from 5' 6" through 6' 6" and capable of handling lures or rigs ranging from a half ounce through 1 1/2 ounces are ideal. A spinning reel loaded with 150 yards of 8- to 15-pound line balances a nice outfit. It's usually better in saltwater to lean towards a heavier, rather than too light a line, as too light a line results in attrition of lures and terminal rigs that become snagged when drifting or casting.

Long rod use prevalent inshore

Saltwater fly fishing tackle is another effective choice for the inshore scene. An 8-, 9- or 10-weight outfit is the choice of many long rod devotees. Armed with a selection of Clousers, Deceivers or Half & Halfs, or the hundreds of popular local patterns, the fly caster will find enjoyable sport for a wide variety of species in bays, rivers and the open ocean.

A traveler far from home will often find conditions very close to those he experiences in home waters. By using his favorite tackle, he can usually enjoy great sport and fine eating with many different species.

Inshore boatmen who enjoy fly casting have many opportunities to score. This cero mackerel succumbed to a mylar-dressed streamer. King mackerel, Spanish mackerel, and wahoo also respond to flies presented on a deep-sinking line.

East features beautiful bays and rivers

The rock-studded coastline of Maine offers hundreds of rivers and bays which empty into the Atlantic. Many have mud, sand or pebbled bottoms where winter flounder take up residence. Anchoring on mud flats or along channel edges and chumming with a mixture of ground clams or crushed mussels, sent to the bottom in a lead-bottomed chum pot, is a good way to attract the tasty flatfish. Small No. 8 or 9 Chestertown or wide-gap hooks baited with sandworms or bloodworms bring strikes from the tasty bottom feeders. It's also not unusual to catch harbor pollock or small codfish on the same rigs, although most are immature fish that should be returned to grow up.

Much the same scene is repeated along the Massachusetts, Connecticut, Long Island and New Jersey coasts. The difference is instead of a rock-studded coastline, there are many barrier islands, with broad bays separating the mainland, and with an abundance of winter flounder that provide fine action each spring and fall.

Anglers who fish from small boats can enjoy superb fishing within 20 miles of the beach on all three U.S. coasts. Boats rigged out like this one are ideal, with two small fighting chairs in the cockpit. Always keep a couple of blocks of ice in the stern fish box to ensure your catch returns in prime condition.

Mackerel a plentiful visitor

The Atlantic mackerel summers in the inshore waters of Maine and the Canadian Maritime Provinces, often traveling in schools of tens of thousands. While generally found in the close-to-shore ocean waters, they'll often invade large coastal bays as they search for food. On any of the three outfits included earlier they'll provide fine sport, striking tiny diamond jigs, bucktails or tube teasers. Flies presented with a sinking fly line will often draw strikes until an angler is arm weary. Not only do the mackerel provide fine sport, but they're delicious when either smoked with hickory chips or as fillets pickled in kosher salt with alternating slices of onion.

These same mackerel, averaging 12 ounces to 3 pounds, usually winter off the Virginia Capes, providing boatmen with fine action as they move north to the Maritime Provinces for the summer, and then again on their return visit in early winter. They're fun to catch and especially well suited to newcomers and youngsters. When you get into a school the action is often fast and furious, and a great deal of skill isn't required.

Stripers and blues both popular

It would be difficult to say whether the striped bass or bluefish is the most popular inshore gamefish along this stretch of middle and north Atlantic coastline. Both species frequent the same inshore waters and are regularly targeted by anglers casting or trolling lures, chumming, bottom fishing, drifting and jigging.

Most of the stripers and bluefish that migrate north to New England have achieved respectable size. Along their mid-range of Long Island and south to New Jersey and through the Chesapeake Bay area, many smaller fish are encountered. Many of the youngsters of both clans spend their first few seasons in the bays, rivers, and creeks near where they were hatched. The inshore nursery grounds have an abundance of grass shrimp, spearing, menhaden and other forage to satisfy their ravenous appetites.

Depending on local state regulations, some of the smaller fish may be undersized, but they provide fine catch-and-release sport for anglers armed with light outfits. Both species are readily caught on plugs, plastic-tailed and bucktail-dressed leadheads and metal jigs.

Striped bass readily respond to live baits such as menhaden, herring, hickory shad, croaker and spot. This beauty being held aloft by Al Wutkowski was caught from his boat "The Flume" by Ian Quarrier. He used light tackle to cast the live herring in among the rocks of a coastal jetty.

Inshore party boat fishing for both stripers and blues has gained increasing popularity in recent years, as it enables anglers an opportunity to catch trophy fish with minimal cost. The most popular way to catch the bass and blues is with a diamond or slab-sided chromed jig, with a plastic or feather teaser 18 to 24 inches ahead of the jig. The schools are often mixed, with the stripers on or near the bottom and the bluefish staying near the surface.

The party boats use their fishfinders to locate the schools and then drift over them. Jigging is accomplished by lowering the rig to the bottom and retrieving to the surface. As a general rule, the slow retrieve concentrated near the bottom gets strikes from the stripers and the fast, jigging retrieve gets the action from the blues near the surface.

Wire line effective for many inshore species

Wire-line trolling with medium-weight tackle is very popular for striped bass, bluefish, king mackerel and wahoo. Anglers spool 200 to 300 feet of either solid monel, stainless steel or stainless cable trolling wire over Dacron backing line. A loop is made in the terminal end of the wire using a haywire twist, to which is tied approximately 10 feet of 50-pound monofilament leader material, with a coastlock snap on the end. This length of leader is primarily to make it easy when letting wire line out and when reeling fish within range of a net or gaff.

A ball-bearing swivel and coastlock snap are attached to the end of the first leader. Depending on the lure used, some anglers attach a 3- to 6-ounce trolling sinker, after which they attach another leader, usually 6 feet in length, with a coastlock snap on the end with which to attach their lure.

When anglers are using leadhead parachute-type jigs that weigh 3 or 4 ounces, they often forego the trolling sinker and second leader. With leadhead jigs, the most effective method of trolling is to move over known haunts of the various species being sought and have anglers positioned in the stern actively jigging the lures. The parachute jig, often with a pork rind tail, resembles a wounded baitfish.

With tube lures, bunker spoons, chromed jigs, and big swimming plugs the sinker adds weight to take the lures into the depths. In most cases the rods are placed in rod holders, with the line streamed sufficiently far astern to get near the bottom.

This technique is also very effective when used with umbrella rigs which feature anywhere from six to 12 tube lures or plastic fish replicas attached to the rigs arms. Usually, there is either one or two primary lures fished 36 inches behind the umbrella rig. The umbrella rigs are effective at catching fish, and it's often possible to catch several bluefish, striped bass, or king mackerel at one time. The system leaves much to be desired as far as sport is concerned, but is included here because there are many times when it is the only way you can troll for these species in deep water.

Trio of bottom feeders are favorite targets

Bottom feeders tautog, sea bass, and porgies are plentiful in inshore waters along the middle Atlantic coast. They're found around most broken, irregular bottoms, particularly rock ledges and around the many artificial fishing reefs built along the coast in recent years. They frequent these areas because there is an abundance of food readily available and the surroundings often provide sanctuary from predatory species.

The most popular technique employed to catch all three of these bottom dwellers is to use a high-low rig, employing a pair of hooks snelled to 12 to 18 inches of leader material. Virginia, sproat, claw or beak style hooks are the most popular. When targeting porgies, which are often only a pound or so in weight, a size No. 8 or 10 hook is used. For sea bass that are generally larger in size, a No. 4 or 6 hook is ideal. With tautog, it depends on where you're fishing. In open ocean waters, where they range from from 3 to 6 pounds or more, a No. 2 or 1, or even a 1/0 hook is preferred.

Small pieces of conch, clam, squid, or seaworm are preferred baits for porgies and sea bass, while the tautog prefer green crabs and fiddler crabs, although they'll take the aforementioned baits as well.

This is relaxing fishing, as it's a matter of finding structure, such as rockpiles, mussel beds, or artificial reefs, and anchoring your boat so it is positioned directly above the structure. All three species stick very close to the structure, and if you're positioned over sand bottom just a few feet from the structure you're apt not to catch a thing.

Once anchored it's a matter of baiting up, using sufficient sinker weight on your rig to keep it perpendicular to the bottom, lowering the rig to the bottom and waiting for strikes. All three fish have reputations as bait stealers, so always be alert, and lift back smartly with your rod tip at the first tug on the bait. You'll be rewarded with a respectable tussle, and some of the finest-tasting fish the sea has to offer.

Anchoring above coastal wrecks, reefs and ridges gives anglers an opportunity to catch fish right on the bottom and at intermediate levels as well. The key in wreck fishing is paying attention to wind and current, either of which can affect your location over a wreck.

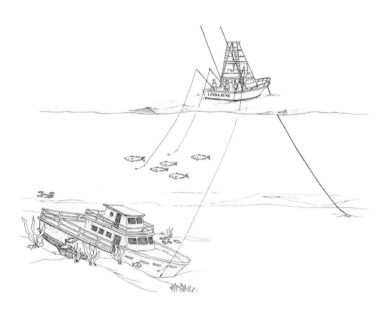

Weakfish and spotted weakfish enjoy popularity

The weakfish is the darling of inshore fisherman because it is plentiful, grows to more than 10 pounds, provides a variety of angling opportunities, and is excellent table fare. Caught from New England through the Chesapeake Bay area, the species is also found throughout the Carolinas and is often called the gray trout.

The spotted weakfish, locally called trout or sea trout, is found throughout the inshore waters of Georgia, Florida, and from the Gulf Coast of Florida all the way to Texas.

The habitat and feeding patterns of the weakfish and spotted weakfish are very similar. In the southern portion of their range it's not unusual to catch both species in a day's outing. The only major difference in appearance are the large black spots that are prominent on the back of the spotted weakfish.

Both are creatures of habit and tend to be lazy when seeking a meal. As a result they're easily attracted to a chum line of their favorite food, which includes the tiny grass shrimp so plentiful in coastal bays and rivers, as well as the larger shrimp that are targeted as table fare.

The technique of chumming for the weakfish and its spotted cousin doesn't vary much along the thousands of miles of Atlantic and Gulf Coast they frequent. Both species spend much of their time in the shallow reaches of bays and rivers, moving across eelgrass and weed beds where there is an abundance of forage. Often the water on the shallow flats ranges from 3 to 6 feet.

Armed with three or four quarts of live grass shrimp or their larger culinary counterparts, it's an easy matter to seek out promising water, and to double anchor— so your boat is held steady and does not swing in the wind—and begin chumming.

Just a few shrimp are dropped over the side at a time, and carried away with the tide over the weedbeds or bottom frequented by the weakfish. It's best to cut larger shrimp into pieces the size of a pencil eraser, and sparingly distribute them to establish a chum line that attracts the weakfish. It's important to not provide too much food, for then they'll hang well back and just feed. You want to get them moving towards the source of the food, where they'll find your hook bait.

Once the chum line is established, it's time to bait up. This can be accomplished by simply tying a No. 1 or 2 claw or beak hook with a baitholder shank directly to the end of your monofilament line or, preferably, fluorocarbon leader. Bait up with three or four tiny grass shrimp, or a small piece of a larger shrimp. Ease the baited hook into the water and permit the current to carry it along, much the same as the current is carrying your chum. Once the bait has drifted off 40 to 60 feet, even more at times, simply reel in and repeat the procedure. Often the strikes will come from as close as a rod's length from the boat. The key is to keep the bait moving naturally with the chum line.

If you're chumming in very shallow water and the weed growth is heavy, the baited hook may sink to the bottom and not drift properly, especially if there is little current. At such times it's very effective to add a float to the line to suspend the bait just above the weeds. A rubber-cored sinker may be added to the line between the float and hook, thus ensuring that it drifts along perpendicular to the bottom. The float and sinker rig is especially popular with children, who take delight in seeing the float pulled under as a big weakfish takes the bait.

While standard plastic floats are popular, veteran weakfish anglers have found that a cork or plastic float with a concave head that emits a popping or gurgling sound as it is pulled through the water attracts the attention of the fish better than an ordinary plastic or cork float.

You can also catch weakfish by working a tiny bucktail jig through the chum line, and many strikes are received on plastic bait tails fished on plain leadhead jigs. Small swimming plugs work, too.

Drifting across open bottom during ebb tide often brings strikes when the weakfish vacate the shallows. At such times a high-low bottom rig with a pair of hooks snelled to 12 to 18 inches of leader material works fine. Use a bank or dipsey-style sinker heavy enough to glide along the bottom. Shrimp, strips of squid, spearing and live minnows are all effective baits.

"Both species of weakfish migrate as seasons change, vacating the protected waters of estuaries, bays and rivers and moving into the open reaches of the ocean and gulf."

Both species of weakfish migrate as seasons change, vacating the protected waters of estuaries, bays and rivers and moving into the open reaches of the ocean and gulf. They travel in huge schools, often moving close to the bottom, feeding on baitfish. On these occasions anglers can catch them on diamond jigs and teasers, bucktails, or natural baits drifted along the bottom.

Not to be overlooked is trolling. Trolling with small plugs, leadheads with plastic bait tails, bucktails or spoons can produce plenty of luck. The small boat angler who trolls can cover a lot of water and once a school is located he can capitalize and continue trolling, or shut down and drift and work a jig through the fish.

Flatfish coveted by bottom fishermen

While the weakfish are favorites of the gamefish set along a long stretch of shoreline, the summer flounder, and its cousin, the southern flounder, more than hold their own in the popularity department.

Both flounders spend a great deal of time in the shallow reaches of bays and estuaries. They're also found in the open expanse of the Atlantic and Gulf, generally close to shore. However, they often frequent humps or high bottom several miles from shore, especially when forage species are plentiful at these locations. Flatfish are a perfect target for boatmen, no matter the size of the craft.

The summer flounder is an aggressive bottom feeder. Unlike the sea bass, porgy and tautog, which stick close to structure, the summer and southern flounder move about searching for a meal. Most often it's over sandy bottom, where their backs take on the color of the bottom over which they're traveling. This chameleon-

Snelling a hook

The uni-knot allows an angler to snell a hook with ease.
First thread 6 inches of fluorocarbon leader through the eye of the hook.
Hold the leader material against the hook's shank, and form a uni-knot circle.
Make five to seven turns through the loop and around the standing leader and hook's shank.
Tighten by pulling the standing line in one direction and the tag end in the other. A pair of pliers will give you a firm grip on the tag end and enable you to pull it up tightly, after which it can be clipped close with nail clippers.

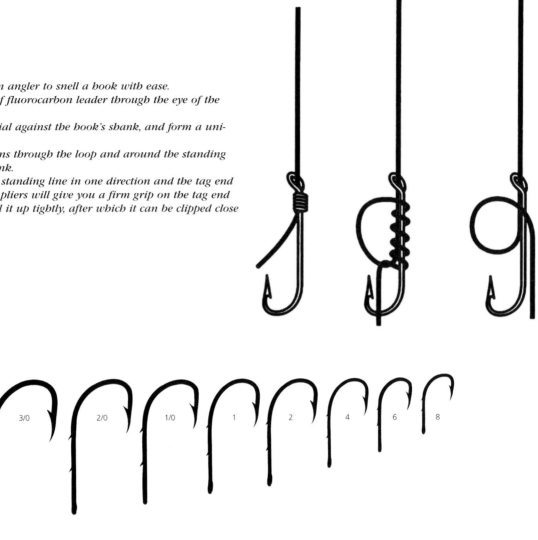

Beak or claw hooks

Beak- or claw-style hooks are effective when used with baits such as sandworms, bloodworms, clams, squid, mussels, shrimp, and other natural baits. Made of fine wire, they penetrate a fish's mouth quickly and hold securely.

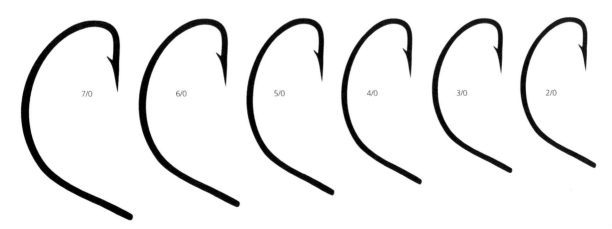

Wide gap

The wide gap has a unique style and hooking quality that makes it particularly effective with flounder and halibut. Most flatfish get hooked in the corner of the mouth, an advantage when undersize fish have to be released.

Party boats sail from most every port on all three coasts for inshore bottom fishing. The "Captree Star II" sails from Captree, Long Island, and spends the pleasant summer months fishing for summer flounder.

like characteristic is very pronounced, with the fish having a very light sandy color when frequenting light bottom, mottled or spotted brown and beige tones when over gravel or pebbly bottom, and dark chocolate when feeding over mud bottom.

When resting the flounder usually stay on the bottom and use their fins to partially cover themselves with sand or mud. If a cold snap develops, they'll lay on the bottom for days without moving about or feeding. At such times the mud will actually stick to their undersides and if you catch one shortly after it emerges from the mud it'll still carry a light covering of the mud on its otherwise snow white bottom.

As the flounder rests on the bottom, its eyes extend upward, watching for baitfish, shrimp or crab. They're extremely fast and strike quickly.

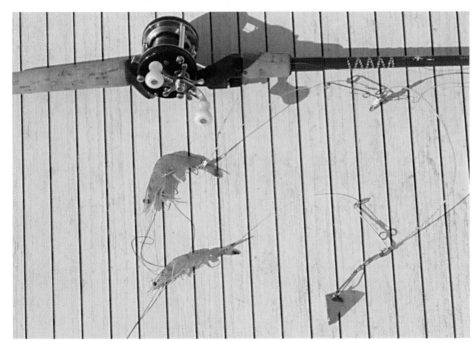

Shrimp are found in all the waters of the world and are widely used as bait. Many anglers employ a high-low rig such as the one pictured here when fishing inshore bay, sound and river waters. Strips of fresh squid, pieces of clam and chunks of fish may also be used with this rig.

Flounder fishermen find drifting to be the most successful technique. While chumming results in strikes from flounder, as does fishing at anchor, you'll catch more of the flatfish by setting the boat adrift and covering known flounder grounds while drifting with the current or wind.

Standard inshore fishing tackle is ideal for seeking flounder inshore, although in open ocean and gulf waters, where you may fish in 25- to 50-foot depths, heavier gear is appropriate.

The most popular flatfish rig is made by tying a small three-way swivel directly to the end of your line. Tie one eye of the swivel to a 6- to 8-inch piece of monofilament line, with a loop in the end. Slip a dipsey or bank sinker onto the loop to hold bottom over the area you plan to drift. Tie in a 30- to 36-inch piece of 20-pound-test fluorocarbon leader material to the other end of the swivel. Snell a Carlisle, beak, claw or wide-gap hook (1/0 through 3/0 sizes are the most popular) to the end of the leader. Many anglers use circle hooks with good results. These hook the flounder in the corner of the mouth and make unhooking and releasing undersize fish less of a chore.

The summer flounder, or fluke, feeds on a wide range of forage species, including sand eels, spearing, crabs, shrimp, squid and the young of almost every species in residence. All of these may be used as bait. Perhaps the most popular bait is the saltwater killie, also known as a mummichog or minnow, which is hooked through the lips and drifted live along the bottom.

Russ Tinsley spends his leisure time fishing the Texas sea coast for redfish. Here he's with Captain Terry Panknin, a veteran Corpus Christi guide, who has mentally cataloged hundreds of inshore spots where redfish and spotted weakfish reside. Inshore fishing along the Gulf Coast shallows is very rewarding just a few minutes run from coastal marinas.

Channel bass has broad range

The channel bass, or redfish, is a formidable target of anglers fishing inshore waters from the Virginia Capes all the way to Texas. Often called the southern counterpart to the striped bass, the channel bass frequents much the same waters, has very similar habits, and grows to the same size.

Perhaps the most exciting method of catching channel bass is to sight-cast to them as the schools travel just off the surf line of the DelMarVa Peninsula on the Atlantic coast during spring. The same technique is employed in Gulf coast waters and in the back-country waters where schools of a hundred or more redfish are encountered.

The Hopkins stainless steel hammered jig is one of the most popular lures for enticing strikes when the fish are on the move. Schools present themselves in different ways. In open ocean waters they often appear as a huge, dark shadow or dark area just beneath the surface. In the shallows of bays and estuaries, their movement often disturbs the surface as the tightly packed schools mill about.

The key is positioning your boat upcurrent from the school and permitting wind or current to move you within casting range. Take care not to approach too close and spook the school while motoring in. Once positioned, place your cast so it goes beyond and ahead of the fish, and then work the lure back towards the school. Properly presented, the Hopkins draws quick strikes. Bucktail jigs and their plastic-tailed counterparts, swimming plugs, and small spoons all prove effective in this exciting inshore sport.

There are also opportunities to catch redfish on live shrimp, spot, pinfish or grunts, or to troll for them using drone spoons. A popular, hard-fighting southern adversary, smaller redfish are considered fine table fare. Make certain to check state size restrictions before bringing any home.

Three gamefish dominate Keys

Inshore fishermen who spend their time in the Florida Keys are treated to three great gamefish that will test their skills to the utmost: tarpon, bonefish and permit. All three are caught using a variety of techniques.

Unquestionably the most challenging and exciting technique is to pole across the shallow flats of the Keys and sight cast to the fish as they move through water barely deep enough to cover their backs.

Bonefish are the most plentiful and generally travel alone. There are times, though, when "the gray ghost of the flats" travels in small pods, and even schools. All flats travelers are spooky, and don't let fishermen get too close. This usually forces anglers to pole along until a fish is sighted, then waiting until the fish moves within range.

Many anglers employ a single live shrimp on a 1/0 beak hook, and cast just ahead of the cruising fish. Tiny delta-shaped jigs and plastic-tailed jigs also bring strikes from this speedy flats resident.

Anglers seeking bonefish will sometimes encounter the prized permit, which also presents a formidable challenge. While the bonefish may weigh upwards of l5 pounds, the permit is often in the 20- to 30-pound range, and is extremely fast and powerful. It, too, will readily take a shrimp, although its favorite bait is a small, live, blue crab.

The tarpon, or "silver king of the flats," weighs l00 pounds or more and is hooked regularly using the same techniques employed for bonefish and permit. However, anglers using spinning or casting tackle usually move towards 15- to 20-pound-test lines and rods rated with a heavier action. Favorite baits include live mullet, pinfish, and grunts.

All three species are regularly caught by fly-rod devotees. A standard 10-weight outfit with at least 200 yards of backing line handles most of the fish, although some anglers who specialize in tarpon, move up to a 12-weight which gives them more leverage on big fish.

Chasing big tarpon in such renowned areas as Key West and Boca Grande Pass in Florida, and the many passes emptying into the Gulf of Mexico all the way to Texas, is usually a bait-fishing proposition. Live crabs, pinfish, grunts, squirrel fish and other small fish are drifted through the area frequented by the tarpon, which moves with the tides searching for a meal. Large pods of feeding tarpon are frequently encountered on the surface and may be coaxed into a strike by casting a live bait to the cruising fish.

The yellowtail snapper, here being swung aboard by June Rosko, is a favorite of reef fishermen throughout the South. It will strike small lures and natural baits fished on the bottom and may also be enticed away from the reef with ground fish and chunks as chum. A sliding egg-shaped sinker, with a 2-foot leader and 1/0 or 2/0 claw- or beak-style hook with a chunk of little tunny is perfect.

Grouper and snapper found in many areas

The many species of grouper and snapper are popular with inshore fisherman from the Carolinas to Texas. They are found on most every patch of rock bottom, coral reef, shipwreck, or ledge where there is an abundance of food.

Inshore small-boat anglers fishing this type of structure employ a variety of techniques to catch snapper and grouper. Anchoring and chumming adjacent to and above the structure is effective for yellowtail snapper and porgies. Fishing live baits in the depths is also productive, particularly with big black grouper, red grouper, mutton snapper, and red snapper. Bottom fishing with a high-low rig and fresh bait such as little tunny and balao can result in good catches of these bottom inhabitants.

An especially enjoyable method is to drift and deep-jig the reef with leadhead, bucktail or plastic-tailed jigs. With deep water and a swift current or strong wind it is often necessary to use jigs weighing from 1 to 4 ounces to get to the bottom and keep the jig perpendicular as you retrieve.

The schools of grouper and snapper can be found by cruising the reef areas and employing an electronic fishfinder. Once fish are located, it becomes a matter of positioning the boat so the current or wind will carry you over the fish and away from the reef. This way, as fish are hooked, you'll be drifting to deeper water or away from obstructions.

Bottom fishing on coral reefs can lead to encounters with an endless variety of species. This beautifully hued yellowfin grouper was landed by Dotty Beyer aboard the "D-D" with a piece of balao bait.

All grouper and snapper are fast. Make no mistake about it. As a result, an effective method of working your jig is to permit it to settle to the bottom, then quickly lifting your rod tip, causing the jig to dart towards the surface. Continue reeling and jigging until it reaches the surface. If a strike isn't received, drop the jig back down and repeat the process.

This technique requires tackle rated at 20 pounds or heavier. Snapper and grouper that weigh 15 to 50 pounds or more will break light lines with little effort. Fish a firm drag, and as soon as a fish is hooked lift back smartly and work hard to get it up and away from the bottom. Once a grouper gets turned back to the coral it can rip line from your reel and in an instant cut you off.

Cobia a tough adversary

Cobia is another great inshore gamefish. Found in nominal quantities along the Atlantic Coast from the Carolinas southward, they are very popular along the Gulf Coast. They're apt to be found cruising around channel markers, buoys, docks, and anchored boats.

While found out in the open Gulf where they move among the anchored shrimp boats, cobia are found in the greatest numbers inshore in most every bay and pass. The most popular methods of catching them is anchoring in a pass and using a sliding-egg sinker rig on the bottom with a live pinfish or grunt hooked through the lips.

Perhaps the more exciting approach is to cruise the passes, visiting known haunts such as buoys, channel markers, and dock areas and casting to cobias once they are spotted. Bucktail jigs and swimming plugs all work, but a live baitfish hooked just beneath the dorsal fin or through the lips and cast within range of a hungry cobia is perhaps your best bet. Many cobia top the 30-pound mark along the Gulf Coast. In those waters it is wise to move up to heavier gear. Twenty-pound-class spinning or casting tackle is preferred.

Chumming inshore kelp beds exciting

Along the southern California coast, inshore anglers are afforded a wide variety of gamefish and bottom feeders. Some of the most enjoyable fishing is found in the waters adjoining the kelp beds.

Kelp can best be described as a giant tree growing up from the bottom, with long, willowy, branches adorned with huge leaves. Unlike the green seaweed of the Atlantic coast, which is carried along by the current, the brown Pacific Coast kelp grows in huge beds, and is for the most part stationary. The limbs of the kelp are often as thick as a man's arm, and the leaves several feet long and a foot or more wide. These kelp jungles provide sanctuary for anchovies, sardines, and a host of small fish and the fry of others, all of which can satisfy the appetites of bigger game.

Chumming is the most popular method of fishing the kelp beds. After leaving dockside, boats commonly stop at the bait barge located in most coastal harbors and take aboard several scoops of anchovies, sardines, or mackerel to be employed both as chum and hook baits. Private and charter boats generally anchor near the kelp beds so anglers can cast their baits near the kelp, or let the current carry lively baits along the edge.

"Kelp jungles provide sanctuary for anchovies, sardines, and a host of small fish and the fry of others, all of which can satisfy the appetites of bigger game."

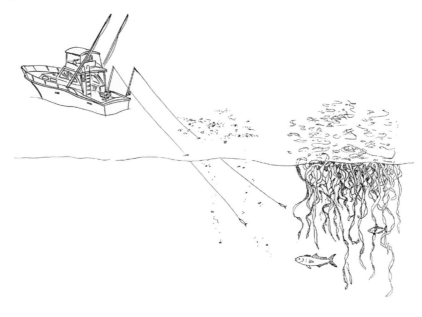

Kelp beds offer sanctuary for baitfish. More formidable gamefish cruise along the perimeter. The key for both trollers, drift fishermen and anglers who chum the kelp beds is to present baits and lures close to the kelp without getting fouled in the undergrowth.

Tiny anchovy baits favored

Because tiny anchovies and other small baitfish are the favored baits, anglers prefer a rod with a delicate tip that can softly cast a bait weighing a fraction of an ounce a fair distance. Correspondingly light lines are used, often only 12- to 15-pound-test, with either a multiplying or spinning reel.

The most popular technique involves a tiny anchovy bait, hooked lightly through the gill collar or lips with a small No. 1 or 2 claw, beak or live-bait wire hook tied directly to the monofilament line or fluorocarbon leader.

As the bait swims along, often swiftly heading for the sanctuary of the kelp, other anchovies are tossed out, sparingly so as to attract and not feed the fish.

With the reel in free spool or with the bail open, the key is to keep the bait moving, struggling to get into the kelp and attracting fish that may be cruising along the perimeter searching for a meal.

There's no mistaking a strike. In fact, you'll know it's coming. As a big fish approaches, the tiny baitfish senses it and furiously tries to avoid capture. When you feel the bait is excited you know you're likely to receive a runoff as the bigger fish inhales the helpless anchovy. Here it's important to keep your rod tip in a lowered position, the tip pointed in the direction the line is moving. As the line moves off quickly, engage your gear or close the bail, and lift back smartly to set the hook. Because you're using a fine-wire hook, set the hook only once.

The key is to maintain sufficient pressure so the fish doesn't reach the kelp. If it does, your line will often become fouled and there's just no way you can work the fish back to the boat. A strong fish that reaches the kelp will usually break your line.

When fishing around kelp, you never know what species may take your bait. Pacific barracuda and Pacific bonito are two of the most popular predators. The Pacific yellowtail and the white sea bass also call this habitat home and are among the prized catches. California's strict enforcement of size and bag limits and sound marine management techniques have resulted in substantial improvement in this coastal fishery, particularly with white sea bass, which have made a remarkable comeback in recent years. Kelp bass also prowl the kelp and are fine table fare.

Bottom fishing also an option

While chumming usually entices strikes from the fish that move through the mid-range and surface waters, you can often score down on the bottom too. When fish aren't cooperating, many anglers simply add a rubber-cored sinker to their line and send the bait right down to the bottom. Often they're rewarded with sand bass, California corbina, or California halibut, all of which are fun to catch and good eating.

Silver and king salmon inshore favorites

Inshore anglers have opportunities for silver salmon and king salmon off San Francisco's Golden Gate on north to Alaska. There the time-proven technique of using cannonball sinkers to get anchovy baits down to the fish is still very popular. Most of the party boats still use the cast-iron breakaway cannonballs which weigh up to 3 pounds. However, many of the small boats employ downriggers to send their spinner-blade attractors and anchovy- or herring-baited hooks down to the fish.

There are times when slow trolling for big salmon brings fast and furious action. Frequently, though, you have to put in the time, searching the fishfinder for schools of baitfish and systematically slow trolling until the bigger blips, indicating salmon, show up on your screen. Once the season gets under way, the fish are usually concentrated, with the professional party and charter boats communicating daily and zeroing in on the fish.

Private boatmen often fish the same areas as the party packets, but common courtesy should prevail. Troll the same area, but keep in mind that the professionals have many anglers on board, and shouldn't be crowded by the small boat fraternity.

Rockfish are a gourmet treat

The many species of rockfish that inhabit the cold Pacific waters from the Golden Gate north to Oregon and Washington are among the tastiest fish the region has to offer and are regularly sought by inshore bottom fishermen. While they are caught well offshore in the deep, sufficient numbers are found inshore wherever there is broken, irregular, rocky bottom.

Drifting chunk baits of herring and using a basic high-low rig with sufficient weight to hold bottom results in fast action when you locate a piece of choice bottom. Often small-boat anglers will drop a marker buoy once a productive area is located and repeatedly drift over it. Another option, of course, is anchoring right above a productive spot.

Famous bridges offer exciting striped bass action

Inshore anglers on the Atlantic Coast have their Verrazano Narrows Bridge spanning the Hudson River. On the Pacific Coast, the Golden Gate Bridge reaches across San Francisco Bay. Both bridges have one supporting tower in the water which causes currents to swirl about it, often trapping baitfish and in turn attracting striped bass. Both bridges are very productive for small-boat anglers armed with bucktail jigs and deep-running plugs.

The most popular technique around these bridges is to position a boat on the downcurrent side of the tower and cast up into the swirling maelstrom of back-eddies that are formed as the tide rushes along. Another approach is to fish the upcurrent, where the current is separated by the tower. The resulting dead spot of minimal current is where stripers take up station to wait for food to be swept their way.

Freshwater anglers, in particular, know that trout hang out near large rocks in a stream, as there is less current. They wait for food to either congregate or be swept their way. The towers of these two famous bridges serve much the same as a rock in a stream, only on a much greater scale.

The waters of the San Francisco Bay delta are home for striped bass of all sizes. The original stocks came from New Jersey's Navesink River and have propagated over the years. While overfishing depleted the stocks, sound fishery management practices have resulted in recovery to a point where bay anglers now enjoy superb sport. Some of the most enjoyable fishing comes with light casting or spinning tackle and plugs and bucktails along the many miles of marsh that border undeveloped areas of the bay.

This nice lingcod was hauled from the bottom with a leadhead jig with a chartreuse plastic bait tail. Lingcod are a favorite of West Coast inshore fishermen, who also have their jigs attacked by a wide variety of rockfish that reside on the same bottom.

Fly fishing from small boats is also becoming popular, with a No. 8-, 9- or 10-weight outfit ideally suited to coaxing strikes from predominately school stripers in the 2- to 10-pound class.

Lingcod a tasty Pacific treat

Lingcod are a target of Oregon and Washington small-boat and party-boat anglers, who often employ a multi-hooked ganion rig with as many as five or six hooks to send their herring chunk baits into the depths. While the lingcod is the favorite because of its great taste, there are dozens of species of rockfish that can be caught as a bonus. Live baits are favored. In fact, many anglers who catch a small fish on the lingcod grounds will often bait up with it, or use live anchovies or sardines. If live bait isn't available, chunks of herring, anchovies, sardines or mackerel may be used.

The ganion rigs are often sent to the bottom with a pound or more of sinker weight to deal with the 150 to 300 feet of water. The multi-hook, high-low rig enables you to present five or six baited hooks and do less reeling. Multiple hookups are often the norm. It's not always as enjoyable as fishing in the shallows, but small-boat and party-boat anglers can wind up with great table fare.

Trolling for silver and king salmon exciting sport

Oregon, Washington, and Alaska anglers who fish the inshore grounds can seek silver or king salmon, or they can send their rigs down to the bottom for Pacific halibut. All three species are fun to catch and great on the dinner table.

Inshore trolling at the river mouths is by far the most popular method of catching all of the salmon species. This is very seasonal sport, with the runs of each species coming at different times of the year. The salmon fishery is highly regulated, which has helped greatly in its recovery in recent years.

Deep, fast water at river mouths and turbulent currents force anglers to employ conventional outfits rated for 20- to 30-pound line. Trolling whole herring baits, with spinner blades attached to your leader ahead of the baits, has for years been a proven method of scoring with these great gamefish. Depending on tidal flow and water depth, the baits are run into the depths with the aid of heavy trolling sinkers, or via downriggers.

Pacific halibut heaviest members of the flatfish clan

The Pacific halibut frequents much the same areas as the salmon. It is not unusual for anglers to fish for salmon when the tides are optimal for them, then switch over to bottom fishing for the Pacific halibut.

Catching this biggest member of the flatfish clan is often work. The most popular rig is a conventional bottom rig, consisting of a three-way swivel, 3 feet of 40- or 50-pound-test leader material and single or double hook in tandem with the beak or claw hooks in 6/0 through 8/0 sizes. Baited with chunks of herring or mackerel, the rig is sent to the bottom with a sinker sufficiently heavy to hold bottom, often 16 to 24 ounces. Then it's just a waiting game as you drift over their known haunts. Once hooked, the halibut shows its strength, using its broad, flat, body stubbornly. Constant pressure is the key. Even when nearly to the boat, it is not unusual for a big halibut to dive for the bottom, ripping line from your reel. It's a good idea to keep a moderate drag and not apply too much pressure and risk breaking the line.

With the halibut, care must be exercised to observe daily bag limits and size limits, both of which have sustained this fishery over the years.

Look for exciting inshore sport close to home

Anglers often travel great distances in pursuit of their favorite gamefish and bottom feeders and overlook fine inshore fishing close to home. There are many species that haven't been included in this chapter that offer fine sport and table fare. The inshore waters are the nurseries where many species spawn. These waters often hold a variety of species to satisfy the most discriminating angler.

DRIFT FISHING

Of all the types of fishing available to the coastal angler, perhaps the most contemplative of all is drift fishing. It has a character all its own, one that is ever changing. There are times when a brisk summer breeze moves you along swiftly over productive bottom. Other times, barely a breath of air in the morning carries your craft.

The tide changes by the minute, ebbing and flowing twice in each lunar day of 24 hours, 51 minutes. A 4- or 5-knot current of a tidal river swiftly swirls along, with rips and eddies crashing so loudly it becomes difficult to hear. On other occasions, the silence on the slack permits you to hear the crickets in the nearby reeds.

A spot completely devoid of fish or activity at one stage of the tide may provide sterling action just hours later. Thus it becomes important to study each waterway you plan to fish to determine how different wind and tide conditions affect the area. Above all, study coastal charts of the area, so you know the bottom conformation. The makeup of the bottom is a major consideration, whether drifting on a broad expanse of ocean or in a meandering tidal creek.

For most inshore drift-fishing situations you don't really need a lot of equipment. A light spinning and popping outfit are ideal. A tackle box should include loose hooks, dipsey- and rubber-cored sinkers, plastic floats, and assorted leadhead jigs. It's also good to carry a tape measure to ensure compliance with size regulations and repellent to ward off insects.

(Left) California halibut, southern flounder and summer flounder are all popular inshore feeders that are caught by drift fishing. June Rosko is unhooking a typical summer flounder that was caught by drifting a sea robin strip bait just a mile offshore by granddaughter Jacqueline Basilio while aboard the "Linda June."

Familiarity breeds success

No two waterways are the same. Water may run swift and silent in some spots, and more turbulent in others. Each hour can present a different set of circumstances. Anglers who spend time studying these conditions can quickly adjust to the changing movements and feeding habits of the fish.

Many species call canal home

One example of an area that offers a wide variety of drift-fishing possibilities is the canal that joins the north end of Barnegat Bay with the Manasquan River. This canal is narrow, with bridge towers and swift currents, especially during moon tides. Its bottom is irregular, with deep holes, wide flats and rocky areas. This canal provides a good cross section of the many kinds of fish and backdrops the drift fisherman may find.

A wide variety of species either call the canal their home or use it as a thoroughfare between the two bodies of water. During spring and fall, winter flounder are in residence, often burying in the sand until tidal conditions suit their fancy. As waters warm, sea bass and blackfish move in, holding forth on the rocky patches of bottom and tight to the bulkheads. Their arrival is followed by summer flounder, who take up residence along the sandy bottom vacated by winter flounder. Arriving early in the spring are striped bass and weakfish, which often share the same deep holes and can be read by fish-finding electronics. Bluefish move in, too, but most often they are on the move, traveling swiftly until they catch up with the plentiful schools of sand eels and spearing.

A light popping or spinning outfit is ideal for this type of waterway. Monofilament line in the 10- to 15-pound-test range is preferred. It is fine enough for a variety of terminal rigs and lures, yet heavy enough to pull off an obstruction or the many mussel beds that litter the bottom.

This canal, which joins a river and a bay, is used by fish as they travel to feed or as a migration path. It's ever changing, as are all waterways of its type.

Because of the canal's swift current, winter flounder often bury themselves in the sand bottom sections of the canal, preferring not to fight the flow during its peak. As the current slows, they begin searching for food. It's at this time, usually during the slack, that they're most active

A popular rig for the flatfish begins with a tiny three-way swivel to the end of a line. To one eye of the swivel tie in a short piece of 8- or 10- pound-test monofilament with a loop in the end, onto which you can slip a small dipsey sinker weighing a half ounce to an ounce. The light connection is so you can easily break free if the sinker fouls on the bottom. A lightweight sinker should bounce along the bottom rather than drag as you drift.

To the remaining eye of the swivel, tie in an 18-inch piece of 10-pound-test monofilament or fluorocarbon leader material. Tie a No. 8 or 9 Chestertown or wide-gap hook to the end. Next, tie a dropper loop into the leader and tie in a second shorter leader, about 6 inches long, with a second hook. Bait up with a 3-inch-long piece of sandworm, bloodworm, clam, or mussel and drift along slightly before, during, of slightly after the slack and you'll be pleasantly surprised how quickly the flatfish will take bait. At both ends of this waterway there is sandy bottom that holds the flatfish and is the most productive.

Species such as sea bass, blackfish, and porgies tend to stick close to the canal's bulkheads, as this is where grass shrimp tend to cling and mussels are abundant. Boatmen find that drifting a sinker close to the bottom often results in snags, especially in the rocky bottom areas. They instead use a float rig that keeps their hook bait just off the bottom.

Water depth important

It pays to know the depth of the water where you'll be drifting. Tie a knot in your line a foot shorter than the water depth (i.e. if the water is 15-feet deep, tie the knot 14 feet from the end). Slip a bead or button onto the line, followed by a plastic

float with a hole in the middle, so it slides freely. Tie a No. 4 or 5 claw or beak hook to the line, and finish off the rig by placing a small rubber-cored sinker onto the line about a foot from the hook. The sinker will help hold the entire rig perpendicular to the bottom as you drift.

The plastic snap float saves the chore of using a knot and button, and may simply be snapped to your line at a desired depth. The float snaps open and slides on the line when a fish is hooked and many prefer it to the aforementioned method of rigging.

Live grass shrimp are a good bait to use, but a tiny fiddler crab, small piece of clam or mussel, bloodworm or sandworm, all work well with this rig. Keep in mind that most of the fish weigh less than 3 pounds, so keep the bait small. Smaller fish will rip a large bait from the hook. Small baits get sucked in and fish are more easily hooked.

This rig enables you to reel in to the sinker, with the plastic float sliding on the line. As you let it back out, the sinker takes the baited hook to the desired depth just a foot or so off the bottom, and the bead and float slide up the line, stopped by the knot, which holds the rig in just the right position.

Because the porgies, blackfish, and sea bass stay close to the bulkhead, the best way to fish is to drift close to the bulkhead, holding your rod tip as close to the bulkhead as possible. Just watch the float and when it pops under—just like fishing for sunfish in a farm pond—lift back smartly and set the hook.

Some species avoid swift tidal flow

When striped bass and weakfish arrive in waterways they'll often school and take up station in a spot that gets them out of the main tidal flow. You can often observe them on your fishfinder stacked like cordwood in the deep holes, where they can pass the time without expending effort fighting the current. As the tide slows, usually an hour before, during and after the change, they fan out searching for food in the form of baitfish, crabs, and seaworms.

Bob Rosko's about to unhook a fine weakfish landed by Jacqueline Basilio, while his daughter Kelsey looks on. Drift fishing from the "Baby Linda June" on the placid waters of Barnegat Bay in New Jersey is relaxing and enjoyable for the entire family. A variety of species are landed during the summer months, including summer flounder, striped bass and bluefish.

A live shrimp, hooked through its back, is a potent bait that will bring a strike from many varieties of fish. When rigging for drift fishing, it's often possible to simply tie a beak-style hook directly to the end of your line, bait up with a shrimp and ease it out in the current.

Use live baits to score

Live bait fishing is an extremely effective way of getting strikes while drifting. Because waterways can have a lot of boat traffic during the day, the best time to drift is often at night, and especially at dusk and daybreak when the tides are right.

This is very easy fishing, and great fun. Rigging is as easy as it gets. Begin by tying a 2-foot-long loop in the end of your line using either a Bimini knot or double surgeon's knot. Then use a double surgeon's knot to tie a 36-inch piece of monofilament or fluorocarbon leader material to your double line. To the end of the leader, tie in a claw, beak or O'Shaughnessy hook sized according to the bait you're using.

Sandworms work extremely well when drifting for stripers and weakfish, and a No. 1, 1/0 or 2/0 beak or claw hook with a baitholder shank is perfect. Simply slip the hook point into the worm's mouth and bring it out about 3/4 of an inch from the head. The baitholder shank holds the worm securely, and it will swim as you drift along.

If larger baits are used, such as live eels, a 4/0 through 6/0 hook is more appropriate. Eels measuring 8 to 15 inches are most often used. The eel should be hooked through the lips, which permits it to swim freely as you drift. The same size hook may be used when live herring, spot, or other small baitfish are used. Small blue claw crabs are also used with success by placing the hook into the white shell on the crab's bottom and bringing it out the top near the point.

With all of these baits it's just a matter of drifting along with the current and paying out 40 or 50 feet of line. When the current is running fast you may have to add a rubber-cored sinker to the line to take the bait down, but as the tide slackens no weight is needed. Most anglers fish with their reel in free spool, and as a striper or weakfish picks up the bait, they permit it to move off. Then, with the rod pointed at the fish, lock the reel in gear, lift back smartly to set the hook, and the fun begins.

These techniques can also bring some big summer flounder, which also cruise along the bottom searching for a meal.

Bluefish play by own rules

When the bluefish move into the canal they create havoc with anglers targeting stripers and weakfish. Bluefish use their teeth to bite through a baitfish to immobilize it, then swallow the pieces, whereas stripers and weaks swallow the bait whole. When you suddenly find your eel bait bitten in half, or a herring chopped to pieces, it's the result of the bluefish and time to switch to lures. If you stick with live baits the blues will continue to cut them in half.

Unlike stripers and weaks, bluefish move along in small schools. Their appearance is often heralded by schools of spearing, baby menhaden and herring leaping into the air to avoid the ravenous attack of bluefish from below.

The most exciting way to catch them is casting a surface popping plug to the breaking fish. This results in great surface strikes and often many jumps from the tough adversary. When the fish are hanging out in the depths, deep-running swimming plugs, bucktails or plastic-tailed leadhead jigs, small spoons, or metal squid can drum up some action.

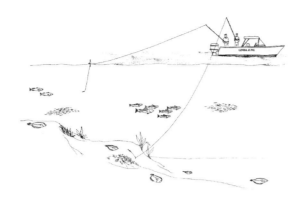

In most bays, rivers, and other inshore saltwater waterways, you'll find there are some species, like the flounder and halibut, that reside right on the bottom. Striped bass and sea trout are often traveling at intermediate levels. It's often wise to fish a rig right on the bottom and a second rig at an intermediate level to pique the interest of both types of fish.

Flounder provide leisurely sport

Drift fishing for summer flounder, or fluke, is perhaps the most relaxed form of drift fishing on waterways.

A very effective drift rig for summer flounder is made by tying a small three-way swivel to the end of your line. Next, tie in a 5 or 6-inch piece of monofilament line with a loop in it to one of the swivel eyes, onto which you'll slip a 1- or 2-ounce dipsey or bank-style sinker. To the remaining eye of the swivel, tie in a 36-inch piece of 15- or 20-pound-test leader material. Wide-gap or long-shanked Carlisle or beak hooks, size 1/0 or 2/0, can be snelled to the end of the leader.

One favorite hook bait is a live mummichog, or killie, which should be hooked through the lips. Some anglers add a thin strip of squid, about the same size or a hair longer than the killie. As the killie swims it causes the squid strip to flutter. It is a combination summer flounder love. You can also use a fresh spearing or sand eel with good results.

Fluke are aggressive feeders, and they'll seize a bait quickly. Veteran anglers will hesitate a few seconds when they feel the initial strike, lowering the rod tip to give the fish slack and time to mouth the bait. When they feel a firm pull, they slowly begin reeling, which often causes the fluke to bite down hard and hook itself. This technique often works better than pulling quickly at the first sign of a bite.

Broad ocean is a big a challenge

Drift fishing on an open expanse of ocean is much different than floating through a canal or other waterway. The water may be all the same, but there can be a big difference on the bottom. Depressions, peaks, ridges, rocks and reefs determine where bait will congregate. Where the bait congregates, you'll find larger game. It is critical to know the bottom conformation, and the direction that your boat will drift as a result of wind or tide.

Sharks first to arrive

Along the middle and north Atlantic coast the first gamefish to arrive on the scene each spring are the sharks. The huge schools of Atlantic mackerel arrive early and are often accompanied by schools of blue sharks. Shortly thereafter the bluefish swarm north, followed by mako sharks, threshers tigers and hammerheads.

With the arrival of the forage species such as mackerel and bluefish, it's often easy to score with the sharks by drifting a live mackerel or bluefish through the area where your fishfinder has indicated an abundance of fish. But as the forage moves north, many of the sharks take up residence locally to feed on the oceanic bonito, Atlantic bonito, dolphin, squid and small tuna.

Drift fishing for shark is great sport and not too difficult to master. To enjoy maximum rod and reel sport with many types of shark, it's best to fish with either 30- or 50-pound-class tackle. Many anglers maximize their chances of landing sharks after prolonged fights by loading their 30-pound reels with 50-pound monofilament line, and their 50-pound reels with 80-pound line. Standard 30- or 50-pound-class trolling rods with throw-lever drag reels are excellent choices for shark drifting. Other anglers prefer the shorter stand-up rods that have become popular with chumming devotees in recent years. Again, it is a matter of personal preference.

Drifting for pelagic sharks is popular on all three U.S. coasts. Al Ristori used stand-up tackle to play this big blue shark that struck a fillet of bluefish bait drifted in the waters off Block Island, Rhode Island. The big sharks often migrate along with schools of mackerel, bluefish, and tuna.

Surgeon's loop
The surgeon's loop is a quick and easy way to make a loop in the end of a line or leader. Begin by doubling the end of the line to form a loop, then tie an overhand knot at the base of the double line. Leaving the loop open, bring the double line through once more. Holding the standing line and tag end, just pull the loop to tighten the knot, which will lay over itself and lay straight. The size of the loop can easily be adjusted by shifting the loose knot before tightening it. Clip the tag end with a nail clip.

Chumming is unquestionably the best way to score with the big sharks. The basic terminal rig begins with a ball-bearing swivel and coastlock snap at the end of a line. This type of swivel will minimize line twist as you drift along.

A haywire twist is used to fasten 5 or 6 feet of No. 10 or 12 stainless steel leader wire, or a like amount of stainless steel cable, attached via crimps. Next comes a single ball-bearing swivel, followed by a like amount of stainless steel leader wire or cable.

Finally, attach a triple-strength, forged offset hook in sizes ranging from 8/0 through 10/0. Note that a pair of swivels are used, and two pieces of leader material, rather than a single piece. This method of rigging makes handling the shark at boatside easier, and it also helps keep sharks from wrapping up in the leader. Blue sharks, in particular, have a habit of wrapping themselves in leader and line, which makes it difficult to release them.

Sharks are the scavengers of the sea. They're quick to seize a struggling fish. They're lazy too, meaning they'll readily pick up a dead bait. For sharks, the old adage of "a fresh bait works best" doesn't apply. Older bait, even partially decomposed, will often get you more strikes, as it gives off a potent scent.

Whole mackerel, herring, and bluefish are among the favorite baits of anglers chumming and drifting for sharks. Often fillets of these fish—two or three slipped on and held secure to the hook with soft copper wire—work extremely well. Some anglers prefer a live baitfish, as it emits sounds as well as the scent. The key with a live bait is to remove its fins and clip its tail, so it doesn't swim about too actively.

Boatmen should position their drift so the tide or wind carries them across known wrecks, reefs or irregular bottom conformations that hold fish on which the sharks feed. One bait should be fished at a 50-foot depth, another at 100 feet and a third at 150 feet. Lock the reels in gear, with the drag backed off, yet with sufficient tension that it doesn't backlash when a shark picks up and runs off with the bait.

The reel's audible click should also be activated to help warn anglers of a strike.

Chumming with ground menhaden, herring, or mackerel is relatively easy. To begin with, drill a dozen 2 1/2-inch holes in a 5-gallon bucket. This bucket is used to hold a block of frozen chum. Place a lid on the bucket, tie it off to a cleat, and as the chum thaws, it will ooze out through the holes as you drift along.

It then becomes a waiting game. If you're well positioned, your chum will leave a shark-attracting trail behind the boat. It may take minutes, it could take hours, but if you cover the grounds, chum correctly, and have your baits set at various depths, your chances of scoring are good.

The first "Linda June" was a 24-foot Wellcraft with an Airslot hull and twin Mercruiser stern drives. The author trailered it from Florida to New England and caught a wide variety of species while drift fishing inshore and offshore. Boats of this size are seaworthy, comfortable fishing machines. They are ideal family boats, as they have a walkaround bow, cuddy cabin and head.

Rock and coral bottoms harbor bottom feeders

In southern waters the tropical grouper and snapper congregate around coral reefs and rocky outcroppings. They usually hold tight to the bottom. At intermediate depths around the reefs and rocks you'll find dolphin, king mackerel, Spanish mackerel, barracuda, wahoo, and little tunny. This combination is ideally suited to deep jigging from a drifting boat.

Deep jigging offers excitement

Most anglers prefer the control of conventional tackle over spinning tackle when it comes to deep jigging. A stiff-action 6-foot-6-inch or 7-foot fiberglass or graphite rod, with a reel loaded with 15-, or preferably, 20-pound-test line, will work nicely for deep jigging. Because many of the species you'll encounter have sharp teeth, it's wise to use a double surgeon's knot to double the last couple of feet of line. Use the same knot to tie in a 3- to 4-foot-long piece of 30- or 40-pound-test leader.

Leadheads, with either bucktail or plastic-tailed skirts, are popular jigs for this type of jigging. Depending on the depth of the reef and the speed of wind or current, hook sizes ranging from 4/0 through 7/0.

The key to successful deep jigging is being intimately familiar with the bottom conformation. This can be accomplished by carefully studying geodetic charts of the area, and then using your fishfinder to view the reef, wreck or ridge. This will show you where the peaks and valleys are, and where the fish are holding.

Drift fishermen along the California, Oregon and Washington coast often use leadhead jigs with plastic tails to coax strikes from bottom feeders. This big kelp bass was hooked while drifting and jigging just a mile off-shore. Sand bass, lingcod and rockfish frequent the same grounds and respond to both lures and chunk baits fished on the bottom. All are fine on the dinner table.

Use a marker buoy

If wind is lacking, a boat will be moved by the tidal flow. If wind is present it may overpower the tide and move you against the current.

Many deep-jiggers move to the high bottom they see on their fishfinder screen and drop a marker buoy. This allows them to bracket the area, and also helps them avoid drifting from deep water into the peaks of the reef, which can foul lines.

The most effective method is to move up to your marker buoy and shut down your engine. Permit your jig to settle all the way to the bottom. As soon as it touches down, lock the reel in gear promptly, lift back smartly with your rod tip and begin reeling. Grouper and snapper cruising along the bottom often view the plummeting jig and then excitedly charge it as it leaps off the bottom and heads to the surface.

As you're retrieving, you can jig with your rod tip, making the lure dart upwards and then falter. Keep in mind that grouper, snapper and other bottom feeders will often strike the jig deep, while intermediate cruisers such as king mackerel, dolphin, bonito, little tunny and other pelagic species will strike at mid-level. Often they'll strike just as you're about to lift the jig from the water.

The key when you receive a strike is to pull back firmly, get a few turns on the reel, and keep the fish away from the sharp coral. If you've positioned your drift properly, the movement of the boat away from the peaks of the reef will help put more distance between the fish and the bottom.

In shallow water the positioning of your drift isn't as critical as it is in places like the Bahamas or the Gulf of Mexico, where the bottom is a hundred or more feet beneath the hull. Often in the Gulf you can catch red snapper on every drop to the bottom if you're positioned properly. But if you haven't done your homework, and are drifting over the sand bottom adjacent to where the fish are holding, you won't receive a strike. You've got to be right on the mark.

Flatfish targeted on open water

Drifting for flatfish is another tactic that enjoys tremendous popularity on all three U.S. coasts. Atlantic coast anglers target the summer flounder, Gulf coast boatmen seek out the southern flounder, and Pacific drifters go after the heavyweights of the clan, the California and Pacific halibut. The habits of all four species are remarkably similar. Were you to close your eyes while drifting any of these three huge bodies of water and felt the telltale strike of any of the three species, it would be difficult to identify just where you were.

Members of the flatfish clan spend most of their time on sandy, soft, or mud bottom. Often they are almost completely buried, using their fins to flip sand or mud over their backs, with just their eyes exposed. They'll do this when storms occur, roiling the water, particularly when there is a quick drop in water temperature. Sometimes they use this vantage to wait for unsuspecting baitfish, crabs, squid, and shrimp to be carried their way by the current. When water clarity and temperature are to their liking they vacate the sand bottom and move about aggressively searching for a meal.

Flatfish will search along the perimeter of rocky bottom, or where wrecks or artificial reefs litter the bottom. For it is in spots such as this that baitfish, crabs, shrimp, and other forage take sanctuary. Here again, the drift fisherman must know the bottom conformation.

Flatfish will also hang out near hills or lumps that break up flat areas as that is where the forage is most plentiful.

With some minor adjustments, the same rig used for summer flounder in canals works equally well on all three coasts. Sinkers must be heavy enough to hold bottom. This may mean using 6- or 8-ounce bank-style sinker. If the wind is strong and the drift extremely fast, and you're in 50 or 60 feet of water, you may need as much as 16 ounces of weight. On the Northwest halibut grounds, a 16-ounce sinker is sometimes on the light side, with sinkers double that weight occasionally needed.

Many party boat captains along the Atlantic coast who specialize in drift fishing for summer flounder contend their passengers who lean towards a heavier sinker catch the most fish. Often during the summer months, in the heat of the afternoon, a strong southeast wind will develop and the speed of drift doubles or triples from the barely perceptible drift of the morning. If you don't add sinker weight and continue with just 3 or 4 ounces of lead, your bait may never reach bottom where a summer flatfish could spot it. The angler who keeps adjusting by replacing a light sinker with a heavier one substantially enhances his chance of scoring.

Hook size should depend on the fish size. Inshore drifters targeting 1- to 2-pound summer flounder and southern flounder may opt for a 1/0 or 2/0 beak, Carlisle or wide-gap hook. If summer flounder on lumps or rocky bottom areas are ranging from 3 to 6 pounds, with occasional "doormats" ranging to 10 pounds, then

Party boats on all three coasts spend much of their time drift fishing, where wind and current carry them over productive bottom. The "Gambler" out of Point Pleasant Beach, New Jersey, drifts for summer flounder during the day and bluefish on evening trips. It also sails to far off canyons where yellowfin tuna and albacore are the target while drifting and chumming.

it's appropriate to use larger baits affixed to size 3/0 through 6/0 hooks. Southern California anglers drifting just off the kelp beds and along the beaches generally target smaller California halibut while using 1/0 or No. 1 hooks with a single anchovy bait. On the Northwest coast, where Pacific halibut often reach 80 to 100 pounds, it's not unusual to rig with 7/0 or 8/0 hooks and whole, or fillet, of herring bait.

While drifting for flatfish, it's not at all unusual to catch sea bass, spot and weakfish along the middle Atlantic coast, while Gulf Coast anglers have red snapper and porgies inhale baits intended for southern flatfish. Even on the halibut grounds of the Pacific there is often a plentiful population of rockfish and lingcod which can make a fine-eating bonus catch.

The rainbow runner is a fun fish to catch while drifting. They readily respond to a chum of ground fish and can be seen in the clear water as they cruise through the slick picking up pieces of fish. A chunk bait eased out with the current will often draw a strike. The rainbow runner will also strike small leadhead jigs. Most are released as they're not a popular table fish.

Bays and rivers offer peaceful fishing

If leisurely fishing is what you enjoy, then drifting the quiet reaches of the coastal bays and rivers of the Atlantic and Gulf coasts is made to order. All you need is a small boat and motor and you're all set. Many anglers just use a 9.5-horse-power outboard motor, small aluminum boat, or a rental boat to seek out the wide variety of species that come and go with the changing seasons.

The majority of the bays are located inside the Barrier Islands that border the coast, such as on the South Shore of Long Island, and the east coast of New Jersey, Delaware, Maryland and Virginia, and south through the Carolinas and Georgia.

These bays are for the most part shallow, often less than 10 feet.

While the summer flounder is the most popular bottom feeder caught in coastal bay waters by drift fishermen, the weakfish and southern weakfish are the most popular gamefish from the mid-Atlantic coast down through the Gulf of Mexico.

To the south, the Florida Bay, the Everglades, Mobile Bay and the hundreds of rivers and creeks that empty into the Gulf all are home to the southern weakfish, known locally as the sea trout or just plain trout. An angler content to be carried by wind and tide in his small boat needs to know the water, where the weed beds are, and where the bait congregates.

Weakfishing is light tackle sport at its finest. A light popping rod with a multiplying casting reel, or a spinning outfit rated for 10-pound-test line, is all you'll need. The same tactics work equally well on the tiderunning yellowfins of Barnegat Bay or the spotted trout of Pensacola Harbor.

Float rig vs. artificials

Anglers may use either natural baits or artificials when drift fishing for flatfish. Perhaps the most relaxing system is the time-tested popping cork-and-shrimp bait combination discussed earlier and used by anglers targeting blackfish, sea bass, and porgies in a canal or river environment.

Any one of the many varieties of shrimp found along the coast work well for bait. If the shrimp are large, just a single one threaded on the hook will do. Either live or dead shrimp may be used. If all that are available are the tiny grass shrimp found along the middle Atlantic, then slip four or five of them on the hook. Absent the availability of shrimp, a single sandworm, hooked through the mouth and slid up the hook a half inch or so works fine. Small, live spot or killies, hooked lightly through the lips or just beneath the dorsal fin will drift along enticingly and bring strikes from the weakfish.

If you're a person that lacks the patience to watch cork floats drifting along, then choose the artificials route. Admittedly, it's a bit more work, casting and retrieving, but it certainly will bring results. The weakfish will readily strike a properly presented swimming plug, bucktail jig, or leadhead jig with a plastic tail.

Drifting and chumming on a broad expanse of ocean or gulf also will often bring great rewards. With modern electronics it's now possible to cruise known haunts of pelagic species. Once a favorable temperature break is located you'll often read schools of squid, mackerel, herring, and the wide array of forage on which gamefish feed. Then, by checking geodetic charts to determine bottom conformation, you can shut down, drift along, and establish a chum line to attract the targeted species to your hook baits or jigs.

Beginning in the spring, huge schools of Atlantic mackerel begin a northward migration from the Virginia Capes to the Maritime Provinces. If you find them, you can enjoy a drift-fishing bonanza. The mackerel schools are often brought close to the surface with the aid of ground menhaden chum, and then pursued with diamond jigs and multi-colored plastic teasers. It's fun fishing, with lots of action.

Much the same techniques are employed with the speedy king mackerel. Once located, the kings will respond to a chum line of small pieces of fish or squid, with a hook bait of a live menhaden, pilchard, pinfish, grunt or other small forage species. It's not unusual to encounter stray dolphin, blackfin tuna, barracuda, Spanish mackerel and amberjack as you drift along.

Offshore drifting can bring surprises

A variety of pelagic species take up residence along the Northeast coast during the summer months from the 30-fathom line out to the canyons, the Continental Shelf and beyond. Along the inshore range the schools of bluefin tuna congregate where the supply of forage is plentiful. They're joined by Atlantic bonito, skipjack tuna, little tunny and dolphin. As you move into deeper water, you'll find yellowfin, with the canyons providing action with bigeye tuna and long-finned albacore, an occasional wahoo, dolphin, white marlin and blue marlin.

All of these species will respond to a drifted bait. While the most popular technique is to troll, many anglers have found that once hookups are received while trolling, it is far more relaxing to shut down, begin chumming operations, and then drift baits.

Depending on conditions and the size of the fish being encountered in an area, the tackle choice will range from 20-to 30-pound gear for inshore drifting, up to 50-pound tackle for drifting along the edge of the shelf and in the canyons.

Terminal rigging is simple. Most anglers use a 6- to 8-foot piece of fluorocarbon leader material, usually the same test as their line, sometimes a little lighter if the fish appear to be leader shy. The leader should be tied to the line with a double surgeon's knot. Live bait-style hooks can range from 2/0 and 4/0 inshore with small butterfish and squid baits, on up to 7/0 and 8/0 where larger fish are encountered or where live mackerel or large live squid are used as bait.

If you stream a bait out 100 or more feet the current may push it towards the surface. This may make it necessary to add a rubber-cored sinker to the leader to keep the hook bait drifting along at the same depth as the chum.

Conversely, when there is minimal current or wind, an inflated toy balloon, cork, or Styrofoam float may be added to the line to suspend the bait at the desired level. Otherwise, the bait might sink directly to the bottom while the light, partially suspended chum particles drift off at intermediate levels. The new plastic snap floats work very effectively on the offshore grounds. They maybe attached any-where on the line, and when a strike is received a spring mechanism permits the float to slide freely on the line.

The suspense and excitement generated in far offshore waters comes partially from not knowing just what will strike your bait. It may be a 20-pound yellowfin tuna, or a 500-pound blue marlin that normally dines on tuna of that size!

(right) Many coastal marinas have live bait tanks such as the one pictured here in Islamorada, Florida. Live baits are popular with drift fishermen on all coasts. This tank has circulating water that keeps the mullet baits in prime condition. Mullet, pinfish, goggleyes, anchovies, shrimp and crabs are just a sample of the baits that are available, depending on the coast.

CHUMMING

Chumming is a common practice in saltwater fishing and involves dropping food or other attractant into the water, to draw fish to your lures or baits. The chum food is usually native to the area and the species sought, such as anchovies, herring, menhaden or other forage species. It may also be composed of chunks of fish or ground fish. The oil derived from fish is also used. But chum is not limited to the food on which fish normally feed. Bread is often an effective chum, as is whole kernel corn, neither of which is in the normal food chain of most gamefish.

Practically every fish will respond to a chum slick. The giant bluefin tuna, occasionally weighing more than 1,000 pounds, will readily circle through a chum line, picking up chunks of herring from the slick. On the other end of the scale, a winter flounder weighing but a pound will just as eagerly dart about for pieces of ground clams or mussels drifting along the bottom.

For a day of successful chumming for tuna and other pelagic species you need an adequate supply of chum. Sail with two flats of butterfish or menhaden, a 5-gallon pail of ground menhaden, a 5-gallon pail of crab shells and cleanings, and a box each of large butterfish and squid as bait. Meat hooks make handling fish less of a chore. Knives, a chum ladle and a cutting board are also handy.

(Left) When chumming where there is a swift current it's often wise to employ both a bow and stern anchor to hold your boat in one position. Shown here in the Savannah River, near Savannah, Georgia, anglers are chumming and baiting for striped bass, sea trout, and redfish.

Maintenance of slick essential

There is a delicate balance that must be maintained to be successful at chumming. You want to attract so they'll respond to a baited hook or lure, but if you chum too heavily the fish will often settle well back in the slick, just gorging on your offering. Conversely, if you chum too sparingly, or fail to maintain a consistent flow of chum, the fish will show little interest or move off. Maintaining that perfect balance is something that isn't difficult, but comes with experience. A good rule of thumb is to drop pieces of chum into the water at regular intervals. When fishing with a group of anglers, and especially aboard a boat, a person should be assigned the responsibility of maintaining the chum line. In the excitement of catching fish, the chumming is often forgotten, which can make the action short lived.

Chumming practices vary by area and species. There are literally hundreds of variations and the sampling offered here is representative of some of the most popular methods. Chumming can be done from boats, jetties, the surf, bridges, piers and bulkheads. Wherever fish are found, and regardless of how you may be fishing for them, chumming should be included in your arsenal of options.

This mackerel (top) and butterfish have been cut into small pieces for use as chum. The chunk chum is then supplemented with a soupy mixture of ground fish and sea water. The key is to attract but not feed the fish. It's best to use hook baits cut from the same species used for the chum.

Chumming in the canyons

Along the middle and north Atlantic U.S. coast, boatmen seeking bigeye tuna, yellowfin tuna, and albacore in the canyons often use a combination of ground and chunked fish with excellent results. Boats are either anchored or drift along with the wind or current, usually along the edges of the dropoff, where an upwelling of currents causes baitfish to congregate and the larger gamefish to feed.

Forage species such as butterfish, mackerel, or herring are cut into pieces, usually about the size of your index finger. Five or six pieces from a butterfish and eight or 10 pieces from a mackerel or herring is about right. This is usually done before leaving for the fishing grounds, so you're saved the chore of doing it on the water. The chummer tosses three or four chunks into the water and watches as they drift away. When they've floated 30 or 40 feet from the boat, several more pieces are tossed over.

After a dozen or more chunks have been deposited into the sea, a ladle full of "soup," which is a mixture of ground menhaden, mackerel, or herring and equal parts sea water, is deposited into the sea. This soup disburses in a cloud, carried along with the current. As the fish pick up the scent of the chum drifting along, they move towards its source, picking up tiny pieces of the ground fish, and also the chunks. It's not unusual to attract a school of the tuna, and see the fish moving ever closer to the boat, as the fish vie for the offering drifting along.

As the chummer goes about his task of attracting the fish, anglers must work their lines to present the bait in a natural drift. Terminal rigging is very basic. Some anglers just tie a size 4/0 through 7/0 O'Shaughnessy, beak, or circle hook directly to the end of their line. Because the various tuna are often line-shy, many anglers

Live baits are very effective during chumming. Anchovies, sardines, mullet, menhaden, spot and goggleyes are just a few of the more popular hook baits. They may be hooked through the back just forward of the dorsal fin, or just behind the dorsal fin. Some anglers run the hook point in one eye socket and out the other, while others run the hook through the lower jaw and out the upper jaw.

are now using fluorocarbon leaders. The hook is tied directly to the end of a fluoro-carbon leader that is 5- or 6-feet long, and the leader is attached to the monofila-ment line using a surgeon's knot.

A whole butterfish is often an effective bait in the chum line, although some anglers prefer to use just half a fish.

Because squid are found in abundance in canyon waters, as are mackerel, some anglers will obtain a live bait and work that in the chum slick with excellent results. A live bait in distress will often immediately attract tuna. If your boat has a live well, live 6- or 7-inch spots or porgies caught from coastal rivers and bays also make an effective bait in an offshore chum slick.

The bait should be permitted to drift back in the chum slick unimpeded 100 feet or more feet from the boat. Then reel in and repeat the procedure. As a general rule, the angler who works at keeping the bait moving along with the chum will catch more fish than the angler who locks his reel in gear and keeps it in one posi-tion. If you don't work the line, the current pushing against the bait will often push it towards the surface and it will spin in a manner not as attractive to the fish as a free-drifting bait.

When there is little or no current, the chum and bait may sink directly beneath the boat. With a moderate current, the bait and chum will usually flow together. This is easily observed in the air-clear waters of the canyons. If you see the chum settling deep and the current carrying your line near the surface, it's wise to attach a rubber-cored sinker to your leader about 5 feet from the bait. Select a sinker that will keep your bait drifting as closely to the chum as possible.

At other times there may be a light current carrying the chum, but your bait may tend to sink too deep. Some anglers insert a tiny piece of Styrofoam into the bait to give it a bit of buoyancy. Another tip is to use a 4-inch block of Styrofoam with a slit cut into it. Place your line in the slit, adjusting it so the bait will be sus-pended at a desired level as you let it drift back in the chum line. Large plastic snap floats are designed expressly for this purpose. An inflated toy balloon may also be used as an effective float.

Some anglers set their baits beyond 50 feet depth, where other fish may be traveling oblivious to the chum far above them. Some anglers set one or two lines to depths of even 200 feet looking for the tuna and occasional broadbill swordfish.

You've got to be alert in this type of fishing. Fish will move up and inhale your bait and be swimming off with it in an instant. A good rule is to always keep your rod pointed in the direction the line is drifting, with ever so light pressure on the line to keep it from overrunning. If a fish takes your bait and begins to move off, lock your reel in gear, and as the line comes tight lift the tip smartly to set the hook. Then the fight is on.

Inshore chumming productive

Chumming on inshore grounds is similar to open-ocean chumming. There is little modification needed to seek species such as bluefish, striped bass, bonito, school bluefin tuna, Spanish mackerel, king mackerel and little tunny. Basically, tackle is scaled down from the 50- to 80-pound outfits used in the canyons, to 20- and 30-pound class equipment. Likewise, hook sizes from 1/0 through 5/0 are more in order. Even the chunks of bait used as chum are smaller, usually the size of your thumbnail, as are the baits. Small mullet, spearing, sand eels and killie baits all prove effective in attracting strikes when drifted back in a chum line.

Proper terminal rigging is essential when the targets are bluefish and king mackerel, both of which have extremely sharp teeth. A 6- to 12-inch piece of No. 8 or 9 coffee-colored stainless steel leader wire, with the hook on one end and a tiny barrel swivel on the other, prevents fish from biting through the monofilament. If you don't care to use a wire leader, a long-shanked hook works well, although occa-sionally fish will still bite through the monofilament when they take the bait deep.

Bays, rivers and estuaries provide opportunities

An angler's chumming tactics don't need to change much when he moves to

Party boats like the "Jamaica" often travel 100 miles offshore, where they anchor along the edges of canyons and the continental shelf to chum for bigeye tuna, yellowfin tuna, albacore, and dolphin. The boats are equipped with bunks and galley, with hot food and beverages available.

protected bays, rivers and estuaries where striped bass, weakfish, spotted weakfish and summer flounder reside. It is essential, however, to chum with the forage most often found in these inshore waters. Common grass shrimp measuring 1 to 2 inches in length are extremely plentiful in inshore waters and constitute a major portion of the diet of these species. Also very plentiful and a major source of food are the many species of crab, most notably the blue, calico, and sand crab. Shrimp and crabs work as both chum and hook baits.

Grass shrimp may be obtained using a seine worked in coastal marshes and around pilings and along bulkheads. A couple of quarts are all that are needed to fish a tide. Crabs may also be seined or caught in traps. As the crabs are larger, they are often cut into small pieces. Some anglers prefer eating the crabs and saving the discarded pieces for later use as chum. Both types of forage can be frozen and used as chum as the need arises.

A preferred method of fishing is to anchor up along the edge of a channel where these species are known to move with the tide as they search for a meal. The same consistent chumming is all that is needed to attract them to your boat. Just drop a few shrimp or a nominal amount of crab overboard at a time. Or use a combination of the two.

Because the shrimp are so small, smaller claw or beak hooks with baitholder shanks work best. A tiny rubber-cored sinker is often used if the current is swift, sometimes in conjunction with a plastic float. In many bay and river waters you'll be fishing in depths of 6 to 12 feet, and the float-and-sinker combo works well. Just let the bait drift out 100 feet or so, reel back in and repeat so the bait moves along with the chum.

The techniques outlined for using grass shrimp and crabs as chum also work from piers, bulkheads, docks and bridges. The key is positioning yourself so you can dispense the chum and have it carried away by the current, along with your baited rig. It's not unusual to see the fish move up into the chum line, especially when fishing night tides from bridges, piers and docks that have bright lights that illuminate the water.

Bottom feeders respond to chum

Bottom feeders such as winter flounder, sea bass and porgies also respond to a chum line, but here it is necessary to get the chum to the bottom. For this anglers use a chum pot. The most popular size chum pot is 4 to 5 inches in diameter and 8 to 10 inches deep. It has a lead bottom and hinged metal top with quarter-inch-square galvanized wire mesh sides.

The pot is filled with a frozen ground chum and eased to the bottom with a piece of cord. As the chum thaws, it oozes from the pot and is carried along the bottom.

Grass shrimp are tiny and may be collected with a seine from most any coastal bay and river along the Atlantic coast. They represent a major portion of the diet of many inshore species. They're an excellent chum, attracting a wide variety of species. Most anglers use a small hook that is baited with three or four of the tiny shrimp, which in turn are drifted out in the chum line.

Frozen ground chum an advantage

There are many kinds of ground chum. Ground menhaden, mussels, clams, conch, grass shrimp and seaworms all have their devotees. A combination of these ingredients often works best. If there is time, it's worthwhile to make up several batches of chum and keep it in your freezer. After a strong northeast storm you can often go down to the beach along the northeast Atlantic coast and collect a 5-gallon bucket of big sea clams that have washed up on the beach. Remove all of the clam meat from the shell and grind it up with a grinding head that produces pieces small enough to pass through the chum pot's quarter-inch mesh. You can also grind up the meat from sedge and black mussels and conch. Be careful of local regulations with regard to shellfish, as some states do prohibit collecting them in certain waters.

Once you've ground the above ingredients, boil up equal quantities of white rice and whole kernel corn. Mix all three ingredients together and place the chum in paper cups that will fit into the chum pot. Then freeze the cups of chum.

When it's time to fish, peel off and discard the paper cup from the frozen chum log and insert the log into the chum pot. Ease it to the bottom and let the current carry the chum to the fish.

You need only use the same bottom rig for winter flounder that you'd use if not chumming, usually a pair of No. 8 or 9 Chestertown hooks baited with bits of clam, sandworms, bloodworms or mussels. In the case of sea bass, porgies and tautog, a high-low rig, with hook size tailored to the fish in residence, works fine. Size

2 to 6 beak or claw hooks snelled to 8 to 12 inches of leader material are ideal. Pieces of clam, conch and strips of squid work well with the sea bass and porgies, while fiddler crabs, pieces of blue crab or green crabs are perfect for the tautog, also known as the "blackfish" or "whitechins" in some areas.

It sometimes pays to give the cord holding the chum pot a good yank, especially if there's little current around slack tide. This will send a cloud of chum streaming from the pot.

Some anglers attach a baited rig to the chum pot. This often gets a couple of bonus fish for the pan and proves the chum pot's attraction. Further proof comes when you clean your catch. Whether it's tuna from the canyons or flounder from bay waters, the fish will invariably have chum in their stomachs.

Still another trick, which attracts winter flounder in particular, is to stir up the bottom with the help of a long extension pole such as those used by house painters, with a plumber's toilet plunger, or a garden cultivator, attached to the end of it. Disturbing the bottom creates a cloud of mud which is carried off by the current. This in turn attracts the flounder, which will be looking for sea worms, crab, and shrimp that have been stirred up out of the mud. This technique is especially popular on the South Shore bays of Long Island.

Whole sea clams, conch, and mussels are used by many middle and north Atlantic Coast bottom fishermen to attract codfish, pollock, sea bass, porgies, flounder, and a host of other bottom feeders. The clams, conch and mussels are crushed with a hammer and the combination of shell and clam meat is dispensed overboard to settle to the bottom around the boat. When the bottom feeders pick up the scent of the chum, they move to the source and pick away at whatever meat they can obtain from the crushed shells. When they spot a piece of clam on a hook, they're often onto it in a flash.

Chumming reefs effective

Chumming also proves extremely effective for reef species. In Florida and along the Gulf Coast, many party boat skippers wouldn't think of leaving the dock without a good supply of chum on board. The accepted technique is to use electronics to determine where on the reef the fish are located. The skipper then positions the boat and places his anchor in sand bottom just off from the reef, easing back and using sufficient anchor line to place the boat at the edge of, or over, the reef.

Frozen ground-fish chum is available in 5-pound boxes. The cardboard is pulled away from the frozen chum and the block is placed in a mesh bag and hung over the side. As the chum thaws it oozes from the mesh bag.

While this gets one phase of chumming going, the deckhands on the party boats—and many private and charter boats, too—prepare a separate chum mixture. It is composed of equal parts thawed chum, rolled oats, and play sand, with just enough water added to enable the chum to be molded into "meatballs" the size of a tennis ball. The sand in the chum takes the meatball to the bottom, where it crum-

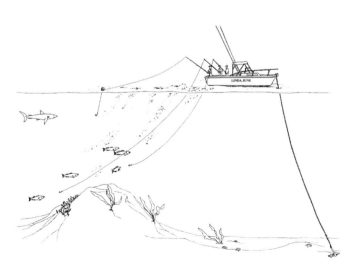

Baitfish tend to congregate on the crown of lumps, ridges and mounts. A wide variety of gamefish stay in an area where food is plentiful. When chumming, anchor your boat so the wind or current positions you so that your chum is carried towards the high bottom. Fish some lines deep and others suspended with a float for species that may be traveling high in the water column.

Weakfish and spotted weakfish readily respond to a chum of grass shrimp or pieces of table-size shrimp. Vin Sparano just netted this beauty for grandson Nick Andelora, who hooked it while drifting a shrimp-baited hook in the chum line. Note the splasher-type float which when twitched creates a surface disturbance a few feet above the bait, attracting inquisitive weakfish.

bles and is carried along the bottom by the current.

To get bigger pieces of chum to the bottom "depth charges" are employed. These are made by taking two brown paper lunch bags. A layer of sand is placed in the bottom of the bag, then a layer of cut-up fish—any fish will do. Last is a layer of rolled oats. This bag, which when filled will weigh several pounds, is placed inside of the second bag to keep it from falling apart on its decent to the bottom. The bags are loosely twisted closed and dropped overboard near the bow of the boat. When the depth charge reaches bottom the paper bag quickly disintegrates. The oats and pieces of fish are carried along the bottom by the current and attract the fish from all over the reef beneath your boat.

Once the chum slick has been established through the chum in the mesh bag, the meatballs and the depth charges, fishing begins in earnest. Some anglers fish with a regular bottom rig. Ohers employ a meatball rig to entice strikes.

Perhaps the most popular bottom rig begins with an egg-shaped sinker sufficiently heavy to hold bottom—usually 1 to 4 ounces—and a tiny barrel swivel. A 24-inch long piece of monofilament or fluorocarbon leader material is tied to the

111

remaining eye of the barrel swivel. A beak or claw hook, usually size l/0, is best, although hook sizes must fit the fish. Baited up with live shrimp, pieces of squid, chunks of bonito or mullet, or live pinfish or blue runners, the rig is lowered to the bottom. From there it's a waiting game until the reef dwellers are attracted to your bait by the chum in the depth charges.

The baited meatball rig is another effective way to combine chum and bait. It works in Bermuda, the Bahamas, Florida and the Gulf Coast, and wherever reef dwellers are found. The rig is made up of the same mixture described for meatballs. The hook is tied directly to the end of the monofilament line. Leaders are seldom used, although those who use fluorocarbon often have an edge. An exception is if very heavy grouper or snapper are in residence. Then leader material up to 50-pound-test may be used.

The hook is baited with a pilchard or a piece of cut bait. Mullet, balao, or a piece of bonito or little tunny are very effective. The bait is buried inside the meatball, which should be the size of a tennis ball. Next, wrap the leader and monofilament line around the meatball for a total of about 10 wraps. Firm up the meatball so it stays together.

The next step is to strip off sufficient line to reach the bottom. The meatball is tossed away underhanded, 10 to 20 feet away from the boat, and permitted to settle to the bottom. The bail of a spinning reel is kept open or a conventional reel kept in free spool. As it is settling to the bottom, the meatball begins to disintegrate and creates its own mini-chum slick. In just a minute or so the meatball will disintegrate.

By watching the line you'll quickly know if the fish has it. You're apt to be hooked to anything from a 2-pound yellowtail snapper to a 60-pound black grouper. The key is always having sufficient line stripped from your reel so the meatball reaches bottom unimpeded. If there is any drag whatsoever, the meatball will disintegrate completely on the way down and lose its effectiveness.

Many party boats chum by placing a frozen block of ground chum in a mesh bag and hanging it over the side. As the chum thaws, it oozes from the bag and leaves a cloud in the water. Small chunks of fish are also tossed over, sparingly, so as to attract, but not feed the fish. Fish are often attracted right to the boat.

Chum productive on tidal flats

There are times when wind conditions make it impossible to pole the flats, or where tidal conditions or a storm have roiled the flats and made it impossible to spot fish. Under such conditions, or even when visibility is good, chumming can be very effective in attracting bonefish within range.

Veteran bonefishermen will stake out their flats skiff on a flat or thoroughfare known to be frequented by bonefish during a particular tidal stage. They prefer a spot that has a patch or two of open sand bottom, within easy casting range of the skiff, usually 25 to 40 feet. Live shrimp are taken from the live well and each is broken into two or three pieces. The pieces are tossed out and targeted to land on the sandy bottom. Then it becomes a waiting game. Bonefish have fixed patterns of movement as they search for a meal, and can be seen approaching the area when they are attracted by a chum scent. It's then that the angler makes his cast, with just a single live shrimp on a size No. l or 1/0 beak or claw hook tied to the monofilament or fluorocarbon line.

Many anglers have used this approach, as do many guides, to put anglers into their first bonefish. Once you've mastered casting to these "gray ghosts of the flats," you can advance to casting tiny bucktail jigs to them. Many even employ a flyrod to present a shrimp fly or crab fly after the bonefish have been coaxed within range with the shrimp chum.

Live-bait hooks

Live-bait hooks are designed expressly for use with live baitfish such as anchovies, sardines, mackerel, menhaden and other forage species. Many anglers tie the hooks directly to the end of their line, although fluorocarbon leaders offer an advantage.

Lori Kelly Parker runs her charter boat "New Wave" out of Key West and specializes in light-tackle chumming for big tarpon, cobia, barracuda and permit. She obtains an ice chest of shrimp dragger discards, called "trash," and uses it to establish a chum line that attracts many gamefish.

113

Offshore draggers periodically lift their nets and empty the contents on deck. The crew sorts the catch, discarding overboard anything that is not salable. This includes crushed fish, crabs, shrimp, and squid, which creates a chum line. Many sport fishermen obtain the discards from the draggers and fish in the area and do very well with tuna, sharks, dolphin and other species.

Shrimping by-catch is high-powered chum

From the Carolinas to Florida and along the Gulf Coast, shrimp trawling is big business. Since most shrimping is done at night, the trawlers anchor during the day, culling their catch and tossing overboard huge quantities of by-catch, or "trash." The trash consists of literally dozens of species of small fish, crushed or broken shrimp, squid and crabs. This smorgasbord, when dropped into the sea, attracts hordes of gamefish in quantities that defy description. At times hundreds of fish gather to feed on this chum line from the shrimp trawlers.

There are several ways to benefit from this phenomena. Boatmen who know the shrimp trawler owners can get permission to tie up to the stern of the shrimp boat and take advantage of the chum slick that is established as the trash is shoveled over. Other boatmen often pull up to a shrimp trawler and, for a few dollars, take aboard a couple of containers filled with trash. Some shrimp boats even retain the trash and, when they return to port, sell it to charter boatmen and private boat owners.

The approach used when chumming with the trash is to cut the small fish into several pieces, much the same as employed by anglers fishing the northeast Atlantic's canyons. The pieces are dropped overboard and in turn attract a multitude of species, most notably yellowfin and blackfin tuna, little tunny (often called bonito in the South), dolphin, wahoo, amberjack and even an occasional Atlantic sailfish or white marlin. The trash chum also accounts for many fine catches of cobia and tarpon along the Gulf Coast.

In inshore waters the shrimp boat trash is regularly used to attract tarpon and permit. There is an extensive fishery for these great gamefish in the waters adjacent to Key West, Florida. The tarpon and permit follow regular patterns, moving with the tide as they feed. The accepted manner of chumming them is to anchor up in an area they frequent. The anchor rope is attached to a quick-release floating red buoy, so that when a fish is hooked you can get off the anchor quickly to chase after the fish.

Large shrimp are a favorite bait when fishing in a chum line of discarded "trash" from a shrimp dragger. The hook bait must be drifted out with the chum unencumbered. Drift a hundred feet of line from the reel, then retrieve and start over again. When a fish picks up the bait, point your rod towards the line, lock the reel in gear, and lift back smartly to set the hook.

Small pieces of trash are dropped overboard and carried away with the tide. Light 20-pound-class tackle is most often employed on these fish, for the permit averages 15 to 35 pounds and the tarpon 50 to 100 pounds or more. A size 6/0 O'Shaughnessy hook is used by many of the guides and tied directly to the monofilament or fluorocarbon leader, which is 50-pound-test or stronger. Mahua baitfish are silvery and, because of their reflective qualities, are favored for the tarpon. Most anything removed from the trash will bring strikes. If permit are the target, a large manta shrimp is an excellent bait choice.

The key, as in all chumming, is keeping the bait moving with the chum. If there is no pressure on the line the bait will drop deep as it moves along in the swift current with the chum. It's not unusual to allow 125 feet of line to pay out. If a strike isn't received, the bait is reeled back in and the step repeated. While permit and tarpon are both big, strikes can be subtle and you've got to be alert and set back quickly and hard, especially with the bony-mouthed tarpon. Many anglers use large circle hooks, which quickly penetrate in the corner of the mouth and make releasing easier.

Veteran tarpon anglers keep their hooks needle sharp. A sharp hook can be the difference between success and failure when it comes to battling tarpon.

Chum attracts giant bluefin tuna

Giant bluefin tuna weigh in excess of 300 pounds and occasionally grow up to 1,400 pounds. These world travelers are believed by many to be the strongest, hardest-fighting fish in the ocean. They require huge quantities of food each day, so when large schools move into an area there has to be a huge quantity of forage nearby.

From New Jersey north to the Maritime Provinces of Canada, these giants roam the sea from June through October, settling into areas where there is an abundance of mackerel and herring, their staples. While these two species constitute the bulk of their diet, they are not adverse to feed on the abundance of squid, bluefish, red hake and silver hake that are found in the area, along with most any other fish they encounter.

This need for food makes them a natural for chumming, and the bulk of the summertime fishing is done by private and charter boats who anchor up in choice locations and use huge quantities of forage species as chum. It's not unusual for a single boat to dispense several hundred pounds of chum overboard in a single day.

Chumming is very effective for all species of tuna, as this fine catch of four different species shows. Richard Hightower landed, from left, a bluefin tuna, yellowfin tuna, bigeye tuna and albacore. Known as a "tuna slam," the haul was made while Hightower was chumming local tuna grounds aboard the "Red Rooster III" out of San Diego.

Catching the giants requires the finest-quality tackle and a crew that works together. When using 130-pound-class tackle, which is the standard when seeking the giants, there is no room for error.

Boatmen have learned over the years that the tuna usually follow a pattern of moving along the coast searching for food. Some believe a tuna may travel a hundred miles in a day, making a massive sweep of an area.

Skippers position their boat by anchoring in spots such as the Mud Hole off New Jersey, Cape Cod Bay off Massachusetts and off Gloucester, Mass. They carry a minimum of two plastic trash containers filled with fresh mackerel, herring, or menhaden, usually obtained directly from a local dragger.

Chumming begins by taking a whole fish and cutting it into three or four pieces. If the mackerel or menhaden are small it's not unusual to chum with a whole or half a fish.

Some chummers use what is popularly called "cod guts" as both chum and bait. They obtain the carcasses of fish that have been filleted by commercial fishermen. Sometimes the carcasses are cod, hence the name, but pollock, haddock, hake, bluefish and other fish heads, carcasses and entrails are used. It's not unusual to have huge tuna swarm into the slick, gorging on the remains of what were 5- to 10-pound fish.

As with all chumming, steady maintenance of the chum line is essential. It's not unusual to spot the big fish on the electronic fishfinder as they move beneath the boat. They swim through the chum line, moving in a big circular pattern, picking up pieces as they go. At times when they move near the surface you can actually toss three or four pieces, at 5-foot intervals and the fish will draw in each piece of chum as it swims along.

There are many ways the basic 130-pound-class tackle can be rigged to present a bait in the chum line. The standard approach is to employ 130-pound-test Dacron line with a 150- to 200-foot piece of 250-pound-test monofilament spliced into the Dacron. Some anglers snell or crimp their hook directly to the monofilament. Others use a ball-bearing swivel and a 10- or 12-foot fluorocarbon leader, to which their hook is snelled or crimped.

A wide range of giant tuna hooks are available and there are many opinions on which are best. Some anglers prefer a size 7/0 or 8/0 forged offset hook, feeling the small hook is more easily concealed in the bait. Others prefer the extremely strong forged size 12/0 and 14/0 Martu models. Circle hooks have also come into vogue, as the tuna are often hooked in the corner of thier mouth, which makes it easier to release the fish without injury.

Tuna fishermen often will bait up with a whole mackerel or herring, although some will use half a fish, so it more readily identifies with the chum being employed. Fillets from a bluefish also bring strikes. When using dead baits, many insert a small piece of Styrofoam into the bait to make it more buoyant as it drifts along in the chum.

Live bluefish, which may be caught on the tuna grounds, are also an excellent bait. Often tuna fishermen will bottom fish for bait, with a live red hake, or "ling," making a fine bait. Silver hake are also very effective. Live baits are hooked through the fleshy part of the back, just ahead of or behind the dorsal fin.

The most effective way to fish baits in a chum line for giants is to work the bait, paying it out with the chum and then pulling it back in and repeating the procedure. Many prefer to coil 100 feet of the fishing line in a plastic trash bucket, and pay the line out hand-over-hand into the slick. This keeps the line from getting tangled and, perhaps most importantly, prevents anglers from getting their feet hung up in the line if a giant takes the bait.

The normal procedure is to pay out the line by hand in the slick, with the rod positioned in the fighting chair's rod holder. Fighting these big fish may require 40 or 45 pounds of drag pressure, a bucket harness and safety line attached to the chair.

As soon as the fish is hooked, the boat is released from the anchor line buoy and the fish is followed by the boat. The idea is to position the angler so maximum pressure may be brought to bear. The objective is to boat the fish as quickly as possible. Experienced anglers may need less than a half hour, although marathon battles have been known to last six hours or more.

While the giant bluefin tuna is one of the world's great gamefish, it is also a highly prized gourmet treat, especially in Japan. Many of the giant tuna caught off the northeast Atlantic are destined for the Tokyo fish market, shipped there via air freight. A single tuna having a high fat content and in prime condition with a dressed weight of 600 pounds or more can bring $50,000. It is this exploitation of the tuna fishery that has caused a drastic decline of tuna stocks in recent years.

During the early 1990s a large population of medium and giant bluefin tuna were located in the waters adjacent to wrecks off of Hatteras, N.C. A fine chumming fishery developed during the January-through-April period. During the course of a day the fish would travel from wreck to wreck or to wherever there were heavy concentrations of forage.

Fortunately, federal regulations limit a boat's catch to one medium tuna per day, which keeps the harvest down. The season on giants over 300 pounds is closed at that time of year and the fish are usually brought to boatside quickly and released. The circle hooks are most often lodged in the corner of the tuna's jaw, and release is simple. Veteran angler Bob Eakes of Hatteras even developed a unique circle-hook remover, which enables a tuna to be released in the water in a matter of seconds.

Live anchovies a potent chum

Pacific Coast anglers successfully chum for a wide variety of species when they're able to obtain and employ live anchovies and sardines. Southern California boats that fish the inshore kelp beds, long-range boats that head far out to sea for albacore, and those who head off the Baja Peninsula for tuna and wahoo, rely on the anchovies and sardines to bring gamefish within range.

The boats sailing from ports such as San Diego, Long Beach, and Newport Beach take on dip nets, or "scoops," full of anchovies from bait barges anchored in coastal harbors. The anchovies are kept in live wells with circulating sea water to keep them in perfect condition until the fishing grounds are reached.

It takes patience and skill to coax fish from kelp. A small dip net is used to remove several anchovies from the live well, and the chummer tosses the anchovies into the air, so they land midway between the boat and the kelp. The excited anchovy does one of two things: It seeks the sanctuary of the kelp, or hurriedly swims back to the boat to seek shelter beneath its stern.

Gradually, the anchovies get the gamefish excited, and it's not unusual to have yellowtail, white sea bass, Pacific bonito, Pacific barracuda and kelp bass vying for the chum.

The most popular technique is to tie a tiny hook, such as a size 3 or 4 O'Shaughnessy, live bait, beak or claw hook, to the end of your monofilament line or fluorocarbon leader. Then a lively anchovy is obtained from the live well, and gently hooked under the gill collar. The anchovies are only 3 to 5 inches long and too large a hook restricts their movement. While the collar-hooking method is most popular, some anglers hook the bait through the lips, the eyes, or place the hook into the back just ahead of the dorsal fin.

The bait is cast away from the boat, using either conventional or spinning tackle, and permitted to swim about freely. An active anchovy will often swim about excitedly, and when gamefish are plentiful the strikes come fast and furious. Always keep your rod tip pointed in the direction the line is moving. When a fish picks up the bait and moves off, lock your reel in gear, and when the line comes taut, lift back firmly to set the hook.

Anchovies and sardines are a popular chum on the Pacific's offshore grounds, as are several small species of mackerel and jacks. Long-range boats sail with a supply of live chum in the tanks. They'll usually stop on productive banks where anglers use jigs and Sabiki rigs to fill the live tanks with a supply of both hook baits and chum.

In some cases, boats anchor over productive banks and kelp beds. Albacore

anglers often troll until either albacore or bluefin tuna strike.

The techniques used with other types of chumming are essentially the same. Maintain a chum stream of the anchovies, tossing them out a couple at a time, but don't feed the fish. When done properly you can actually see the albacore picking the anchovies right off the surface. They "boil" as they swirl on the surface moving ever closer to the boat. Keeping the bait drifting back unimpeded is very important.

Tackle and hook size must be tailored to the species sought. When huge 250- to 300-pound yellowfin tuna are targeted by the long-range boats, the short stand-up outfits are favored, with fluorocarbon leaders gaining in popularity in recent years.

Tailor hook size and style to the bait being used, with the smaller bends ideal for anchovies and larger hooks for sardine, mackerel, and jacks.

Chumming is a waiting game. You can chum effectively while drifting or at anchor. An ideal situation is a moderate current to carry the ground chum and chunks over a wide area. The key is assigning the task of chumming to one person. An unbroken slick must be maintained, especially once fish have moved in and are taking baits and being fought.

Sand bass respond to a chum line of live anchovies. A live anchovy fished on a 1/0 size live-bait hook may be used while chumming. A chromed jig or plastic-tailed leadhead worked through the spread of chum also works well.

Chumming works if you work at it

Regardless of where you fish, you'll find that chumming is an exciting challenge. You've got to plan and work at it to be successful. While chumming isn't always essential to enjoy a good day's catch, there are times when it will make the difference between success and failure. The key is experience. Knowing where to anchor, or whether to drift; how frequently the chum should be dropped over the side; if weight should be added to your line to take the bait deeper, if a float is necessary—these are the questions that are answered with experience, trial, and error. But make no mistake, chumming is something every serious saltwater angler should know how to do.

(Right) Live-bait barges are located at most every port along the California coast. This barge's live wells are filled with live anchovies and other forage species, which are sold to boats by the "scoop" or net full. Many boats fish at the kelp beds, where they sparingly toss live anchovies towards the kelp, attracting Pacific barracuda, Pacific bonito, sand bass and kelp bass to waiting hook baits.

FLY CASTING

Perhaps the most graceful method of presenting a lure to a fish is through fly casting. Often it's sight fishing, where the quarry is spotted cruising across an air-clear flat, perhaps rushing at a hookless teaser trolled close astern, streaking through a chum line, or slicing through breakers crashing onto the sand.

While with many other types of fishing the same scene unfolds, the difference is that the fly fisherman is presenting an almost weightless tuft of feather and bucktail. A conventional or spincaster is casting a lure that has weight to carry it to its target.

In fly fishing, the delicate fly is presented by skillful execution. It is the fly line, which has the weight, that is actually cast. The leader joining fly and fly line tapers down from the line's butt end and has sufficient diameter and stiffness to turn the fly over as it reaches the target. When a cast is executed properly, the fly line, leader, and fly finish in a straight line, directly on target ahead of and within the vision of the quarry.

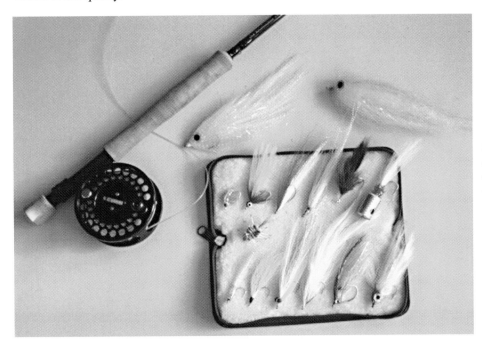

This international selection of 15 saltwater flies was tied by renowned tier Bob Popovics of Seaside Park, New Jersey.

A balanced outfit essential to success

Having a fly rod outfit that is balanced is critical because it enhances your ability to cast effortlessly. It also plays an important role when fighting and landing fish, which may range from bonefish on the flats to big sailfish and even marlin on the offshore grounds.

Fly fishing outfits are assigned a numerical classification, with the lightest weight being 2 and the highest 15. The lightweight outfits ranging from 2 through 7 are most often employed in fresh water, and are suitable for trout, bass, panfish, and small salmon and pike. Weights 7 through 15 are employed by saltwater

(Left) Tom Ohaus often fished the same Mantoloking surf with the author in New Jersey. He now makes his home in Alaska and relishes catching silver salmon on a fly rod when they move from the ocean into the many river systems. Tom also has plenty of success trolling and drifting the river mouths.

anglers, with the 9- and 10-weight outfits being the most versatile and lending themselves to the widest range of applications. Thus, when purchasing any component of the outfit, the weight should always be the same, for the rod, reel, and line

Mark Sosin fishes in many of the great locations throughout the world as host of "Mark Sosin's Saltwater Journal." He enjoys fly fishing and loves the challenge of coaxing big snook to take his fly while casting in the Florida Everglades.

Fly line the most critical component

The line is without question the most critical element of the fly outfit. Fly lines have undergone a tremendous evolution over the years. It was in 1945 that Leon P. Martuch, Sr., Paul Rottiers, and Clare Harris teamed together to form Scientific Anglers. The three set out to develop fly lines that would be easy to cast and suit the varied needs of the fly caster. Up until that time they suffered with poorly made lines that required great care.

Originally most fly lines were made of silk. They would float, an important consideration in most fly-fishing applications, but only for a short time. They required care and drying each time they were used. With the advent of nylon, the water absorption problem was solved, but the problem of flotation still existed.

It was in Leon's kitchen that he, Clare and Paul discovered that polyvinylchloride could provide a supple and durable coating for braided nylon. It took them until 1959 to develop and introduce Air Cel Supreme, a floating fly line that became the standard for fly fishermen everywhere.

In the intervening years fly lines have changed dramatically, thanks to the continuation of the pioneering efforts at Scientific Anglers. The concept of fly casting in saltwater, and the equipment and flies used in this fishing, could in itself warrant an entire book, as could many of the chapters in this book. Included here are the fundamentals and some of the advanced techniques that saltwater flyrodders employ. It is important to acknowledge that this is a style of fishing that can capture the imagination and turn into a lifelong pursuit.

While developing lines that floated was important for freshwater fishermen, saltwater anglers have always required lines that floated, sank slowly, sank at a moderate speed, and sank quickly. While each of the four types of lines were available, you really had to have four different reel spools, with each type of line, and then had to change spools every time you targeted fish at a different depth.

Today's fly fishermen have available Quad Tip lines that come with one each of a floating tip, slow-sinking tip, moderate-sinking tip and fast-sinking tip. The tips have attached loops for easy changing, a small-diameter running line, and an extra-stiff, braided, monofilament core that proves extremely helpful when casting larger flies or in windy conditions. All of the tips are available in a handy wallet, and may be changed in less than a minute, enabling a caster to have versatility never before possible.

Graphite fly rods have become the standard

Saltwater fly rods utilize a variety of materials, including bamboo, fiberglass, graphite and various composites. Graphite and graphite composites are by far the most popular. They're extremely light and have enormous lifting power. Most importantly, they have an inherent stiffness that enables an angler to lift a fly line from the water, execute a false cast, double-haul if necessary, and shoot the fly line, leader and fly 100 feet or more to a cruising fish.

The reel's primary function is to hold line

Fly reels have also gone through an evolutionary process. Today's models are lightweight, most often made of anodized aluminum, and have a removable spool. Braking systems now use unique aviation braking carbon, which minimizes the overheating that occurs with cork or other synthetic drag materials.

Many major manufacturers of fly fishing equipment produce quality products, each with their own unique features. As always, it is wise to deal with a reputable tackle dealer who has loaner outfits or sample models available that an angler may borrow and try out for a day or two. Quality saltwater fly fishing tackle is costly, and it is risky to purchase an outfit without first experiencing its performance in your hands.

Leader must be tapered and turn over fly

You might think that by simply tying a light leader to the end of your fly line you'd be able to neatly present it. That may be true where using other types of salt water tackle, where the lure weight carries the line and leader to the fish, but not in fly casting.

The leader, where it attaches to the fly line, must be of practically the same diameter as the line. Made of stiff monofilament or fluorocarbon, the leader is tapered, using short pieces—18 to 24 inches long—of gradually thinner-diameter material over the entire 6- to 18-foot length of the leader. Many fly casters tie their own leaders to suit their particular style and needs.

There are, however, tapered fly leaders manufactured for each type of application.

A saltwater fly leader tapered to these dimensions and tied using blood knots will turn over a large saltwater fly or popper with ease. It should be constructed of stiff fluorocarbon leader material for best results.

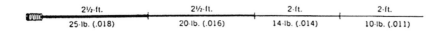

2½-ft.	2½-ft.	2-ft.	2-ft.
25-lb. (.018)	20-lb. (.016)	14-lb. (.014)	10-lb. (.011)

125

Blood knot

The blood knot easy to tie and is used for a line with different diameters, or for a tapered fly leader. Begin by laying the leader and line parallel with each other. Wrap one strand of line around the other five times and double back and insert the tag end where the two lines meet. Repeat the same procedure from the other end, wrapping the remaining strand of line or leader around the other five times and double back. Insert the tag end where the two meet, in the opposite direction of the first tag end. Pull the tag ends reasonably taut and then gradually exert pressure on each section of line or leader and snug it up tightly, causing the turns to neatly form around each other, resulting in a neat, clean, strong connection. Trim the tag ends with a nail clipper.

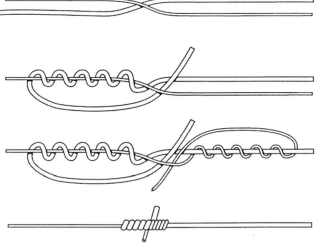

Tarpon fishing with a fly rod is a challenge that many anglers enjoy as a lifetime pursuit. Here, veteran fly caster Spider Andresen holds aloft a beauty he landed in the Florida Keys while sight casting. Tarpon of this size are landed with the aid of a release gaff placed in the lower jaw. This chrome-plated gladiator was quickly released.

Countless flies available

It is safe to say there are thousands of fly patterns in use along the coasts today. Fly tiers often dedicate themselves to tying patterns that closely resemble most every type of food found in the sea. Their creations are often true works of art. Simply stated, if the fly resembles food on which a fish feeds, you can catch that fish on the fly. This includes bottom feeders such as the flatfish, and sea bass that feed on crabs and shrimp.

The number of fly patterns that are available presents a dilemma of sorts, for you can only use one fly at a time. While it is important to match a certain fly to a baitfish found in a particular area, this can be overdone. Too many anglers use hundreds of patterns and waste time experimenting in hopes of finding the "perfect fly."

Basic patterns often suffice

Newcomers to fly casting in saltwater would be best served by first selecting a basic 9- or 10-weight outfit. The next step would be to pick 12 to 15 basic fly patterns and master their use and develop a confidence level in them. In time, patterns that prove unproductive could be discarded, and replaced by more appropriate patterns. In this way you keep a selection of proven performers, rather than boxes containing hundreds which you use haphazardly.

I have great confidence in the Clouser fly in olive and white color, tied on a 2/0 stainless steel hook. It resembles a nearly transparent baitfish with a big eye, typical of most small forage species. For a period of several months off the Jersey and Long Island coastline, it was the fly I used to the exclusion of all others, and it landed more than a dozen different species of fish. Included were: striped bass, weakfish, bluefish, summer flounder, Atlantic bonito, little tunny, school bluefin tuna, yellowfin tuna, dolphin, herring, mackerel, and sea bass.

The same fly has also accounted for redfish, ladyfish and sea trout on the Gulf Coast and bonefish, snook, jack crevalle, amberjack, cero mackerel, Spanish mackerel and yellowtail snapper in Florida's picturesque waters. Off the kelp beds, Pacific bonito, Pacific barracuda, and yellowtail assaulted the Clouser, too.

The key is confidence, and skill in presenting the fly at the right depth in the water column—utilizing a line with the proper sink rate—and retrieving it in such a way as to convince a hungry gamefish to strike.

Throughout this book many species of saltwater fish and the techniques used to catch them are discussed. Practically every one of these species can be caught on a fly. The angler may use a fly-casting outfit to present his offering from a boat while a teaser is trolled to attract fish to the surface, after which a fly is presented. He may work his fly with a fast-sinking line through a chum slick. Along the surf, where stripers, bluefish, and weakfish prowl, strikes are often received when the fly almost reaches the sand on a retrieve. There is flats fishing, too—perhaps the most exciting fly rodding of all, where you may either cast from a boat or wade the shallows.

Just drifting and blind casting on the shallow flats of bays and rivers will bring a response from almost any species that is swimming along and searching for a meal. Fly fishing can open up a whole new dimension in saltwater fishing.

Plenty of line needed

Saltwater fish are often big and may strip far more than the normal 100-foot length of shooting head and running fly line from the reel. Thus it becomes important to load the reel with approximately 200 yards of fine-diameter backing line.

Saltwater fly fishermen generally use either 20- or 30-pound-test Dacron line in bright orange or optic yellow color. The colors prove helpful in tracking the line when a fish has stripped many yards of line from the reel and the boat is being maneuvered.

It's important to have a properly tied knot to secure the backing line to the running line. Many anglers employ a nail knot, which is extremely strong and not bulky. The knot is then lightly epoxied, giving it a smooth, tapered look that will slip through the rod's guides easily. Make certain the knot is small and has no loose

Mark Fernandez spent many hours at his fly-tying vise while designing Mark's Prober, a saltwater fly that has an action much like that of a lead-head jig. The fly has a weighted plastic nose that causes it to dart to the bottom during any hesitation. It closely resembles a frightened bait-fish, darting towards the depths to avoid capture.

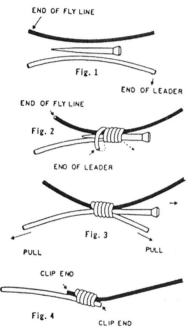

Nail knot

Fig. 1 Begin by holding the end of the fly line and leader alongside each other and use either a nail or piece of plastic or metal tubing, such as a ball-point pen cartridge.

Fig. 2 Allow ample overlap. Then wind the leader downward around both line and tube or nail six times. Run the end of the leader back along the nail or through the tube up under the loops.

Fig. 3 Pull both ends of the leader tight. Slip the knot down the nail or tube, tightening by pulling both ends of the leader as it goes. Slip nail or tube out and retighten by again pulling the leader ends.

Fig. 4 Pull the line and leader tight and clip the end of the line and leader close to the knot.

ends that could hang up on a line guide while a fish is making a speedy run.

The same knot may be used to tie the leader to the tip of the fly line. Take care to make the knot as inconspicuous as possible.

Once your outfit is assembled, it's wise to tie a small fly to the end of the leader. Use a pair of cutting pliers and cut the point and barb from it at the curve of the hook. It's best for newcomers to practice fly casting without a hook, as it's very easy to hook yourself.

Practice casting skills

Casting skill is best developed on the water, rather than the lawn or driveway. Water provides drag on the fly line, a key consideration when lifting a line from the water to execute a cast, and plays a role in the timing of your casts. A park pond is an ideal place to practice.

A newcomer is best served by trying to handle a short amount of fly line for starters. This is best accomplished by stripping 30 or 40 feet of line from the reel, and permitting it to rest at your feet. Pull 10 or 15 feet of line through the line guides of the rod, so the fly, leader and line are loosely resting in the water in front of you.

While holding the rod with one hand, grasp the line with the other and slowly pull back with the rod, causing the line to lift from the water and carry back over your head. As the line straightens behind you, bring the rod forward smartly while still holding the line, pointing straight ahead. This will cause the 10 or 15 feet of line and leader to rest on the water directly in front of you.

Begin by executing short casts. Use a floating-tip line for starters, as this is easier to handle. With the line laying limp on the water in front of you, and holding the fly line with your left hand, lift back slowly with the rod tip, and when it reaches a near vertical position, push forward sharply. As you are executing what will be a roll cast, the line will slide across the water, dragging as it goes and will lift from the water and then be rolled over. Then you can extend the length of the line, by permitting the loose line resting at your feet to slip through the fingers of your left hand.

With the line resting on the water in front of you, the next step is to slowly strip line in, pulling with your left hand, while using the index finger of your right hand as a line guide. With the fly still in the water and sliding along, lift back smartly with your right hand, so that the rod tip reaches the near-vertical position. You want the line to lift smartly from the water and straighten in the air behind you.

As soon as you feel the firm pull of the weight of the line, bring the rod forward, shooting the line out in front of you, and releasing the grasp on the line with your left hand. Permit the weight of the line to carry the loose line at your feet as the fly travels to its target.

The key is to develop a rhythm that permits you to lift the line from the water, shoot it behind you, hesitate until it straightens and pulls at the rod, then shoot it out in front of you. Begin by casting just a few feet of line at a time. Relax and let the rod do its task of lifting the line and shooting it back on the backcast, and exerting power on the forward cast. It's all a matter of timing, with more line requiring a longer hesitation.

Striped bass are very responsive to a wide variety of saltwater flies. The author hooks many stripers on a Clouser weighted fly. Many bass are hooked right at the edge of the dropoff, often not more than 20 feet from the sand. It's along the dropoff that stripers cruise and search for unsuspecting forage species in the shallows.

Stu Apte chose to release this Pacific sailfish he landed while using a 9-weight fly rod and 16-pound tippet. It was estimated to weigh 140 pounds and would have established a world record, but Stu turned it free. Sailfish such as this are attracted to trolled hookless teasers, which are pulled in as the fish surfaces. The caster then presents his offering of feathers and bucktail.

The double-haul cast popular in saltwater

The roll cast and normal short cast are essential to all saltwater fly-rodding applications. In saltwater, however, the cast must often be extended to 50 feet or more. Many proficient casters are able to lay out a perfect straight cast of 100 feet with uncanny accuracy, presenting it within 5 feet of a feeding fish.

To cover greater distances, many anglers employ what is popularly called a double-haul cast. In this method the caster uses his left hand and arm to cause the line to move through the air at an accelerated speed, resulting in more distance to the cast. It is easily and smoothly executed. With just a minimal amount of practice, newcomers using a properly balanced outfit can cast 50 feet or more with ease.

Whether fishing from boat or beach, the caster should determine just how far he feels he'll be able to cast, taking into account wind direction and sea conditions. Assuming the target is 60 feet away, the caster strips approximately that length of line from his reel, permitting it to rest on the deck at his feet, or in a stripping basket attached to his waist.

To begin the double-haul it's important to have the fly and some line resting in the water in front of you, ideally with 20 or 25 feet of fly line, with the balance at your feet or in the stripping basket.

With the line resting limp in the water and the rod pointed in the same direction, grasp the line near the rod's stripper guide and hold it firmly. Lift back smartly with the rod, and at the same time pull down hard with your left hand on the line. Continue back with the rod until it is at about 1 o'clock. As you lift back with the rod to this position, look up at it, and imagine you are shooting a basketball into the hoop. Actually, you're throwing the fly line back, and you want to keep that backcast high, for a high backcast permits you to execute a good forward cast.

As the line shoots back, let your left hand sweep upward in front of your body. As the line begins to pull at the rod, permit line to pull out through the fingers of your left hand, being careful not to let too much line slip through, which will cause you to lose power.

Then quickly, and with one smooth movement, stop the line by grasping it with your left hand. As you start pushing forward with the rod, pull the line downward with your left hand across the front of your body. This will give speed to the fly line and shoot it forward. With your right hand, thrust the rod forward as though you were hammering a nail into a wall at eye level. As the rod comes forward and the line begins to shoot out, let go of the fly line with your left hand. If your timing is right and you've properly executed the cast, the forward motion of the line will be such that it will pick up the loosely coiled line at your feet or from the stripping basket and carry the line, leader and fly to the target in a straight line.

While the double-haul may sound difficult, once you get out there and slowly begin to extend line, you'll find that you quickly pick up the rhythm and timing that is so essential in the execution of this cast. Each person develops a style of their own. It should come naturally, and the length of your casts will extend as you develop the timing. Be patient and distance and accuracy will come in time.

"Experienced fly casters often find they have a distinct advantage when fishing for bonefish, tarpon, barracuda and permit."

Jim Cary always keeps a fly rod handy when he's chumming on the offshore grounds. He's about to release a nice little tunny that inhaled a white Deceiver fly worked through a chum line. Many fly casters use chum to attract offshore species and present their fly as the fish move into the slick.

Casting tough in some places

Some types of fishing do not, however, lend themselves well to fly casting. Pier and bridge casters are often too high off the waters to execute casts properly, although dock casters often score with a variety of species that reside in the shadows. Fly fishing from party boats is another awkward situation, both because of the number of passengers on board and the height off the water. Some long range party boats anglers do employ fly fishing in limited applications.

Otherwise, the opportunities are almost unlimited.

Sight casting on the flats a challenge

Experienced fly casters often find they have a distinct advantage when fishing for bonefish, tarpon, barracuda and permit from a boat being poled across the flats. A cast with spinning tackle and a leadhead jig may spook wary flats residents, but the fly rodder is able to deftly present a fly with barely a ripple.

Often it's possible to be within 50 feet of a targeted species, and here is where accuracy plays a critical role. The target is that angle of vision, a window of approximately 45 degrees ahead of the moving fish, ideally 5 to 10 feet in front of the fish.

Flies tied to resemble small crabs and shrimp are favorites of casters seeking bonefish and permit. The key is making your cast, permitting the fly to settle and then making a retrieve by stripping line so that the tuft of feather and bucktail looks alive. Slow and irregular is best.

When targeting tarpon and barracuda, big, gaudy, brightly colored flies often produce best. It's often possible to have a half dozen tarpon in the 50- to 100-pound class slowly circling about on the flats. When a tarpon does move towards the fly, just keep stripping in a normal manner until the fish inhales the fly and begins to turn away. The tarpon has a very tough, bony mouth, and you want the fly well in, so that the hook point can quickly penetrate as you set back to strike. Some flies are now tied on circle hooks, which catch the corner of the jaw as a tarpon turns away.

Make certain to come back smartly with the rod tip to firmly set the hook, while holding the line taut with your left hand. An exception is when using flies tied with circle hooks, where it's best to hesitate and wait for the fish to turn and come tight on the hook.

Timing is important. A fish will quickly streak off and you've got to permit the loose line to slip through your fingers, clearing off the deck or out of the stripping basket, until all the loose line runs through the guides. After that the reel's drag takes over and you can settle down to fighting the fish. Remember that you can control drag tension not only by the amount of pressure on the reel drag, but by adjusting the position of your rod. Holding the rod nearly vertical exerts maximum pressure, while lowering the rod tip, or "bending," minimizes pressure.

If you like the idea of wading the shallow flats, don't hesitate to use a fly rod. Wading, which is discussed in detail in Chapter 9, is very enjoyable. Because it becomes difficult to cast when you've got a lot of loose fly line coiled in the water at your feet, it's best to employ a stripping basket, into which the fly line is placed as you retrieve.

Casting to kelp beds offers excitement and variety

Small-boat anglers enjoy superb fly casting sport off the California coast while cruising just off the inshore kelp beds. There are times when Pacific barracuda, white sea bass, yellowtail, Pacific bonito, kelp bass and sand bass can be seen in the shadows of the big-leafed kelp.

This environment offers sight-casting at its finest. Often you can spot excited schools of tiny baitfish leaping skyward as they're herded from below, especially when bonito are on the prowl. While anglers casting lures are often frustrated, the fly caster presenting a small fly tied to resemble the nearly transparent anchovies and other fry will find his offering regularly receiving strikes.

Chumming gets fish in a feeding frenzy

When gamefish are attracted to a chum line and are excitedly feeding, the fly caster can outfish other anglers using most any type of tackle and lures or baits. Fish attracted to a chum line of ground and chunked fish get whipped into a feeding frenzy, and streak through the chum picking up every piece of food they can find.

It doesn't matter where you're chumming. Anglers targeting albacore and

Bob Hutchinson does much of his fly fishing after dark. Here he's just landed a school striper while casting to the shadow line of the Chesapeake Bay Bridge and Tunnel.

bluefin tuna with their anchovy chum lines many miles off the California coastline often find dozens of these speedy adversaries streaking in. A streamer tied in white and silver and a trace of mylar, and fished with a fly line with a fast-sinking tip, will draw strikes from fish accustomed to feeding on the silvery anchovies.

Bluefish, striped bass, and weakfish all respond to a chum line. The key is presenting a fly that resembles what they're feeding on. A mossbunker fly being stripped through a chum line of chunks when blues are on the prowl is deadly, as is a fly tied to resemble the tiny grass shrimp on which weakfish feed.

Surf and beach fly casting can produce bonanzas

Flatfish are among the most popular species found on all three of our coasts. Most often they frequent inshore waters, often swimming along the edge of the dropoff where forage species congregate. In bays and rivers, and along the Gulf Coast they frequent the shallows, too, where they're apt to find an easy meal.

This lifestyle makes the flounder an ideal target for fly casters. The key is recognizing that the fish normally feeds on the bottom. To reach them you'll need a fly line with a moderate-sinking or fast-sinking tip. You've also got to remember to hesitate before you begin your retrieve to give the line's tip sufficient time to sink.

You may also want to stand back from the edge of the surf, so that as you retrieve you can literally snake the fly right onto the sand. Often the flounder will be feeding within a rod's length of the sand, and you want your fly working through the strike zone. Employ flies that resemble the sand eel, spearing, mullet, or other small forage that frequents the surf and beach areas where you plan to fish.

Obstructions offer opportunities

There's hardly a section of our vast coastline that doesn't have some type of obstruction that extends seaward, be it groins to hold back the ravages of the sea, jetties that flank coastal inlets, or natural promontories so prevalent in both the Northeast and Northwest. Fly casting from these structures can be tough. If wind or wave action is heavy, it's difficult to control the fly line among not only the rocks, but the marine growth, barnacles, and mussels that cover them. Should you elect to fish from these structures, you'll find a stripping basket most helpful.

It is often best to fish from the beaches adjacent to the rocks, wooden groins, and jetties. Where the structure and beach meet there can be a concentration of forage species that seek what little sanctuary is offered by staying close and in the shallows.

Weakfish, striped bass, flounder, redfish, barracuda, and a host of other inshore feeders regularly cruise along, searching for a meal, and a properly presented fly, worked right in the midst of the frothing white water crashing across the structure, can work wonders.

Pacific Northwest fly casters pursue king salmon and silver salmon

Northwest fly fishermen targeting silver salmon as they move in from the Pacific often enjoy super results wading the mouths of coastal rivers, working their offering through the rips and eddies where salmon often hold as they move upriver. The fish often hold deep in the swift waters, and fishing a fast-sinking fly line, cast up and across the current, and permitted to sweep downcurrent as it is retrieved, is often the way to success.

Any fly that imitates a silvery baitfish can be effective for salmon. Flies with weighted heads, such as the Clouser, work well when combined with a fly line and fast-sinking tip that takes them down to where the salmon are feeding.

Saltwater fly fishing a different challenge for freshwater anglers

Millions of American fishermen live to present their flies to a wide variety of freshwater species. Their targets are usually trout and bass, both of which provide

sterling sport and an exciting challenge.

But these fishermen should remember that the welcome mat is always out to visit the sea coast. It is the natural extension of fishing inland lakes and rivers. The tackle is a little heavier, the fish a bit bigger, and the speed is awesome. It's the kind of fly fishing that every long-rod devotee should experience.

Silver salmon move in from the Pacific Ocean and invade almost every river system from California to Alaska. Most casters employ 8-, 9- or 10-weight outfits and sinking-tip fly lines to shoot their bright, gaudy patterns to the salmon. Often the salmon will rest in pockets and eddies, out of the swift current, before moving upriver, and present a challenge to fly casters.

135

JETTIES, ROCKPILES, BREAKWATERS & INLETS

Along almost every section of coastline are natural rocky outcroppings that extend seaward and provide anglers with a platform from which to cast. There are also many manmade structures, which are usually strategically placed to limit erosion from the sea. These, too, provide anglers with a casting opportunity.

Anglers who climb around coastal jetties and rockpiles most often use medium-weight spinning or conventional outfits. This type of fishing is perhaps one of the most challenging found along the seacoast, for everything depends on the angler's skill. A surf bag should include a good selection of lures, leaders and teasers, a tape measure, and nail clip.

Jetty fishing a challenge

Sportsmen who have participated in most types of fishing know that "jetty fishing," is perhaps the most challenging. There is no boat, guide, or comfortable beach location from which to fish. The angler must depend on his dexterity, moving about moss- and mussel-covered rocks, sometimes in the dead of night, presenting a lure or bait to gamefish that are often tough adversaries. Then, after having successfully hooked up, the angler must have the skill to land the fish in the face of crashing waves and flying spray. This is the challenge of jetty fishing, an exciting, rewarding pastime that tests your skills every inch of the way.

Rockpiles and jetties found on all coasts

The "jetty jockies" who climb around the rockpiles of the Northeast are challenged by such bottom feeders as summer and winter flounder, tautog, sea bass, pollock and cod. Also presenting a challenge are striped bass, bluefish, weakfish, and the little tunny that occasionally come within range.

(Left) Jetty fishermen experience fine fishing within an hour of sunrise, when many species that frequent inshore waters are active. Position yourself near the water's edge and bracket the area with casts. Then move a short distance and repeat the same steps until you find a pocket of feeding fish.

Anglers who traverse the rockpiles and coral outcroppings of the Southeast and Gulf coasts encounter flounder, a variety of snapper, sheepshead, grouper and croaker. The gamefish caught from these structures include channel bass (redfish), bluefish, tarpon, snook, barracuda, and spotted weakfish (trout).

Pacific casters who fish from the coast's many picturesque rocky outcroppings encounter surf perch, rockfish, California halibut, sand bass, and tough adversaries like the Pacific barracuda, yellowtail, and Pacific bonito.

From bonefish on the coral breakwaters in the Bahamas, to big cobia in Alabama's Mobile Bay, jetty anglers have no shortage of targets.

Many surf beaches are littered with boulders. At low tide, anglers wade out and stand atop the rocks. Many anglers have golf-shoe soles cemented to their waders, or use golf rubbers over the wader feet. Strap-on ice creepers can also keep you from slipping.

Spinning tackle is most popular

The tackle arsenal available to the jetty fisherman is extensive. However, for the normal range of casting situations, a few basic outfits serve the rock-based caster well. In spinning gear, which is by far the most popular gear used by the rock hoppers, the choice is a one-handed spinning outfit. A stiff 6- to 6 1/2-foot fiberglass or graphite rod with a reel loaded with 200 yards of 10- or 12-pound-test line is ideal for the smaller bottom feeders

For gamefish, heavier gear is in order. A rod measuring 7 to 8 feet generally works well. Select one with a stiff action that is capable of casting a 3- to 4-ounce sinker, or bucktail jig, metal squid or lighter plug. Reels should be of intermediate size and handle 200 to 250 yards of 12- to 17-pound line. If a fish cleans you out of line when you're using a reel of this size, then the fish deserves to get away!

Fly fishing from jetties is difficult, but it's manageable with the help of a stripping basket. A 10-weight outfit with a shooting-head sinking-tip line is the outfit of choice of most long-rod devotees who fish from the rockpiles. The Deceiver, Clouser, Peanut Bunker, Honey Blond and Half & Half patterns tied on 1/0 through 3/0 size hooks are the flies of choice, with colors to match the baitfish in residence. As always, though, there are literally thousands of fly choices.

Specialized footwear essential for jetty safety

There are a number of equipment items that are essential if you're going to enjoy this sport and fish safely. Safety is unquestionably the most important consideration. You'll be walking on a variety of surfaces, from solid rock, to concrete, to wood, all of which may be wet, covered with slippery marine growth or sheathed in mussels. Peculiar configurations are the norm and one must often negotiate angles and crevices before reaching a flat spot to cast from.

Wearing ordinary footwear while fishing from jetties, or even rubber-soled boots or waders, is sheer folly. This type of footwear does not give you the traction to hold at peculiar angles, or to hold securely on slippery, slimy, marine growth.

There is a variety of jetty footwear available with special soles, or "jetty creepers." Ordinary golf-shoe soles with replaceable metal spikes are ideal. The golf shoes may be worn as is, especially when fishing from jetties where you're situated well above the water and don't have to wear boots or waders to gain access. You may also employ golf rubbers, which may be slipped over regular boots or waders.

Another option is to have a shoemaker remove the rubber sole from a pair of boots or waders and cement a pair of golf soles to the bottoms. This method is by far the most popular among jetty fishermen. Over time the aluminum golf cleats wear down, but they are easily replaced using a wrench made expressly for that purpose. Always lubricate the threads of the cleats when inserting them to prevent them from becoming corroded.

Strap-on ice creepers are also used, but straps tend to bind and are often uncomfortable to wear. There are also jetty creepers made to slip on over boots and footwear. Some anglers even use felt-soled boots and chain slipovers on their boots. None of these options are nearly as effective, safe, and comfortable as golf soles.

Many beaches are covered with big stones and boulders and have treacherous footing. Golf soles or strap-on ice creepers are used by many to secure their footing. Here Al Ristori unhooks a nice bluefish that walloped a darter plug cast from the rock-strewn shoreline at Shagwong Point near Montauk, Long Island.

Suits, bags, lights all essential

A storm suit is another piece of essential gear. In most jetty-fishing situations there are waves crashing against rocks and wind-blown spray. It isn't always necessary to wear it, but the suits are especially nice to have during cold or windy days.

Mobility is essential while jetty fishing, which rules out carrying a tackle box or bucket. Newcomers sometimes learn the hard way. They place their tackle box on a rock, only to have it slip off into a crevice and lose its contents, or have it showered by a crashing wave.

A shoulder bag is the only way to go. Carry a minimum of essential gear and use plastic zip-lock pouches to keep items accessible and dry.

There are many fine-quality shoulder bags available in tackle shops, some even compartmented with plastic tubing for plugs, and sleeves for metal squids and bucktails. Always store the bag in a well-ventilated spot after each jetty fishing excursion. Leaving a wet shoulder bag in a damp place is a good way to turn your lures into a rusty mess.

If you elect to fish from jetties at night, and often that is when the fishing is superior, you'll want a miner's-type headlamp. This can easily be strapped loosely around your collar, so the light hangs under your chin. This makes changing lures, moving around the rocks, or putting your beam on a fish, relatively easy. Forget penlights and regular flashlights. They will just get in the way.

Check local regulations before using gaff

Veteran jetty jockies who target large gamefish generally employ a long-handled gaff to land their catch. The gaff handle is usually the same length as the rod— 7 or 8 feet with a 2-inch stainless steel gaff hook. The gaff enables you to reach a fish without getting too close to the water, an important consideration in heavy surf.

There are some states that prohibit gaffing of gamefish that are covered by minimum size restrictions. Even if a state doesn't prohibit gaffing, but has minimum size limits on gamefish, it's wise to only employ a gaff if you're absolutely certain the fish is well beyond the minimum size restriction.

Jetty fishermen have the option of using natural baits or artificials. While each area has specific lures and terminal rigs that are popular, there are several choices that are time tested.

Bottom rigs

The basic bottom-fishing rig used with natural bait is simple to construct and effective no matter where it is used. Begin by tying a small, three-way swivel directly to the end of your line. Next tie in a 3- or 4-inch loop of monofilament line to one eye of the swivel, onto which you loop your sinker. If the surf is rough, a pyramid-style sinker is most appropriate because of its good holding qualities. Sinkers of 2 to 4 ounces are more than adequate. If the surf is light, some anglers prefer a bank or dipsey style, which offer less resistance in the sand. It all comes down to conditions.

Tie about 3 feet of 20- or 30-pound-test leader to the other eye of the swivel. Select a hook to fit the fish and bait. Anglers often tie in a dropper loop about a foot from the swivel, onto which they loop a second hook. In some cases, Styrofoam floats measuring a 1/2-inch in diameter by 2 inches in length are attached to the leader where it meets the hook. This suspends the hook and bait off the bottom, within range of cruising fish and away from the bait-stealing crabs on the bottom. When targeting summer flounder, weakfish, striped bass, redfish, rockfish, and species that average a couple of pounds or more, a size 2/0 or 3/0 beak, claw or wide-gap hook is appropriate. These hook styles work well when used with seaworm, shrimp, squid, killie or other small baits. If you're using large, 2- to 4-inch-long chunks of menhaden, mullet, mackerel or other fish, or whole squid or clams, move up to a 4/0 hook or larger.

Work the bottom in the waters surrounding the jetty, breakwater or groin from which you're fishing. Assuming you're fishing from a rockpile that extends several hundred feet seaward, it's appropriate to make your initial casts from along the side of the jetty just outside the surf line. The churning surf often exposes sand fleas, crabs, shrimp, sand eels, and other forage and fish move in to feed. While patience is important, move farther out on the jetty and make another cast into new water if you have waited 10 to 15 minutes without a strike. Keep moving and covering new ground until you find success.

You usually don't have to cast far while fishing from a jetty or rockpile, as the natural forage is often in close. A good practice is to make a cast of nominal distance, perhaps 100 to 150 feet, and periodically reel in the bait several feet, thus bracketing the entire area.

Protective rocks have been placed around the cliff beneath famous Montauk Light to keep the seas from eroding the beach. The rocks are a favorite of casters, who regularly post fine catches of striped bass and bluefish. It's treacherous fishing, however, as the seas are often heavy and the rocks slippery.

Visit jetties and breakwaters at low tide

The ravages of the ocean often displace rocks and tumble them about away from the jetty. Because of these rocks, it's wise to visit jetties you plan to fish when the tide is low, so you can see what spots to avoid. Often the fronts of jetties are in disarray. At high tide the jetty appears straight and intact, while on the ebb the front of the jetty takes on a mushroom effect with boulders tumbled about.

While casting away from the jetty works for most species, there are exceptions. Tautog, often called blackfish, sea bass, grunts, snappers, rockfish and sheepshead are among the species that crowd the rocks, often swimming right into crevices for crabs, shrimp and mussels. To catch them you've got to present your baits in close, with the rig resting right among the rocks. The fish will never find it if it's 10 or 15 feet from the jetty.

Because it's so easy to snag your rig when fishing in the rocks, it's often best to simply tie a loop into the end of the line with small half- or 1-ounce dipsey or bank sinker. Next, tie in a dropper loop a foot or so above the sinker, and tie that to a 10- to 12-inch leader with a small No. 1 or 2 claw- or beak-style hook. This is a compact rig and less apt to get snagged than a multi-hook rig with a swivel.

The hook is baited with small pieces of seaworm, shrimp, squid, clam, mussel, snail or cut mullet and cast out just far enough so that it rests either on the rocks or the sand immediately adjacent to the rocks where these species are searching for a meal. Most of the species that feed among the jetty rocks are quick to take a bait, so it's important to be alert. A delay in setting the hook will often result in a lost bait, or a hooked fish that dives into a rocky crevice and cuts your line or leader.

This scene is typical of those found on all three coasts, for there are thousands of rock jetties and groins in place to keep the sea from eroding the shoreline and to protect harbors. Marine growth and mussels attach to the rocks. Many species seek the small forage species that seek the sanctuary rocky crevices offer. As is evidenced by this angler, jetty fishing is relaxing on a warm summer day.

Live baits score with heavyweights

When targeting some of the bigger gamefish, live baits are often used and free-lined without a sinker. This permits the bait to swim out and away from the jetty. A tiny barrel swivel is tied to the end of the line, after which a 3- or 4-foot leader of 20- or 30-pound-test fluorocarbon is tied in. The leader is heavier than the casting line because the fish often ingests the leader when it takes the bait, and a light leader may break as you attempt to land the fish.

Beak- and claw-style hooks are the favorites for live baits, although some anglers employ the O'Shaughnessy bend, and circle hooks are finding more devotees all the time. The size is tailored to the bait being used. Anglers employing live crabs for tarpon often use size 5/0 through 7/0. They are honed needle sharp, with the hook placed through the crab's hard shell. The crab should be hooked so it can swim about freely, but its pincer claws should be clipped off so you don't get nipped while handling it.

Anglers targeting striped bass employ menhaden, mackerel and herring. They lightly hook the bait just beneath the dorsal fin, cast it out and permit it to swim away from the jetty. Properly hooked, a live baitfish will swim a half hour or more, quickly becoming excited as a striper, weakfish or bluefish homes in on it. Live baits such as these can be transported to the jetties in 5-gallon buckets. This is just about the only practical way to carry live baits onto jetties, although it breaks the rule of not carrying buckets onto rockpiles. Carry only a couple of baits in the bucket at a time, so that all of the oxygen in the water isn't quickly depleted. Live eels are fished in much the same manner, except that they are usually hooked through the lips or eyes.

Live mullet are also used to tempt strikes from tarpon, snook, and redfish in southern waters. Some anglers add a sliding float to their line, positioning it so the bait works from 3 to 5 feet beneath the surface with the float signalling precisely where the bait is.

These basic terminal rigs will work for the great majority of species that haunt the waters surrounding coastal jetties. The key is tailoring the size of the hook and bait to the species being sought. If targeting 1-pound winter flounder with blood-worms as bait in Maine, you'll have to go down to a No. 8 or 9 Chestertown hook with a 2-inch piece of sandworm bait, as the flatfish have very small, rubbery mouths. If line-shy Pacific bonito are your target, a No. 4 or 5 beak-style hook and anchovy may be the way to go.

Fishing activity affected by tide

Tides are another consideration when you're fishing natural baits from jetties. At high tide there is often 8 or 10 feet of water where only a sand flat exists at low tide. At other jetties, the rockpile isn't even accessible at high tide, and you can only get onto the rocks after the tide has ebbed for a couple of hours. Experience is the best teacher. Visit the spots you plan to fish. If you're new to an area, visit the local tackle shops and ask for advice on the tides. Keep in mind there are no set rules, for many of the species move about with the tides, feeding for just a short while and then moving on. It's not unusual for a jetty jockey to visit several jetties in the course of a tide, capitalizing on the movements of the fish.

Artificials offer exciting sport

Trying to coax gamefish to strike lures sent from coastal jetties is exciting and a challenge so great that many anglers forego all other techniques. The spinning or conventional outfits used with natural baits work just as well with a wide range of artificials.

The most popular lures at the disposal of the jetty fraternity are metal squids, plugs, and bucktail jigs. Within these three lure categories there are dozens of com-binations. A case in point: Metal squids include the time-proven molded-block tin squids, the hammered stainless steel jigs, chrome- and gold-plated jigs, and assorted variations of the diamond jig. Some of these lures are fished plain, others by adding a plastic bait tail to the hook, a plastic tube tail, feathers, bucktail skirt, or a piece of pork rind. Some are painted exotic colors to resemble baitfish. The lures are avail-able in sizes ranging from a quarter ounce to 3 or 4 ounces. Again, it is a matter of choosing the size lure that best imitates the baitfish in residence.

Dozens of plug models also coax strikes from a wide variety of species. Perhaps the most popular plug in use today is the swimming plug, which has a side-to-side swimming action. These plugs are available in surface-swimming, interme-diate and deep-diving models. Some models are solid, others are jointed. They are available in every color of the rainbow. Sizes range from a mere inch in length—to imitate tiny fry—on up to 7- or 8-inch models that resemble menhaden and mullet.

There are also popping plugs, darters, flaptail plugs, bullet plugs, mirror plugs, pencil plugs and a host of other variations of these basic models. All are fun to use and each requires a different retrieving technique to maximize its action. Mastery of retrieving techniques is crucial. It's not just a matter of casting out and reeling in, which is a trap many anglers fall into. Each lure works differently. Some require an extremely slow retrieve, some a fast retrieve, and some with an irregular retrieve.

Many combinations can produce good results

The basic bucktail jig, as its name implies, consists of lead head molded around a hook, with a bucktail skirt. They're made in a wide variety of shapes. Some are left unpainted, while others are painted solid colors, with white and yel-low the most popular. Still others are air-brushed to replicate a variety of baitfish, right down to the mouth and eyes.

Plastic bait tails have replaced the bucktail and feathers used on many jigs because they are easier to produce. With the plastic tails it's just a matter of select-ing a size and finish, and slipping the tail onto the hook of the leadhead. The plastic tails mimic baitfish such as sand eel, herring, and mullet. Some tails are made in

"There's no way of knowing precisely where the fish will be feeding. This makes it very important that you thoroughly cover all the water surrounding the jetty."

multi-colored shades. Others have sparkles, to resemble most any fry.

Jetty fishermen regularly employ some of these lures in combination, with a plug or metal squid as the primary lure and a plastic-bait tail as a teaser 24 to 30 inches ahead. This teaser combination is rigged by tying a small barrel swivel to the end of a lure, followed by a 30- to 36-inch leader with a duo-lock snap for the primary lure. The teaser, which can also be a saltwater fly or even just a strip of pork rind on a hook, is then snapped to another duo-lock snap tied to the end of the 6-inch dropper off of the barrel swivel. The teaser sometimes gets strikes, and sometimes it's the primary lure. It's not unusual to hook a "doubleheader" with a fish on each lure, especially with bluefish, sea trout, and striped bass.

While live eels are effective for striped bass, weakfish, cobia and other species found around rockpiles, many anglers prefer dead rigged eels. The common eels ranging in length from 6 to 18 inches are killed in salt brine. They are then rigged on metal squids designed expressly for this purpose. The metal squid's hook is placed in the head of the eel, and a second hook run through the eel with a rigging needle, so that it comes out near the eel's anal vent. Rigged in this manner, the eel is a combination lure and bait. It is cast out and retrieved much the same as a plug or metal squid and is very effective along many areas of the coast.

Anglers generally keep six to a dozen eels rigged and stored in kosher salt brine in one gallon plastic mayonnaise jars. These jars can be obtained at most delicatessens. Prepared in this manner, the eels are tough and keep for months.

With an extensive variety of lures at your disposal it's often easy to make the mistake of carrying a massive selection with you and constantly changing lures. It's best to select two or three lures of each basic type and build confidence in using them. When the surf adjacent to the jetty is running high and the wind is onshore, break out a heavy metal squid to reach out into the stiff wind. On a calm, windless night, a small swimming plug worked in close to the rocks may be just right.

Try to cover lots of water

No two jetties are alike and it takes a while to master all the techniques involved. Keep in mind that fish are attracted to a jetty because forage species often seek the protection of the rocks, and crabs, lobsters, sand fleas and shrimp are readily available. There's no way of knowing precisely where the fish will be feeding. This makes it very important that you thoroughly cover all the water surrounding the jetty. This is best accomplished by making your first cast just outside the curl of the breakers and working in towards the beach. Often the churning action of the waves exposes sand fleas, crabs and shrimp and fish will move right into the heavy water to feed. After several casts, move out onto the jetty and bracket your casts, making a cast in towards the beach, so the retrieve almost parallels the jetty. Next place a cast at a 45-degree angle from where you're standing, then straight in front of you, out 45 degrees, and finally almost parallel to the jetty. Then move out and repeat the procedure.

As you approach the end of the jetty you'll often find waves crashing onto the rocks, making it difficult to cast over the submerged rocks. But this is a spot where the fish often feed and you should work it carefully. Complete the circuit and work the remaining side of the jetty to the beach. You'll find that on each jetty you'll receive strikes at different spots. Sometimes it's the location of submerged rocks and the way currents swirl around them that determine where fish will feed. In time you'll accumulate a wealth of information about each jetty and, instead of working the entire rockpile, you can concentrate your efforts on the spots and lures that regularly produce strikes.

Make the first cast count

It's important to make each cast count. If a fish is feeding in a pocket adjacent to a jetty it will often strike on your first cast. Working your lure properly means working it right to the very edge of the rocks before lifting it from the water. Newcomers often reel fast as their lure approaches the rocks, to avoid getting fouled. This is a big mistake, as by far the greatest number of strikes come in close.

Sometimes the fish are feeding in close, but more often than not the gamefish follows the lure and makes a last-second lunge to prevent it from getting away. Huge stripers, tarpon, and snook will startle you when they crash a lure only a few feet away. It's an exciting experience that really gets the adrenaline moving.

When you're fishing for smaller fish it's not too difficult to reel them within range or simply lift them onto the rockpile. With bigger fish it's important to let the hooked fish move well away from the jetty, where it can't get the line caught on the rocks and mussels. Let the fish have its head, take drag and tire itself well out from the rocks. As the fish tires, work it in close and position yourself so that you can get it within range of your gaff or a fishing partner. Avoid spots where tumbled rocks or pilings or other debris are in front of you.

A piece of plastic clothesline makes an excellent stringer, especially when the targets are small- and medium-size fish such as bluefish, sea trout, weakfish, and redfish.

Inlet jetties require different techniques

Along most sections of coast where inlets or breachways empty into the ocean, there are rockpiles constructed on each side of the inlet. These slow down the ravages of the ocean and prevent shifting sands from causing the inlets to shoal. These jetties often provide excellent fishing. However, the conditions at inlet jetties vary considerably from other coastal jetties. Where most coastal jetties have currents working up and down the beach adjacent to them, in the inlets the tidal flow presents a different set of challenges.

The height of the tidal flow in and out of inlets ranges from just a few feet to 10 feet or more. As this water moves, strong currents develop, often carrying huge quantities of bait with them. Most often this occurs on the ebbing tide, when forage species found in bays and rivers are carried along. Gamefish and bottom feeders will gather in the inlets, usually along the bottom and out of the heaviest current, and wait for a meal to be swept their way.

The techniques involved in casting and retrieving is different because of the current. Often the currents are so swift that any lure or the heaviest sinker and bottom rig is just swept along.

The jetty fisherman using natural baits with a bottom rig must constantly cast out his rig, permit the current to carry it along, and then retrieve and cast again. Bottom fishermen usually enjoy their best results within an hour or so of either high or low tide. The current moves more slowly just before the slack. It is then that fish that may have taken up station in the quiet water ahead of or behind rocks, ledges or depressions in the bottom, begin to move about in search of a meal.

Heavy artificials essential

Lightweight lures customarily fished from jetties, especially the surface and intermediate depth plugs and the keeled, high-riding metal squids, just don't work as effectively in the swift, often deep, water of the inlets.

Many inlets are more than 20 feet deep. Fish holding at the bottom, where they try to avoid fighting heavy currents, rarely rise to the surface for a lure. They may not even realize it's there.

The single best lure in inlets is the lead-headed bucktail jig, or its feather or plastic-tailed counterparts. These lures sink fast and get to the bottom quickly in even the heaviest current. They can then be worked along the bottom as the current carries them along.

In many inlets the norm is to use bucktail jigs weighing 2 to 4 ounces, often with a pork rind or a plastic bait tail attached to the hook.

Stay low to the water with tip low

To effectively cover all of the bottom in an inlet that may be a couple of hundred feet wide by a quarter mile long requires a methodology all its own.

Most successful inlet jetty jockies position themselves low to the water on the rocks and cast out and across the current, beginning with a short cast of perhaps 25

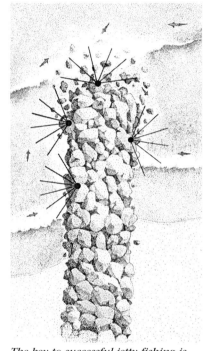

The key to successful jetty fishing is knowing where the fish are apt to be feeding and completely bracketing that area. This is a typical structure extending into the sea, with fish traveling along the surf line, the sides of the jetty and among the tumbled rocks on the front. Climbing around the rocks can be tiresome, but the angler who covers every spot where fish may be feeding will often be rewarded.

145

to 40 feet. Permit the lure to settle on a slack line. As soon as the jig touches bottom, the line will pull taut, at which time the bail is closed or the gears engaged. The lure is permitted to be lifted, bounced, and carried by the current, where it will often lift off the bottom again, move some more and then bounce. As it moves along it is being carried in towards the rocks, and as it nears the end of the swing, the current will sweep it off the bottom. This is where the strikes most often occur, although they may feel like a snag.

Each succeeding cast should be lengthened by 15 or 20 feet, thus enabling the bucktail jig to bounce and sweep across a progressively longer stretch of bottom. Continue extending the distance of your casts as far as you can. If you receive no strikes, just move out along the jetty rocks 20 or 30 feet and repeat the same procedure. In this way you cover all of the bottom. You may receive multiple strikes on successive casts as your jig works into an area where a pod of fish are schooled up.

The author loves to climb around coastal rockpiles in the dark of night. On night tides striped bass, bluefish, weakfish and other species move in to feed. Forage species such as sand eels, spearing, menhaden and mullet move close to the rocks to seek shelter. When casting with plugs, leadhead jigs and metal squids, always make certain to work your lure close to the rocks. That's where you'll receive the most strikes.

Work leadhead jig as ebb tide begins to slacken

To get the feel for bouncing a leadhead jig along the bottom, get low to the water and keep your rod tip pointed downward. As the tide begins to slack, especially on the ebb, which is when the bulk of the forage is in the inlet, you'll find the jig moving more slowly. You can enhance its action by working your rod tip, causing the jig to dart ahead, then falter and be again carried by the tide. At the end of the sweep you can then work the jig back to you, alternately lifting your rod tip, hesitating, then sweeping it upward, reeling, and repeating until you've completed the retrieve.

As the tide slackens in the inlet you can often get strikes on metal squids, rigged eels and plugs. Most often the intermediate- or deep-running models will bring more strikes than surface lures.

An exception to the deep-lure approach occasionally comes into play when the tide is swiftly ebbing, and rips are formed to the seaward end of the inlet jetties. On occasion tarpon, jack crevalle, snook, redfish, striped bass, weakfish and bluefish will gather in these rips and feed on the baitfish that get trapped in the whirlpool-like eddies. Sea gulls and other birds will usually spot what's happening and pick baitfish from the water. This is when a big surface-swimming plug, cast out into the rips and just held in the current where it swims as the current pushes against it, can bring exciting surface strikes.

Safety should be primary concern on the jetties

Jetty fishing is among the most challenging, physical types of fishing anglers can experience. Care should always be taken as you move about the rockpiles. Jetty fishing often develops into a lifelong challenge that can be enjoyed at nominal cost. There are breakwaters, jetties, rockpiles, groins and inlets practically everywhere along the sea coast, all with a population of bottom feeders and gamefish waiting to test your angling prowess.

Herring are found in great numbers in many areas, particularly during the winter months, when they congregate around the mouths of coastal rivers. They'll readily strike tiny shad darts and Sabiki rigs worked ahead of a metal squid of a leadhead jig. While fun to catch, the herring are a great treat when pickled, which is what makes them so popular with jetty casters.

SURF AND BEACH CASTING

Webster's describes surf as "the swell of the sea which breaks upon the shore." But each section of coastline varies substantially. Huge rollers travel across the broad Pacific crashing on the Washington and Oregon shore, while the gentle lap of the often placid Gulf of Mexico results in an almost gentle surf. On the Atlantic side, the warm surf of the Florida Keys is more relaxed as a result of the coral reefs that soften the swells, with beautiful flats extending to the shore, while to the northeast the storms called nor'easters often pile awesome surf onto the sand beaches.

Surf casting is very demanding upon the angler. It ranks closely behind jetty fishing as the most challenging, for it often tests an angler's physical endurance, casting skill and angling prowess to the utmost. Conversely, there are times when the surf is calm, short casts are more than adequate and the fish being sought are cooperative, all of which makes for pleasant, relaxing days on the beach.

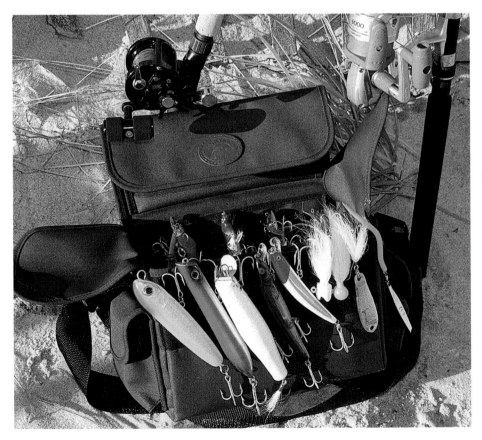

Medium-weight gear is often the most practical choice for surf fishing. Carry a surf bag filled with a small assortment of lures.

(Left) When you walk the beaches and fish night tides you're all alone with nature. Typical of the rewards is this fine weakfish landed by June Rosko while casting a surface swimming plug on a pleasant autumn evening.

149

Tackle selection a key ingredient

Properly balanced tackle is more critical in surf casting than in many types of fishing. Some surf situations are ideal for light, one-handed spinning outfits. More often, though, heavy surf conditions require a two-handed casting outfit that can deliver your presentation 200 to 300 feet.

Many people mistakenly believe bigger is better, and that a long, heavy rod, big reel and huge amount of line is the proper outfit for surf casting. Nothing could be further from the truth. The key is employing a balanced outfit from which an angler can obtain maximum power to execute the cast. The average angler of average build cannot handle some of the very heavy outfits available in most coastal tackle shops. Outfits that are too heavy take away from the fun and sport of surf casting.

Surf-casting outfits fall into three basic categories: heavy, medium and light. Keep in mind that there are extremes at both ends of the spectrum, and what is included here are those outfits that accommodate the widest variety of conditions.

These outfits may be readily handled by an angler of reasonable build and skill. The choice of reel comes down to personal preference. A spinning reel is generally easier to master than a multiplying reel.

Heavy surf for heavy water

Heavy-surf rods range in length from 9 to 12 feet. They're built for two-handed casting, with butt sections measuring from 24 to 36 inches, depending on the action of the rod and whether it is designed for a spinning or multiplying reel. Spinning-rod devotees generally prefer a longer rod.

The tip section of heavy surf rods are somewhat stiff and powerful, for they're called upon to deliver weights of 10 ounces or more. While fiberglass was the material of choice for saltwater rods for many years, graphite and graphite composites have slowly became the standard. They're stronger, lighter, and capable of delivering the power needed for long casts. Kevlar is also gaining prominence as a rod material because of its strength and weight, although such rods are expensive. As with most new technology, given time, Kevlar rods will eventually become more affordable.

In surf casting you're holding and physically handling the entire outfit for long periods of time, casting and retrieving and fighting fish. Thus, weight becomes a critical factor. Take care not to purchase an outfit that is so heavy it will quickly wear you out. Most of the better quality heavy-surf rods weigh between 14 and 20 ounces. Some weigh twice that and should be avoided.

Look for a rod made with quality, lightweight components. Those with through-butt construction are preferred by many. Graphite reel seats with anodized aluminum hoods are lightweight, impervious to saltwater and hold the reel securely. Aluminum oxide or ceramic line guides, mounted to evenly distribute the strain over the length of the rod, help in executing casts and fighting fish. Several manufacturers provide roller guides on their surf rods. These rollers are particularly effective in the northwest, where long casts and heavy sinkers and baits are the norm. The best quality rods have guides that are wound and secured with epoxy, ensuring many years of trouble-free use.

Another innovation is a rod with exterior guides. The line runs within the wall of the rod and exits at the tip. The line travels along the smooth inside of the rod, and its action is evenly distributed.

For the most part there is a direct correlation between cost and quality. Many of the best rods are costly, but the workmanship is apparent, and invariably the rod will last longer than a cheaper model.

Several national manufacturers provide dealers with sample rods to be used expressly for trial purposes. You may stop by a local tackle shop, borrow a rod and matching reel and line, and have the opportunity to take it out and cast with it, and even fish with it for a day or two. Admittedly, these are the high-end quality rods, but these loaners can help you find an outfit you know you'll be happy with.

Most of the spinning reels designed for heavy-surf spinning are capable of holding anywhere from 250 yards of 20-pound-test line to 300-yards of 30-pound monofilament. They weigh 25 to 32 ounces and are often much heavier than the rod. You can lean towards the smaller line capacity and lighter-weight reel, as there are few surf species you're apt to encounter that will clean you out of 900 feet of line. The big reels are overkill for most surf fishing.

When selecting a reel, ask your dealer to permit you to try using it with the rod of your choice, just to get the feel of how it casts and how it feels in your hands.

The better reels have machined, anodized-aluminum skirted spools, into which are built smooth, powerful drag systems. The reel should have a main shaft of quality stainless steel. While stainless steel components are admittedly heavy, in the case of the shaft, gears, ball bearings, and bail mechanism, they're especially important. The majority of the heavy surf reels have 4-to-1 or 4.5-to-1 gear ratios for a fast retrieve and substantial power.

It takes a while to master the thumb discipline when casting with a multiplying reel, but many surf casters swear by these popular reels. In recent years the quality of surf reels has made the thumb less important in controlling the fast-turning reel and preventing the line from an overrun and resulting backlash.

The multiplying reels used for high surf are generally lighter than spinning reels. They have a line capacity ranging from 200 yards of 30-pound-test monofilament or braided nylon up to 350 yards of 20-pound-test. Casting from the surf with a multiplying reel loaded with 30-pound test is very difficult and the heavier line is seldom used or needed.

Many surfcasters now opt for smaller reels and lines of Spectra fiber. The microfilament lines have diameters one-fifth those of monofilament line, enabling an angler to use a heavier test, with a smaller reel. This can be overdone, however. A small reel might not have a strong enough drag system for some bigger fish.

Here again, sampling a rod and reel combination is critical. You are likely to know if an outfit is right for you when you make a few casts or fish with it for several days. Even if you've got to borrow a friend's outfit, don't purchase a rod and reel until you're comfortable with them. Remember, you'll be walking the beach, often encumbered with waders and a surf bag, and the last thing you want is to be burdened with an outfit that doesn't suit you, your frame, and your ability.

Many of the newer surf-casting reels are made of space age composites, with graphite among the most popular because of its light weight. Some surf reels have a throw lever that disengages the gear by moving it backward prior to the cast. Others have a button that is depressed prior to the cast and engages as the reel handle is turned. This eliminates the need to engage the throw lever. The quality reels are impervious to saltwater and will give you years of service when properly cared for.

You can't tell what kind of a drag a reel has in the store because the reels usually don't have line on them. A good way to check the smoothness of a reel is to fill the reel with line and mount it on the rod you plan to use. Tie the line off to a post, and walk off line with various degrees of drag and rod pressure. Regardless of the setting, the reel's drag, usually adjusted via a star wheel adjacent to the handle, should relinquish line evenly and consistently, with no jerking or binding. Just the slightest hesitation or binding in a drag can result in a broken line, which is the last thing you need to happen after hooking a big one from the beach on a day of hard fishing.

Stainless internal components are just as important in multiplying reels as spinning reels. Cheap reels often have minimal stainless steel and will rust. Many better reels have a quick take-apart feature that enables you to easily change spools and clean the reel.

It is certainly appropriate to adhere to the manufacturer's line recommendations for a specific reel. It is also appropriate, however, to adjust to what makes you comfortable. When fishing bottom where there are many obstructions, it may prove wise to spool a heavier line, enabling you to pull your line free with ease should you become fouled. In heavy surf a bit heavier line, within reason, may help you

"When selecting a reel, ask your dealer to permit you to try using it with the rod of your choice, just to get the feel of how it casts and how it feels in your hands."

land a big striper or channel bass that might otherwise get trapped in the strong current.

These heavy, high-surf outfits are used throughout Washington and Oregon, where heavy surf is the norm. They also serves casters who fish from the beaches of Cape Cod, Massachusetts and Montauk, Long Island, where long casts are often required. Cape Hatteras anglers fishing from the famed Outer Banks of North Carolina regularly use heavy-surf outfits to carry 4- to 6-ounce sinkers and heavy menhaden baits seaward.

These outfits are also popular among anglers who employ heavy natural baits and place their rods in a sand spike to await a strike.

June Rosko walks a desolate stretch of surf, fishing a dropoff where gamefish often gather.

Medium-surf outfit ideal for general surf, beach and bank

The medium-surf outfit is suited to almost all surf conditions. It's heavy enough for many rough situations, yet light enough that it can still be fun to catch small fish. It is an outfit that is ideal for the surf caster who only wants to buy one rod-and-reel combination.

The medium-surf rod is a two-handed casting outfit measuring anywhere from 7 to 8 1/2 feet in length. It has a rather stiff action, basically designed for handling 1/2- to 2-ounce lures, although it can be used for lures or rigs twice that weight. This is especially true with many of the graphite rods currently on the market which, although light in weight, have a tremendous amount of backbone.

Graphite is the most popular rod choice among veteran anglers. Fiberglass, or fiberglass graphite composites, and Kevlar also have a following. At just 8- to 12-ounces total, the medium rods are about half the weight of the heavy surf models. This makes a big difference in a day on the beach, especially when casting and retrieving artificial lures for hours at a time.

Many of the medium-weight surf reels are made with graphite frames, as opposed to cast aluminum used in the heavy models. The medium-surf models handle 275 yards of 12-pound-test line or 250 yards of 15-pound-test, yet weigh just 14 to 24 ounces. Lines are being made in increasingly finer diameters, which means you can often load a quality 17-pound-test line and fill the spool with the same yardage the manufacturer recommended for 15-pound-test.

With medium weight surf casting reels, anglers now employ what are really enhanced versions of the time-proven freshwater bait-casting reel. This basic multiplying reel has been made stronger and larger, yet carries the same smoothness of the original.

The reels are manufactured with precision-machined aluminum frames and side plates and lightweight aluminum spools. An anodized aluminum finish adds to their longevity. The reels feature a centrifugal-brake casting control system to help prevent the line from over-running and causing a backlash. Where the old bait-casting reels required thumb pressure to control a fish, the new saltwater models feature a star drag system that is as smooth as silk, enabling you to set the drag with a maximum amount of pressure without fear of a line break due to binding.

Most of the newer models have a button that is depressed to disengage the reel spool at the time of the cast. The reel is then engaged by turning the handle during the retrieve. A level-wind mechanism ensures that the line is wound back on the spool evenly. These reels hold approximately 250 yards of 15-pound-test monofilament, which is more than adequate for most medium-surf situations.

The medium-surf outfit is a favorite of California anglers and on the beaches of Long Island and New Jersey, where fish often feed inside sand bars that parallel the coast. In such situations long casts aren't required, and the surf is minimal.

Light-surf outfit a one-handed model

Along the Gulf of Mexico, the light-surf outfit is ideal. It's a featherweight model designed for one-handed casting. It's also favored by anglers who choose to wade the many miles of shallow flats in the Florida Keys. Miles of Atlantic and Pacific beaches have light surf, too, especially with an offshore wind.

With a one-handed outfit you can walk or wade along your favorite stretch of beach, bank or flats for hours on end, casting endlessly without the fatigue encountered when using the heavier surf outfits.

Anglers who fish freshwater will recognize the spinning and multiplying outfits used in light-surf and beach situations as being essentially the same as those used on their favorite lake or river for bass, trout and pike. The difference is they have a little more power to handle the bigger fish.

"By selecting the pack-rod format for either a baitcasting rod or a spinning rod, you can carry your rod and reel with you whenever you travel."

The two most popular light outfits are basically built around pack rods—portable three-piece rods that are stored in a case measuring just 30 inches in length. They can be easily transported, including aboard planes, where they easily stow in the overhead compartment. By selecting the pack-rod format for either a baitcasting rod or a spinning rod, you can carry your rod and reel with you whenever you travel.

Pack rods are available in three models: those capable of handling 3/8-ounce through 2 1/4-ounce lures, 1/4- through 1/2-ounce, and really light 1/16-ounce through 5/16-ounce lures. The two heavier models are suitable for most saltwater applications, especially beach casting and light surf situations.
Made of graphite, fiberglass or a composite, these rods are extremely light. Once you become accustomed to one-handed casting you might not want to return to the heavier two-handed models.

There are also one- and two-piece models. If these are your choice, select one with a fast tip action, capable of shooting light lures, or small baits such as shrimp or crabs, into a breeze.
Many manufacturers now have small reels, both spinning and multiplying, designed expressly for saltwater use. This is a big plus, for in the past it was often necessary to employ freshwater reels, which simply did not hold up when exposed to saltwater conditions.

In the spinning category, select a reel capable of holding 220 yards of 10-pound-test monofilament, or about 180 yards of 12-pound-test mono or micro filament line. This is more than adequate for most applications. If in doubt, go a little heavier. If you go too light, say 6- or 8-pound-test, you'll find yourself being cut off on seaweed, shells or other debris.

The majority of light saltwater bait-casting reels hold 240 yards of 15-pound-test monofilament. Here too, a multiplying reel on a lightweight pack rod will let you fish with all day long with little fatigue.

Learning conformation of beach is essential

It helps to scout an area you plan to fish. If you have an intimate knowledge of the water you can work a productive stretch of beach and score whether you fish day or night, high tide or low tide, rough surf or calm. This is easier than it sounds, as all that is required is for the angler to invest a couple of hours to learn the lay of the beach.

Select a bright, sunny day to do your beach survey work, and be on the beach at dead-low tide. You'll be surprised how much you can learn just by looking. Make it a point to work a mile-and-a-half to two miles of beach. In a stretch of this length you'll find some spots that drop off abruptly. Other spots will just gradually slope into the ocean.

Many sections of coast have bar formations paralleling the beach. No two bar formations are alike, but most have some common characteristics. At low tide the sand bars are occasionally exposed and the surf crashes in on them, rolling across the bar and dumping tons of water inside the bar, into sluices.

Picture two sandbars several hundred feet long, extending parallel with the beach and approximately 100 feet from the beach at low tide. At some point the center of each bar formation will often extend towards the beach, where the water is only a foot or two in depth. Assume the break in the bar is 50 to 75 feet wide, which is usually quite deep, with 5 to 8 1/2 feet at low tide.

As the waves crash across both bars, the water crashing across the bar to your left will flow to your right towards the break in the bar, while the water crashing across the bar to your right will flow left towards the same break, or exit. You'll notice this as you cast and retrieve, for your lure will be carried along with the current formed as the water rushes to exit through the break.

The same current forms even at high tide, for the onrushing water continues to move and exit through the submerged breaks.

All of the species that frequent the surf move extensively as they feed during various stages of the tide. At extremely low tide there may not be sufficient water inside the bars for them to feed, and they'll work along the outer edge of the bar, or in the deep holes and cuts between the bars. As the tide floods the fish will often move through the breaks, inside the bars, and work up and down the sluices to feed on the abundance of forage that seeks the sanctuary of the shallows. It's here that spearing, peanut bunker, rainfish, sand eels, mullet, crabs, clams and sand bugs are found in abundance.

By thoroughly understanding the beach formations you'll know just where to apply your efforts at various stages of the tide.

Surf fishing can be very pleasant when there's little wind and the water is calm. Jacqueline and Jennifer Basilio often accompany the author, their grandfather, to a stretch of picturesque beach. Using light casting tackle with plugs, metal squids or leadhead jigs, they frequently catch striped bass, bluefish, weakfish, and summer flounder.

Surf bag or bucket ideal for carrying gear

If you elect to use natural baits you most often will be spending the better part of a tide at one location. A good surf bag with a shoulder strap, or a 5-gallon plastic bucket, which can also serve as a seat while you're waiting for a strike, work well for hauling gear. The new plastic Lurebox, designed with five trays that fit inside a 5-gallon plastic bucket, is ideal.

You'll need a sand spike in which to place your outfit, as you certainly don't want to lay it on the sand. Many anglers cut two holes for sand spikes into the lid of their bucket.

Bring along a pair of round, plastic, hardware organizers designed to fit the diameter of the bucket. They're available at most hardware stores. Sinkers are placed in one compartment, terminal rigs in another, a folding knife, long-nosed pliers and a dehooker in another, and finally, a small cutting board and towel.

In another organizer include packets of bait. Zippered plastic bags are ideal. Chunks of fish are popular as surf baits, with bunker, mackerel, mullet, spearing, herring and anchovies among the most common. Many anglers prefer to use the head of a baitfish, for the crabs can chew on the head of a bait for a long while and there's still enough bait left to tempt a strike from a hungry fish.

Some anglers carry several packets of clams, squid or fillets of forage species that have been brined in kosher salt. This hardens the bait, keeps it from ripping off the hook when casting, and makes it tougher for fish and crabs to strip bait from the hook. The small cutting board makes it easy to cut baits to size right on the beach.

An especially good time to both collect bait and fish is right after a coastal onshore storm. Often the surf is churned up and clams are exposed. It's often easy to fill up a 5-gallon pail with clams—enough to last for a couple of months in the refrigerator after being brined.

The Gulf Coast, from Florida all the way to Texas, has hundreds of miles of beautiful beaches. Many of the beaches slope off gradually and an angler can wade for miles. This is Bill AuCoin's favorite kind of fishing. Here he used a leadhead jig and plastic bait tail to land a big channel bass, popularly called redfish throughout the South.

A favorite light rig uses a 36-inch piece of 20- or 30-pound-test fluorocarbon leader material. A duo-lock sinker snap is attached to one end of the leader, and a tiny barrel swivel to the other. A pair of 4-inch dropper loops are tied in with about 18 inches between the loops. A small cork is then slipped onto the loop. A 1/0 through 3/0 claw baitholder hook is then slipped onto each of the dropper loops. This hook size works with a wide variety of baits when fishing for striped bass and bluefish, weakfish, rockfish and channel bass. When small surf species are in residence, such as surfperch, kingfish, croakers and spot, use smaller hooks. Double-loop the hooks by passing the hook through the leader loop twice. This way you can snug up the hook to the end of the loop and it stays there. If you loop it just once, the loop will often slide down the shank of the hook.

With this two-hook rig the sinker carries the bait, preventing the leader from falling back on the line and causing a tangle.

Vin Sparano checks the air pressure of his tires prior to moving onto the soft sand for a day of cruising along the surf beaches. Many surf fishermen have their vehicles equipped with oversize tires and are rigged out with all of their gear as beach buggies. The rig includes rod racks, tackle chest, ice chest and all the amenities for a pleasant day on the beach.

The pyramid-style sinker is favored and holds well in the surf. Use as light a weight as will hold. Even in an onshore wind, the 4-ouncers will normally hold.

The general pattern is for the fish to move from the deep, outside the bar formations, through the breaks or into the holes, and then to move either north or south on the inside of the bar. Position yourself where there's a break, and fish in the deep water of the hole, perhaps 100 feet or so from the beach. If that doesn't bring results, cast at an angle in the shallow water between the bar and the beach. In this way you've got a shot at fish moving through the cut, and those traveling up and down the beach in the sluice inside the bar.

It's often wise to use a combination of two baits. On one hook slip on half of a big sea clam, passing the hook through the bait three times so it stays on securely, with the soft stomach and muscles hanging free. Onto the other hook use the head of a bunker, mullet, mackerel or herring. Slip the hook into the lower lip and out the upper, with the head section cut diagonally from just behind the head to the mid-stomach area and entrails hanging freely from the bait.

You can use a small whole squid as bait, or just a small piece of head section. For the smaller species, use pieces of clam or mussel, squid or shrimp.

Next it's just a matter of casting out, setting a very light drag, and either holding the rod or positioning it in one of the sand spikes. Then it's just a waiting game. Make certain the drag is set lightly. If it's set too tight a big fish may take the bait and move off, dragging your rod out of the sand spike and into the surf. This can happen very easily. Turn away for a couple of minutes to talk to someone and you may turn around you see your sand spike has been dragged over and your outfit is gone.

Even if you prefer holding your rod, fish with a light drag for starters. Most often a big fish prowling the surf line will be drawn to the bait by its scent, inhale it and hook itself in the process. Then all it takes is a sharp lift of the rod tip to ensure the barb is set. Let the fish make its run without excessive pressure. Once you get to judge the size of the fish, adjust for a bit more pressure, but never so heavy as to risk a break-off.

Another popular surf bait setup consists of a single-hook rig that suspends the bait off the bottom, a particular advantage when there are crabs stealing your bait in the surf. The basic rig is made by tying a small three-way swivel to the terminal end of your line. To one eye of the swivel tie in a 6- to 8-inch dropper loop, onto which you can slip a regular pyramid-style sinker, or a Hatteras-style pyramid if the surf is rough.

To the remaining eye of the swivel, tie in a 36-inch piece of 20- or 30-pound-test fluorocarbon leader material. Snell a 1/0 or 2/0 claw-style hook with a bait-holder shank to the leader. Finally, employ a small cork float on the leader two-thirds the distance between the swivel and hook. This will suspend the bait off the bottom and make for a better target for a fish searching for a meal.

This rig is especially popular when using sandworms or bloodworms as bait. The worms hang suspended just off the bottom with the movement of the surf current giving them an enticing, lifelike action as they move back and forth. A small whole squid fished on this rig also makes an attractive bait, as does a fillet of most any forage species.

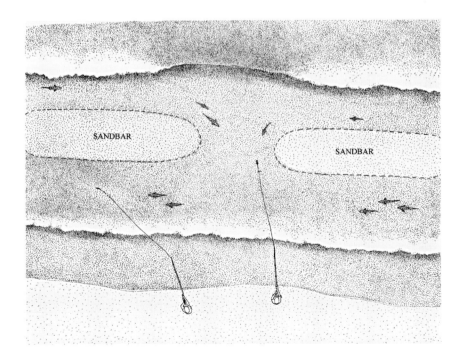

Many areas of surf have offshore bar formations. There are deep holes or cuts between the bars and fish moving along the outer bar enter the sluices inside the bars through these holes. The fish move up and down the sluices inside the bars, often right along the edge of the dropoff. It's wise to always work your lure right to the edge of the sand, as fish are often searching for food in the very shallow water at the edge of the dropoff.

Did you ever realize how few people ever get to experience a sunrise on the beach? Surf fishermen experience the beauty regularly, with no two sunrises alike. This is a particularly productive time to be on the beach, for during that magic period of an hour before to an hour after sunrise many surf species are very active.

Cast-and-retrieve technique best for flounder

Members of the flatfish clan often move about along the edge of a dropoff and are a target for the angler that casts and retrieves his bait.

A favorite rig of surfmen has been popularized by Ernie Wuesthoff, whose tackle shop is in Normandy Beach, on the central Jersey coast. Called the "Sneaky Pete," it is made by first tying a small three-way swivel to the end of your line. A short sinker loop is tied to one eye of the swivel, for use with a light dipsey-style sinker sufficiently heavy to cast.

To the remaining eye of the swivel, tie a 24-to 36-inch piece of fluorocarbon leader material. Slip on a couple of glass beads and a thumbnail-size Colorado spinner. To the terminal end of the leader a pair of size 1/0 claw-style hooks are snelled about 2 inches apart. The head hook is used as bait holder with the trailing hook placed in the center of the bait.

A strip bait cut from squid, sea robin or flounder belly is used. Cut the strip approximately 1/2-inch in width and 3 or 4 inches in length with a torpedo shape.

This rig can be fished with any outfit in any kind of surf. One-handed rigs provide more sport and are ideal for flounder and halibut fishing. Cast the rig out a short distance, as the flatfish are usually working close to the edge of the dropoff and may be feeding within a couple of rod lengths from where you're standing.

Retrieve by drawing back on your rod tip, hesitating, lowering the rod tip to take up slack, and then repeating the procedure. The strike of a flounder will often feel like a snag on the bottom. Don't pull the bait away from the fish. Instead, just keep repeating the procedure. This will cause the flounder to be more aggressive as it tries to subdue the bait.

This technique may also bring strikes from weakfish, bluefish, spotted weakfish, and redfish.

Casting bait into heavier surf can call for a little ingenuity. The baits are heavy and the surf tends to push them back toward shore. The answer can often be found in breaches buoy rigs used by many surfmen to present a live menhaden, herring, mackerel, mullet, spot, pinfish, or other baitfish far from the sand.

The rig is made up by tying a 4- or 5-ounce pyramid sinker to the end of your monofilament line (preferably at least 20-pound-test for heavy-surf outfit). Next use a small combination barrel swivel and coastlock snap and tie it to 24 or 30 inches of fluorocarbon leader material. Snell a 5/0 through 7/0 size beak or circle hook to the end of the leader. Next, take a live baitfish and hook into the fleshy part of the back just ahead of the dorsal fin. With a live eel, place the hook in its lower jaw and out the upper jaw.

Cast the sinker as far out into the surf as possible. With just a sinker on the line, it is simple to cast 100 to 200 feet. Then take the leader with the live baitfish on the hook and use the coastlock snap to secure the leader to the line. Holding the rod high in the air, permit the coastlock snap, leader and live baitfish to slide down the line into the surf, breeches-buoy fashion. As soon as the fish reaches the water it will most often continue swimming down the line, moving in and out, far beyond any distance you might have been otherwise able to cast it. When a cruising channel bass, snook, striped bass, cobia or tarpon picks it up, the big fish will often swallow the hook bait in an instant, and as it moves off the rig will slide down to the sinker, where it comes tight, and you're able to strike the fish and hold on!

Lures can work in the surf

Fishing with lures from the surf can be an exciting dimension and is especially good the angler who likes to move about. Again, knowing the configuration of the surf you plan to fish is important. Each formation, be it a steeply dropping beach, shallow sluice, deep hole or offshore bar, presents a different opportunity. Each requires a different technique to coax strikes from hungry gamefish.

Selection of a basic outfit will in large part be determined by the fish being sought and the surf conditions you expect to encounter. Medium and heavy outfits are popular in the Northwest and Northeast, while casters fishing Gulf beaches usually opt for light tackle.

Tommy Melton loves to fish the surf and spends his leisure time as a surf guide. He travels the beaches in his beach buggy and enjoys superb action on night tides. This big bluefish walloped a darter plug cast into the teeth of a northeaster at Shagwong Point, Long Island.

"Fluorocarbon leader material is effective because of its refractive index when used with natural baits for tuna, bonefish, and other cautious species."

Several types of leaders may be used

Terminal rigging is essentially the same, regardless of the tackle employed. In each instance, a leader is employed that is heavier than the line being used. This is contrary to accepted freshwater techniques, where often the leader tippet is light, so as to fool the quarry. In saltwater, many of the species have sharp teeth, bony mouths and sharp scales, any of which could sever a light leader. The heavier leader also proves helpful when beaching a fish in the surf, as it gives you something to grab hold of.

Fluorocarbon leader material is effective because of its refractive index when used with natural baits for tuna, bonefish, and other cautious species. Only recently have casters who employ lures begun to realize that fluorocarbon also works extremely well as a leader material, for the fish only see the lure and not the leader.

Begin by first doubling a foot or two of the terminal end of your line, employing a double surgeon's knot. Tie in a small black swivel, using a uni-knot or improved clinch knot. Next, tie in a 36-inch piece of fluorocarbon leader with 20- or 30-pound-test appropriate for heavy-surf tackle, and 15-pound-test ideal for a one-handed outfit. Tie a duo-lock snap to the end of the leader and you're all set to go.

There are several variations to this leader, including substituting No. 8 or 9 stainless steel wire in the event toothy bluefish or barracuda are the targeted species. Some anglers also prefer to avoid using a swivel, and simply join their double line to the leader using a surgeon's knot.

Another effective rig is one designed for use with a teaser. Begin with a 42-inch piece of fluorocarbon leader material with a small duo-lock snap at the end for the primary lure. Next, tie in a tiny black swivel inside a dropper loop about 30 inches from the duo-lock snap. Tie another duo-lock snap to the remaining tag end, making the finished tag end for the teaser approximately 6 inches long.

Fish your primary lure at the terminal end, and off the dropper loop fish a saltwater fly or a plastic grub or plastic bait tail. The idea is that the fish is attracted to the primary lure and will strike the smaller teaser lure, especially when tiny baitfish are present.

Mullet are one of the most popular natural baits used by surf fishermen. With a float rig such as this, the hook is inserted into the mullet and attached to the float, which in turn is attached to a 24-inch-long leader with a pyramid sinker. The mullet is suspended off the bottom, where the wave action of the surf moves it back and forth.

A variety of lures available to surf casters

As with seemingly all types of fishing, anglers who cast from the sand have literally thousands of lures from which to choose. The wide assortment breaks down into three basic groups: plugs, leadhead jigs and metal squids.

Plugs are most often constructed from wood or plastic. Some are designed to "swim" on the surface, much like a menhaden, while others swim into the depths, like a mackerel or herring. The swimmer, popper, darter, pencil popper, needlefish, flaptail and mirror plug are all popular styles. Each plug requires a different retrieve technique to maximize its action.

The swimming plugs have a lip which imparts a side-to-side swimming action during retrieval. Some are designed to swim on the surface, while others probe intermediate depths or dive to the bottom. Poppers have a concave head scoop and gurgle and chug along, their action enhanced with a smart pull of the rod tip, causing the plug to "pop" as it throws water ahead of it. The pencil popper is long and thin. By imparting a continuous dancing action with your rod tip, the plug dances across the surface much like a scurrying baitfish. Darters do just that, they dart back and forth, much like an excited baitfish seeking to avoid an adversary. The flaptail has a metal swiveling tail that flaps and spins as it is slowly retrieved, leaving a surface commotion and V-wake much like a mullet cruising on the surface. The mirror plug has the shape of a small baitfish. There are models designed for surface, intermediate, and deep diving, with action imparted by the rod tip during the retrieve.

The combination rig uses a teaser fly ahead of a the main lure. The setup works well for a variety of fish.

Metal squids include a wide variety of models

For many years the metal squid, molded of block tin, was undisputed choice of surf casters. Molded in a variety of keel-shapes, most have a fixed hook molded right into the squid, while some have a swinging hook. Made of pure tin, it has a soft silver color, much like many baitfish, and resists tarnishing. It is often dressed with feathers, bucktail, or a piece of pork rind to enhance its action.

Many enhancements have been made to this lure over the years. Some are cast of lead and chrome plated. Inlaid scale-like finishes enhanced the appeal of some, while others sport fish-like replicas carefully painted on them. Stainless steel squids, often called jigs, were also developed, with a hammered finish and soft luster that is almost impervious to saltwater. Many different versions popped up, all with their own characteristics when cast into the foaming surf.

Plastic tube tails were added to the trailing hook that swings on a split ring of many of the newer models. There were reflective pearl finishes added, too, all to enhance the appeal of the lure. While still a popular lure today, the metal squid now shares the lure bag with many other lures it helped inspire.

Many small metal spoons are cast and retrieved using the same techniques as the metal squids. A lure that has little if any action of its own is the leadhead jig. Cast of lead, with a fixed hook, and sometimes a swinging hook, the leadhead jig may be dressed with either bucktail or a plastic tail, or a combination of the two. Often not even painted, and other times air-brushed exotically to resemble tiny forage fry it, too, comes in a wide variety of shapes and sizes.

There are lima bean shapes, torpedo, bug-eye, ball, smiling, and delta wing models. Few have any action of their own, but are effective with the help of an active rod tip.

There are also lure and bait combinations that prove effective. A good example is the rigged eel of the Northeast surfcaster. A dead common eel is rigged on a metal squid designed expressly for that purpose, and when retrieved the squid imparts a swimming action to the trailing eel. Gulf Coast anglers often rig a dead needlefish on a leadhead jig—a deadly combination for snook.

The combination rig, which uses a primary lure such as a plug, metal squid or leadhead jig with a teaser rigged 30 inches ahead of it, can be a winner regardless of where you fish. By slipping a saltwater fly such as a Clouser, Deceiver, Half & Half, or most any fly resembling a small baitfish, on the leader's dropper, you can really improve your chances. Teasers hook sea trout, Pacific barracuda, yellowtail, striped bass, rockfish, bluefish, and most all the members of the flatfish clan. Occasionally, one fish will strike the primary lure while another hits the teaser. There are many surf casters who wouldn't consider fishing with a single lure and always use a teaser.

All-terrain vehicles are popular along the coast. Mary Healey has her tackle box attached to the hood with a fish box and rod racks on the back. She keeps a pair of binoculars on hand to scan the surf for gulls and terns, which often point to feeding fish.

Flatfish feed along the bottom, right at the edge of the breakers, where food is often plentiful. The author landed this summer flounder on a bucktail teaser fished 30 inches ahead of a leadhead jig. While all of the flatfish are fun to catch, they're an excellent dinnertime treat when filleted and deep-fried.

Control of lure when casting is essential

Surf fishermen have a number of factors to contend with as they fish from the beach. Control of their lure is essential, and the roll of the surf and its impact on a lure must be taken into account when retrieving, as must the current that parallels the beach at various stages of the tide.

Waves generally roll onto the outer bar or directly onto the beach at regular intervals, except in the stormiest of conditions. It's best to time your cast to go beyond the crest of incoming waves and avoid having the breaking wave crash down on your lure and wash it towards the beach. By so this, you begin to control the lure as it splashes in beyond the crest of the wave and perform a retrieve that fully utilizes the lure's action without having it tumbled about.

You also want to time your casts so they not only reach beyond the cresting wave, but land at an angle into the current. Position yourself on the sand, so that the lure is worked right through the edge of the dropoff and onto the beach.

Striped bass are caught on all three coasts and are without question the most popular target of surf fishermen. The author landed this beauty while casting a leadhead jig with a plastic bait tail. Stripers often cruise along the edge of the dropoff, just a few feet from the sand, where forage species such as sand eels, spearing, mullet and menhaden seek sanctuary in the shallows.

Wading is often helpful, especially when the fish are feeding far off the beach. Always keep a balance, however, as all too often anglers are wade right where the fish would normally be feeding.

There are no hard-and-fast rules as to which lure you should fish at any given time, although there are a few general guidelines. In a roaring onshore wind and rough surf it's very difficult to properly fish most plugs. At such times either a metal squid or leadhead jig is easier to cast, controls better in the rough water, and work at deep or intermediate levels.

With a dead-calm surf and clear water that is the result of an offshore wind, a plug becomes a good choice because it is easy to cast and may be worked right up to the sand.

In moderate surf it pays to alternate and try each basic lure type as you work a stretch of beach. Remember that, particularly with leadhead jigs and many plugs, you increase the effectiveness of the lure by working your rod tip.

Many surf fisherman fall into the bad habit of casting and reeling without any regard to the push of the waves or the effect of currents that parallel the beach.

With any lure it's important that you always have the feel of the lure. If the wave pushes your lure and the line is slack, you're not in control. Nor are you in control if a strong wind catches your line and puts a big belly in it. Keep the rod tip low in the wind as you execute your retrieve, so as much line as possible is in the water and you're able to feel the plug working.

If the surf is rough and pushing right at you, do the opposite. Raise the rod tip

*June Rosko uses a lightweight pack
rod to probe the Atlantic Coast surf
for striped bass like the beauty she's
just landed. Light tackle provides
maximum sport for the wide variety
of gamefish that may be caught from
the sand beaches.*

high in the air, keeping the line above the waves where possible and always adjusting retrieve speeds. Reel fast as a wave pushes, slow to a crawl as a wave recedes and pulls against the lure.

If the tide is extremely low you can often fish the water outside the bar by carefully wading out onto the bar Exercise caution, however. If the tide is beginning to flood you may have trouble returning to the beach.

At mid-tide, work the sluices behind the bars. They're often loaded with fish, as are the breaks or holes in the bar where fish often congregate waiting for the water depth to get to their liking.

When fishing the sluices behind the bars, work the current much the same as you would work a trout stream. Cast up into the current and permit it to sweep your lure as you retrieve, all the time maintaining a taut line and control of the lure.

While much has been written on the effects of tides, the moon, wind direction, water clarity and other variables, the most successful anglers are those who fish whenever an opportunity presents itself. Given the choice, an hour before and after first light, and again for an hour before dark are the usually the best times to fish. Many species are nocturnal feeders, and fishing in darkness from the beach can be exciting.

Surf fishing is demanding. The angler who walks the beach and probes each hole and sluice with his lures and bait will catch a wide variety of species. The beautiful sunrises, quiet moonlit nights, and gently rolling waves make it among the most peaceful settings a saltwater angler can experience.

PIERS, BRIDGES, DOCKS AND BULKHEADS

Piers, bridges, docks and bulkheads provide some of the most leisurely fishing available to coastal anglers. These structures are readily accessible, and while there is often a fee for using fishing piers, anglers can enjoy the relaxed atmosphere and camaraderie associated with this type of fishing for little or no money.

The majority of species caught from coastal piers, bridges and bulkheads are panfish, such as this fine catch of croakers. A light popping outfit is ideal. Many of the panfish that frequent the waters of coastal piers are known for their bait-stealing ability, so being alert and striking promptly is important.

Many species are targeted

While at first blush this may not seem particularly challenging, man-made structures can provide exciting fishing for a wide variety of species using a wide range of tackle, baits and lures.

Huge tarpon are regularly taken from bridges in the Florida Keys, along with snook and redfish. Anglers casting from New Jersey piers often encounter big striped bass, bluefish and weakfish, which strike a variety of lures and natural baits. San Diego anglers often receive strikes from fast-moving Pacific bonito and barracuda. To the north, king salmon often reward Oregon and Washington anglers.

While the gamefish attract many, it is the bottom feeders that are the bread-and-butter fish of anglers who practice their skills from the various structures located in bays, rivers and sounds. The miles of structures located along Long Island's North Shore attract both summer and winter flounder and tautog, while dock fisher-

(Left) There are countless spots along the sea coast where you can enjoy a pleasant afternoon catching panfish. This nice porgy was caught from the bulkhead at Shinnecock Canal on eastern Long Island. More than a dozen delicious species frequent these waters each season.

men in Maine tussle with harbor pollock and small cod. DelMarVa Peninsula structure fishermen can often catch spot, croakers and sea trout until they're arm weary. The broad expanse of Pacific coastline offers many species of surf perch, rockfish, sand bass and California halibut. All of these species are excellent table fare.

This type of angling is an excellent way to introduce children to fishing. It's rather easy to master, you don't have to worry about seasickness, and it's economical when compared to other types of fishing.

Tackle is a matter of choice

It's safe to say there's no perfect all-around outfit. If you're targeting big fish such as tarpon, redfish, striped bass, and bluefish, you need heavier gear than if you're seeking bottom feeders.

Fish are most often attracted to the structures because of the forage species that take up residence around them. As a result, casting becomes less of a consideration than while fishing from jetties or the surf.

You can always spot a veteran pier caster. They come equipped to spend the day. This angler built a cart to carry all of his gear. Included is a compartmented ice chest, a tackle box, bait bucket, rods and reels, towel, and a knife and cutting board for cleaning his catch.

Rods and reels

For the heavier gamefish, a rod measuring 6 1/2 to 8 feet is ideal. Because you'll often use big baits and heavy lures for tarpon, stripers, blues and redfish, a rod having a stiff action is best. Rods built of fiberglass, and especially graphite, are preferred. Conventional gear is generally preferred for heavier fishing, and spinning tackle for lighter species.

Because you'll seldom encounter snags or other obstructions, you can usually get by with lighter lines. A spinning or conventional reel holding 150 to 200 yards of 12- to 15-pound-test line is more than adequate. Keep in mind, however, that big tarpon and striped bass have been known to strip all the line from a reel, especially when hooked from a bridge where there is a swift current and you're unable to follow the fish.

For the bottom-fishing enthusiast, the one-handed 6-foot spinning outfit is made to order for piers, docks and bulkheads. The popular popping outfit, consisting of a 5 1/2- to 6-foot bait-casting rod with a long handle for two-handed casting, is also a good choice.

Because the bottom feeders you'll encounter usually range from a half-pound to 5 pounds, there's no need to use big reels. A spinning or conventional casting reel capable of holding 100 yards of 8- to 12-pound-test monofilament line is more than adequate. Anglers whose reels hold several hundred yards of line often place a plastic filler on the reel spool and limit the amount of line they actually place on the reel to approximately 100 yards.

When the Chesapeake Bay Bridge and Tunnel was built it was proclaimed one of the engineering marvels of all time. The planners didn't forget the fishermen and built this beautiful pier, where ship traffic passes close by, but the fish and fishermen don't mind. During the course of a season more than 20 species of fish are landed by anglers fishing from this structure, situated in prime waters of Chesapeake Bay.

Bottom bait rig effective

From most piers, bridges and other structures you'll be elevated from the water. While on occasion you may cast out, often your line will be nearly perpendicular to the bottom. This differs from surf and jetty fishing, where your line is laying parallel with the bottom as you cast out.

There are dozens of bottom rigs used from the structures and each area has its favorites. There are, however, a few standard outfits that perform well no matter where you use them.

The fish-finder bottom rig may be used to present a natural bait to anything from a half-pound spot to a 100-pound tarpon. It's built around an egg-shaped sinker with a hole through the middle. You slip the sinker, of sufficient weight to hold bottom, onto your line and tie in a tiny barrel swivel, which will prevent the sinker from slipping off the line but still permit it to slide on the line. To the barrel swivel tie in a 12- to 36-inch piece of monofilament or fluorocarbon leader material. If you're fishing for winter flounder, spot or croakers, a No. 6 or 8 claw or beak-style hook and 12 inches of 8-pound-test leader is fine. If the target is channel bass or snook, a 5/0 or 7/0 claw or beak hook and 36 inches of 30-pound-test leader material is appropriate.

This rig rests on the bottom, and a feeding gamefish is able to pick up the bait and move off with it without feeling the weight of the sinker. This gives the fish an opportunity to get the bait well into its mouth before you set the hook.

"The high-low rig enables you to fish one bait directly on the bottom, and a second, or high hook bait, 24 to 30 inches off the bottom."

There are several variations of this rig on the market, some with a plastic sleeve that you slip onto the line, with a sinker snap attached to the sleeve. Others have a metal ring through which the line is slipped, with a sinker snap attached to the ring. All three methods are very effective.

A popular single-hook rig is built around a three-way swivel. Tie the swivel to the end of your line and attach a snelled hook to one eye of the swivel. To the remaining eye of the swivel either tie in or use a small duo-lock snap to attach your sinker.

High-low rigs can also be used from many structures. The high-low rig enables you to fish one bait directly on the bottom, and a second, or high hook bait, 24 to 30 inches off the bottom. Many tackle shops have ready-made high-low rigs available, but with a little effort you can tie up your own right on the fishing grounds.

Begin by using a double surgeon's knot to tie a loop in the end of your line, onto which you'll slip your sinker. Just a few inches up from the loop, tie in a dropper loop so that when it is completed the loop extends 10 to 12 inches from the standing part of the line. Next slip a turned-down eye claw or beak hook onto the loop, looping the hook through the loop twice. If you loop it once it will slip and slide, but putting it through twice will firm it up tight. The result is a double leader leading to the hook. Repeat the same procedure where you want to place your high hook, which should be anywhere from 12 to 36 inches up from the low hook.

These three rigs will work effectively in most situations where you want to present a bait to a bottom feeder. They work effectively when either cast or dropped to the bottom from the structure.

Cast and retrieve effective

With some species a cast-and-retrieve approach works best. This is especially true when you're seeking summer flounder and halibut. Cast as far as you can from the structure and permit the rig to settle to the bottom. Then lift your rod tip, causing the rig to slide along the bottom, then hesitate, and slide forward again. This technique also works well with weakfish and spotted weakfish.

With other species, a motionless bait gets the most strikes. This is particularly true with spot, croakers, rockfish, surf perch, and other species that move about searching for seaworms, shrimp, clams and other forage on the bottom.

Keep baits among rocks for some species

Some species, such as tautog and sheepshead, often feed close to the pilings that support piers, bridges and bulkheads. They search for crabs, shrimp and other forage that cling to these structures, and they'll also use their teeth to rip mussels from the piles. To score you've got to present your bait just inches from the pilings or concrete. It's not unusual to see veteran pier and bridge anglers moving from piling to piling, carefully lowering their high-low rig and permitting it to rest motionless for a few minutes. If no hits are received they move on to the next piling. The sheepshead and tautog are extremely fast, and you've got to strike immediately or they'll strip your bait from the hook.

Fishing live bait

Live baits can be very effective when fished from piers, bridges, docks and bulkheads. Unquestionably the simplest technique is to tie a hook directly to the end of your line, bait up, and lower the rig into the water. As simple as it is, it is among the most effective live-bait rigs.

Wherever striped bass are found, anglers use this rig with excellent results while using a size 1/0 or 2/0 claw or beak bait-holder hook. Insert the hook into a sandworm's mouth, and exit the hook an inch down on the worm. This enables you to lower the worm into the water and drift it out with the current moving about the structure.

This rig is also effective for striped bass and weakfish when used with live eels, which are hooked through the lips and fished in the same manner, except with a 5/0 or 6/0 hook. Live spot account for many big weakfish when fished in this manner, and both grunts and pinfish are very effective when live-lined for snook and redfish. The spots are either hooked through the lips, eyes, or just forward of the dorsal fin, permitting them to swim about freely. Many anglers are employing circle style hooks for these species when using live baits, and enjoying fine results.

Because many live baits are small, and will invariably stay close to the structure you're fishing from, some anglers prefer to add a float to the line a few feet from the hook. The float rig is particularly effective wherever weakfish are found along the middle and north Atlantic Coast. The favored floats are made of cork or plastic, with plastic easily snapped anywhere on your line.

Many bridge and pier fishermen chum for the weakfish and sea trout, using tiny grass shrimp sparingly. A favored float of those seeking weakfish and sea trout has a scooped-out head that pops and gurgles.

Croakers are a favorite of pier casters from the middle Atlantic Coast down to Florida and across the Gulf Coast to Texas. This bottom feeder is fun to catch and is especially popular as a table fish. Most anglers use a high-low rig, with a pair of No. 2 or 4 snelled claw hooks with a bait-holder shank and a dipsey sinker. Shrimp is a popular bait, as are pieces of clam, sandworms or bloodworms.

Unique breeches buoy rig produces results

Live baits will often stay very close to the structure you're fishing from, seeking what little sanctuary it offers. Because big baits are difficult to cast, and are easily ripped from the hook, many pier and bulkhead fishermen employ a unique approach to get their bait far from the structure.

A 2- to 4-ounce pyramid-style sinker is tied to the end of the line and a 36-inch piece of 20- or 30-pound-test fluorocarbon leader material is tied to a barrel swivel with coastlock snap on it. Tie a live-bait, claw, beak, or treble hook to the end of the leader.

The pyramid sinker is then cast to the general area where you want your bait to be. Once the sinker is firmly secured into the sand or mud bottom, the coastlock snap is slipped over the line, and closed. A live baitfish is then placed on the hook, usually hooked through the back, and the rig is permitted to slide down the line, and into the water, working on much the same principle as a breeches buoy.

Once the bait enters the water it can only swim from its entry point down to the sinker, and often it will move back and forth, often excitedly fluttering on the surface, where it attracts striped bass, bluefish, snook, tarpon, redfish, king mackerel, barracuda, and other large gamefish. If sharp-toothed species are in an area it's often wise to use a 6-inch piece of No. 8 or 9 stainless steel leader between the hook and the monofilament leader with a tiny barrel swivel joining the two.

The hook is usually set as the fish mouths the bait. Quickly reel the sinker up until it comes taught with the coastlock snap, then lift back to ensure the hook is set and hold on!

Chumming is an option

Chumming often enhances your fishing opportunities from these structures by attracting fish within range of your natural baits.

Many operators of commercial fishing piers regularly chum from their structures. Ground menhaden is often used to attract baitfish, which in turn attract a variety of species.

A weighted chum pot filled with ground menhaden, herring, mackerel, mussels, clams, or crabs, is regularly used to bring fish within range. Almost all bottom feeders will move towards the source of chum when it is carried along by the current.

Chumming with live grass shrimp can bring weakfish and sea trout to dock areas. Pacific bonito and rock bass will respond to small pieces of fish disbursed from structures. The same is true for bluefish, striped bass, snapper and grouper.

A light casting outfit, a bottom rig and some shrimp or clams as bait is all you need to enjoy a day of pier fishing. Both bottom feeders and gamefish often frequent the areas around the piers, providing casters with lots of action. Many of the fish caught are excellent table fare, hence the popularity.

Lure casting from bridges and piers

Bridges and piers often position you high off the water and there are usually currents moving through beneath these structures. As these currents reach the pilings, towers, or other supports, they cause "dead spots" just before or behind the structure. These spots are often where fish congregate, waiting for baitfish to be swept along by the current.

The most popular lures in the arsenal of the bridge caster are plugs, bucktail or plastic-tailed lead-headed jigs and metal squids and jigs. Lures ranging in weight from 1/2 to 1 1/2 ounces are among the most popular because they are heavy enough to be easily cast from the structures. They also don't require heavy tackle.

Many gamefish like to face the current in the quiet water. If the structure permits, position yourself so you can make your cast to position the lure 20 or 30 feet up from where you expect the fish to be feeding. This enables you to work the lure and to swim it with the current to within range of the fish. Often this will require a faster rate of retrieve because the current is pushing the lure. You've got to speed up for the plug to have a swimming action or a jig to be darting and faltering as it moves along.

If you don't receive strikes casting directly upcurrent, move to the left or right of where you feel the fish are holding. Cast up and across at a 45-degree angle, with the lure dropping in past where the fish may be feeding. Work it across and downcurrent, within view of the fish. Sometimes it's possible to work a swimming plug or lead-headed bucktail or plastic-tailed jig so it comes within the sight line of the feeding fish.

When tides or current slow down, fish will expand their range, and you should adjust accordingly. Don't hesitate to move about. Most veterans look for spots devoid of anglers, so they can work their lures through new territory.

When crossing to the "downstream" side of the bridge (be careful of bridge traffic when doing so) you experience an entirely different set of circumstances. The current is running beneath the structure, often forming rips and eddies, with the same dead spots of minimal current. In this situation it's often possible to cast out a swimming plug and just "swim" it in the current. Often only a very slow retrieve or a twitching of the rod tip is necessary to keep the plug working. Many anglers just "walk the plug," moving back and forth along the bridge or pier rail, permitting the lure to move in and out of the spots holding fish, much as a struggling baitfish would do in order to stem the current.

Lead-headed jigs work effectively in this situation, too. The lighter jigs will often work near the surface and the current will do tricks with them, permitting them to settle, be shifted to the side, and then swept towards the surface as they ease into the fast current. The addition of a strip of pork rind or a plastic bait tail does wonders to enhance the action in the current. Twitch your rod tip, and move back and forth, ensuring that the lure resembles a struggling baitfish.

Low bridges, docks and bulkheads provide opportunities for anglers to use a wide variety of lures. A new delivery system uses a spinning reel and rod with no guides. The line feeds into a tunnel ahead of the reel and travels within the rod blank, exiting at the tip.

Vary your delivery

Don't hesitate to switch to a heavy jig that will get down in the current. That old saying that "If there's a fish feeding on the surface there's often a dozen down on the bottom," holds true with structure fishing. too. A heavy jig, in the 1 1/2-ounce range, can be worked deep either while working upcurrent or downcurrent. The key is using the current to your advantage and always maintaining control of the jig's movement.

Bracket the entire structure

It's important to thoroughly fish all the water surrounding the structure. Anglers tend to bunch up at the end of a pier or the middle of a bridge. It just happens as a matter of habit. Veteran anglers avoid the crowds and work the perimeter. This is especially true where a pier extends out from the beach. Often there are eel-grass beds, marsh grass, or reeds extending out from the beach that hold baitfish, and the predator fish know this and move in close.

After dark, shadow lines develop from the lights of bridges and piers and even the moon. With the water flowing towards the "front side" of the bridge or pier, gamefish often wait facing into the current, in the darkness, with their noses tight to the shadow line. On the opposite side, or "back of the bridge," the opposite often occurs, with the fish in the brightly lit area, but still with their noses tight to the shadow line, facing into the current or darkness. It's not unusual to see 100-pound tarpon lined up side by side in the shadow line of the bridges in the Keys, or to see striped bass doing the same in the waters of the many bridges that join Long Island to its South Shore beaches.

When fish are bunched like this, cast up into the current and retrieve the lure within the vision window of the fish, or cast at an angle and work the lure across and toward the shadow line where the fish are holding. The key with either plugs or leadheads is to work the lure parallel with the surface, whether working them on the surface or in the depths. Strikes often come as deep-running lures lift off the bottom at the conclusion of a swing with the current.

Cast under bridge into current

You have to work extra hard to properly present a lure to fish holding on the back side of a bridge. Often the shadow line is tight to the bridge and if you permit a lure to work in the rips and eddies it's many yards behind the line of vision of feeding fish. By pointing your rod tip downward and properly timing your cast, you can flip the lure up into the current beneath the bridge. Then quickly take up the slack as the lure is swept along by the current and to the shadow line and waiting fish. The technique can feel awkward at first, but it can pay off.

Don't overlook the corners, where structure meets land. Often you can fish from the rock rip rap that is often adjacent to the bridge foundation. Sometimes it's just beach or even bulkheaded. Frequently the bridge is located at a narrow point of a bay or river, with an open expanse of water funneling through beneath the bridge structure. This causes back eddies, tidal-rip lines and currents of varying speed, all of which can trap forage and attract gamefish.

By positioning yourself in the corner and using a bracket approach, you can cover a lot of water and catch some beautiful fish. Spots such this often provide exciting tarpon, redfish and snook fishing throughout Florida and along the Gulf Coast. Anglers plying their trade along the middle and north Atlantic Coast are regularly rewarded with striped bass, bluefish, weakfish and summer flounder. Pacific Coast anglers target Pacific barracuda and striped bass that move in under the lights.

Many species are nocturnal feeders and your success ratio may be better at night than during daylight. The only added equipment you'll require is a miner's headlamp, which many bridge casters wear loosely around their necks.

Use a net to land big ones

Many of the species caught from these structures can be reeled in with little difficulty. But should you have the good fortune to hook a big striper, bluefish or tarpon, landing can present a problem. Sometimes you can walk a fish to shore and beach it. But bridgetender facilities, light poles, bulkheading and other obstructions often make this impossible. Many public piers have landing nets comprised of a heavy, round, metal rod with a net bag fastened to it. A length of 1/8-inch cord is attached to the metal rod. The net is lowered into the water, hopefully by a helpful fellow angler, and the fish maneuvered above it. When the fish is in position, the net is lifted up and the fish brought up to the structure.

Large treble hooks with lead molded around their shanks are often lowered to the water with one-eighth inch nylon cord and used as a gaff to snatch the fish when it is brought within range. This gaffing method has lost popularity in recent years as a result of the various size limit restrictions in coastal states. No one wants to make a mistake and gaff an undersized fish.

Anglers fishing for snook and tarpon, which are often released, regularly bend back the barbs of the hooks on their lures. Once a fish is brought within range they give it slack line, and when the fish either jumps or rolls, it can often rid itself of the hook.

Bridge fishing is a relaxing pastime along the sea coast. It's important, however, to only fish from bridges where it is permitted by local ordinance. Many states have built fishing platforms, such as this one, parallel with the roadway, so anglers do not interfere with traffic.

175

Docks and bulkheads get you close to water

Somewhat different techniques are brought into play when you're fishing low to the water from docks and bulkheads. Both structures provide good fishing because they offer sanctuary for forage. Shrimp tend to cling to bulkheads and dock pilings, and hungry bottom feeders and gamefish regularly cruise along these structures, inhaling these tasty morsels. Crabs often cling to the pilings, too, or are observed swimming beneath the dock lights. When there is a seaworm hatch, it's not unusual to observe literally millions of inch-long squirmers swimming just beneath the surface. At such times the water boils as practically every species in residence gorges on the plentiful food.

A single sandworm or bloodworm drifted along with the current can quickly bring strikes. Its modern-day counterpart, the plastic worm, also bring strikes. The key is presentation. The most successful bulkhead casters often "walk the worm," permitting the current to carry it along, just inches from the bulkhead.

Work tight to bulkhead

Plastic-tailed lead-headed jigs also produce excellent results when worked tight to the bulkhead. Cast out and permit the current to carry the lure along. Walk along the bulkhead or dock, working your rod tip. Work the jig just 6 inches to a foot from the bulkhead or pilings and you'll be surprised by exciting strikes.

Many dock and bulkheaded areas come alive at or near slack tide. Many gamefish wait anywhere they can get out of the swift current, which may be in the middle of a bay or river. As the current slows they move about, searching for forage around the docks and bulkheads.

Knowledge of tides essential

Try to time your visits to key locations an hour before to an hour after either the flood or ebb tide. By timing your movements, you can often cover three or four spots, in different areas, capitalizing on the slow-moving water in each location. As you gain experience you'll no longer be surprised to see a quiet area suddenly erupt in a maelstrom of crashing, feeding gamefish. Then, as the current begins to boil, the bonanza shuts off as quickly as it begins.

This phenomenon proves that gamefish often move several miles per day. Boatmen often observe huge schools of fish before, during and after the slack tide. As the tide begins to boil, their fishfinders go blank as the fish promptly vacate an area, rather than fight the current.

Some of the techniques employed by bridge casters can be used by dock fishermen. As current flows to the pilings or supports of the dock, there is a dead spot in the current, as is the case on the downcurrent side of the dock. Work these spots diligently, with swimming plugs and lead-headed jigs.

Shadow lines hold fish

The same can be said for a shadow line from the dock lights. The difference is that you're usually close to the water. Keep your rod tip low, so the plug or jig works parallel with the surface, and work it right up close to the pilings.

Piers, bridges and docks are not glamorous structures from which to fish. They do, however, provide a platform and an opportunity to present your lure or bait to many species, from small bottom feeders to many very formidable gamefish. Day or night, sunshine or rain, these structures are there. You can enjoy many leisurely hours pitting your skills against the adversaries that live in the shadows and depths of the structures.

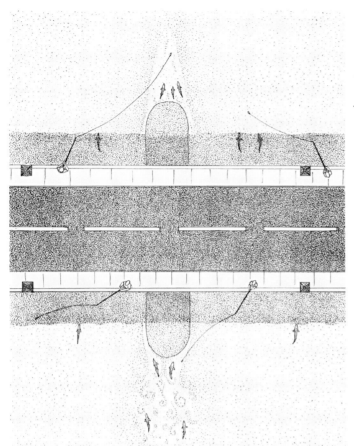

Bridges provide exciting casting opportunities. Illustrated here are the four key spots to concentrate your efforts when night fishing. On the up side of the bridge, the current splits as it reaches a tower, forming a dead spot where fish congregate. The fish also congregate along the shadow line, waiting for bait to be swept their way. On the down side of the bridge, there's another dead spot where eddies form. The down-side shadow line should also be worked carefully, with a cast either beneath the bridge or parallel with it, so the current carries the lure towards the shadow line.

Many old structures are left in place and provide valuable sea access to fishermen when new structures are built. A wide variety of bottom feeders and gamefish take up residence around the bridges, as forage species congregate in the rips and eddies.

177

CASTING ON THE FLATS

Throughout south Florida, its Keys and across much of the Gulf Coast there are miles of shallow flats that offer a variety of exciting fishing opportunities. The flats have water that ranges from just a few inches deep to about 6 feet. As the tide rises and floods, the flats are invaded by hungry gamefish, eager to feed on the abundance of crabs, shrimp and small baitfish that seek the sanctuary the shallows offer.

Bonefish, tarpon, barracuda, sharks and permit are prime targets in the Florida Keys, while Gulf anglers cast to redfish, spotted weakfish, flounder, tarpon and occasional cobia.

Most fishing is done from shallow-draft boats that are poled across the flats, with anglers sight casting to cruising fish. This takes considerable skill, with one angler doing the poling of the skiff from the stern, usually from a raised platform, while one or two others stand in the bow of the skiff and search for fish.

Flats fishing can also be enjoyed by anglers who don trunks and a pair of sneakers to protect their feet.

A light, one-handed spinning outfit is ideally suited for wading in the flats, with a tiny delta-winged leadhead jig an excellent lure choice.

(Left) Stu Apte has fished all over the world and always travels with his favorite fly rods. This tarpon was caught on a 9-weight fly-fishing outfit and was estimated at 140 pounds. This great acrobat of the Florida Keys flats was released. During a good day of flats fishing it's not unusual to see a dozen fish over 50 pounds.

Knowledge of terrain, tidal movements and fish habits is essential

Timing is more important in flats fishing than in other types of angling. If you go during low tide, you may not find water where you've previously enjoyed fine fishing. Thus it becomes important that you know the area you plan to fish. The best way to become familiar with an area of flats is to spend some time either from your boat or while wading the area at low tide. Many flats have depressions where the water is deeper, and fish use these channels to both exit the flats on the ebb and return to the flooding flats on incoming tide.

Long-sleeved shirts and wide-brimmed hats can help shield you from the sun's harsh rays. Be certain to wear sunblock and a good pair of sunglasses, too.

If you like to wade you should always carry along a small plastic box of essential terminal tackle. A light spinning outfit and a selection of loose hooks, tiny rubber-cored sinkers, a cutting razor, nail clip and an assortment of delta-winged and bucktail leadhead jigs is all you'll need for an afternoon of wading.

Light tackle provides maximum enjoyment

A one-handed spinning outfit is standard for flats fishing, although some veterans, especially along the Gulf Coast, employ a light popping outfit. Monofilament line in 8- or 10-pound test is perfect. Those who wade carry a very small shoulder bag with an assortment of lures and natural baits. Some anglers have such a great confidence in a few leadhead jigs and delta-wing bucktails that they just carry a few in a plastic pouch tucked into a pocket.

Fly fishermen often strap on a stripping basket to keep their lines from tangling. They cast a variety of flies tied to resemble shrimp and crabs and small forage species found in the clear shallows.

Florida Keys anglers often encounter gamefish such as tarpon, bonefish, barracuda, permit and sharks, all of which are released. Gulf Coast anglers frequently target gamefish that are destined for the dinner table, such as redfish, sea trout, flounder and snook. Those who wade pull a long stringer with a float attached, rather than carrying their catch.

In the thin water of the flats small lures are the order of the day. You want to make a delicate presentation without spooking the fish. Leadhead jigs 3/8 of an ounce or smaller are popular. The leadheads may be dressed with either a bucktail skirt or a plastic tail. Some anglers use a plain leadhead and add a shrimp to the hook. Delta-winged leadhead jigs with a tuft of bucktail, and the jig head painted to resemble a shrimp or crab, are also very effective. The keel and delta-wing design enable the jig to swim from side to side as it is retrieved, which prevents it from digging into the shallow bottom. Small, shallow-running plugs also attract tarpon, jack crevalle and barracuda.

The gafftopsail pompano is very plentiful on many coastal flats. They're often caught while just walking along and casting a small pink delta-winged leadhead jig with a bucktail skirt.

Florida Keys water clear as air

The water of Keys flats is among the clearest water you'll ever fish, making the sighting of fish relatively easy once you learn to look through the water. The clear water works to your disadvantage as well, for the fish can easily spot you. Move slowly and quietly and work towards the deeper water. This is where the gamefish will enter the flats. An ideal place to position yourself is midway between the beach or mangrove-lined bank and a dark dropoff into deeper water of a channel. From here you can see both left and right as you move along, and target any fish either crossing in front of you or moving directly towards you.

Move slowly and be patient. Look for moving shadows. Once you spot a fish that is within range of a comfortable cast, say 40 to 60 feet, make your cast to position the lure in the direction the fish is traveling. It's better that the lure be too far ahead of the fish than too close.

Don't hurriedly begin a retrieve if you've miscalculated a cast. Sometimes you can just permit the lure or bait to settle to the bottom and let the fish continue moving along. Once you feel the lure is within its range of vision you can then begin your retrieve.

Bonefish and permit usually root along the bottom, where they feed on the small crabs and shrimp that are so plentiful. Their tails often extend from the water as they nose down to root in the sand, so keep alert, as often this will be the first indication of feeding fish.

Bonefish often swim in water so shallow it barely covers their backs. The key in sighting bonefish and permit is watching for a shadow moving across the flat. Sometimes you can spot their tails as they dip down to probe in the sand for crabs and shrimp.

181

The small jigs when worked with a light jigging movement can bring a lightning-fast strike. Permit and bonefish are extremely strong fish. Once you set back and strike them, keep your rod tip high and fish with a firm, pre-set drag, ensuring the maximum pressure the outfit will bear, as the fish will often take 100 yards of line or more in a single run. By keeping the rod tip high you'll avoid fouling the line in grass or other debris on the bottom, for often the fish will circle after its first run.

It's wise to make several casts before fish are sighted, so you can control the amount of line you're handling. When a fish is sighted you can then target the vision window of the fish and present your fly right on target. A smooth, quiet execution and presentation is critical in the clear water of the flats to avoid spooking the fish.

Tarpon, barracuda, jack crevalle and sharks will also strike a leadhead or delta-wing jig, or a small plug. The barracuda will also strike a plain, plastic tube lure, with red or green the preferred color, with a single treble hook extending from the tail of the tube. When retrieved, the tube spins enticingly, and 'cuda just go wild, grabbing it and jumping repeatedly in the shallow water. Be careful when handling and releasing barracuda. They have vicious teeth.

This is how the bottom appears as you're poled along a coastal flat. The water is breathlessly clear, with the weed growth taking on a golden color. Sharks such as this one are easy to spot. It's just a matter of concentrating and looking just beneath the surface. Often the first inkling of a fish is what appears to be a shadow, just gliding along.

Chum can bring the fish to you

Still another exciting way to catch these warriors of the flats is by staking out the boat and chumming an area that fish are known to frequent. This is where intimate knowledge of a section of flat and the travels of its residents is important.

Many skiff casters position themselves by placing their push pole into the sand, and tying off a short line at the stern so that the chumming, sighting, and casting may be done from the bow casting platform.

Tiny pieces of shrimp or conch can be used as chum. Some veteran flats anglers even crush blue crabs to a pulp, so there is really nothing left to eat, but the scent is there and can be carried by the current. Many anglers like to position themselves where there is a patch of clear sand bottom, surrounded by grassy flats. Then it's a waiting game.

You've got to be alert. Often you'll watch the sandy bottom for a half hour with nothing happening. Suddenly, the shadows begin to move, as bonefish, permit, and other flats marauders get the scent and move about to search for the pieces of chum.

This stationary setup is especially good for newcomers, who are afforded the opportunity to make several casts to the area of the chum before fish move in. Then it's simply a matter of executing a good cast into the vision window of the cruising fish.

The most reliable method is to use a live shrimp tied directly to the line and cast it towards the fish. Even if your cast falls short by a few feet, just let it rest, for the fish will quickly pick up the scent. Small pieces of conch or whole blue crabs may also be used. A very small delta-wing bucktail also works wonders when the fish move in on the chummed area.

As the tide begins to ebb, the water often gets so shallow that the fish vacate the flats and move to the adjoining channels. And while it isn't true flats fishing, you can enjoy superb action by anchoring up along the edges, where the clear water of the flats drops off into the deeper blue water of the channels.

Often you can observe the muddy patches as the fish root in the bottom in the channels adjacent to the flats. Casting a shrimp or crab into the muddied water can bring immediate action. It's also effective to slowly work a delta-wing leadhead jig with a plastic tail or bucktail through the muddied water.

The author hooked this nice barracuda while being poled across the flats. Barracuda of this size provide exciting action on the flats, with a frenzied strike and repeated jumps. Moments after this photo was taken, the barracuda was again roaming the flats.

Gulf Coast shallows stretch for miles

The water takes on a darker color along the Gulf Coast and it's often difficult to spot fish when poling the flats. Sometimes you can see schools of redfish pushing water as they cruise about, and sea trout can occasionally be observed as they swim just beneath the surface. Tarpon will move into the shallows, too, pushing water across their backs as they roll just beneath the surface film.

This photo clearly shows the difference in water coloration between the flats and the channel. As the tide ebbs, the fish move from the shallows into the deeper, darker-blue water. Casting a shrimp or small jig into the deeper water can bring strikes from fish that you're unable to see. Bonefish will often cause an area to appear muddied as they feed, and you should always make several casts into the discolored water.

Because of the difficulty in sighting fish, blind casting is often practiced along the Gulf when tides flood the flats. Leadhead jigs with bucktail or plastic tails, delta-wing leadheads and small darter or popping plugs all bring strikes. Many casters tip their jigs with a piece of shrimp, finding the scent of the shrimp attracts redfish, sea trout, snook, croaker and flounder.

It's often possible to score while casting into 3- to 6-foot depths with a splashing or popping cork-float rig. The rig is made by slipping a popping cork float onto the line and setting it 3 feet or so from the terminal end, and then tying a No. 1 or 1/0 claw or beak hook with a baitholder shank to the terminal end of the line. The hook is baited with a live or dead shrimp and cast out, where the bait drifts along, suspended just off the bottom by the float.

Periodically twitch the rod tip to cause the concave cork head of the float to pop and gurgle. This often attracts the attention of sea trout and redfish in particular.

Fishing the flats is fishing at its most intimate. Whether you're poling or wading, you're right down at the level with the fish. You can see them moving, watch them strike, and see them vacate when the tide drops. You'll observe tarpon that may be bigger than you are, and permit that streak away so quickly your eye can barely follow. The chance to be part of this quiet, peaceful scene is what keeps anglers coming back to the flats.

Sight casting, where you first locate the targeted species cruising in the shallow water, provides exciting fishing for many species, including bonefish, tarpon, permit, striped bass, weakfish and channel bass.

RELEASING FISH PROPERLY

Various international, federal, and state regulations require anglers to return fish to the water unharmed. You may have to practice catch-and-release fishing if you hook a fish during a closed season, if your catch exceeds the daily bag limit, or if a fish is below a size limit.

Bonefish are usually netted as they're brought boatside. It's important to handle them as carefully as possible, keeping your hands away from their delicate gills. If the fish appears exhausted, it's better to first revive it by holding it in the water until its gills begin to circulate water through them.

(Left) Fish that are to be released should be held firmly alongside the boat to enable them to regain their strength and have an active flow of water through their gills. This big tarpon is ready to be turned free minutes after being brought to boatside by the author, who was fishing near Key West, Florida.

Unquestionably, these regulations are for the protection of the species and have done a great deal to improve the quantities of fish that are available in coastal waters. What is distressing is the poor survival rate of many fish that are released. Most often it's because anglers are extremely careless in the way they land, handle and ultimately release fish.

Some of these situations can be attributed to downright poor sportsmanship. But I suspect most improper releases come from just not thinking. Fish are delicate creatures and must be handled carefully. For years people thought it best to use a landing net so as not to injure a fish prior to release. It seemed the logical thing to do. But recent studies have dispelled that myth, proving a net often harms fish that are to be released.

A study on fish mortality prepared by R. A. Ferguson and B. L. Tufts of Queen's University in Ontario, Canada, proved very enlightening on this subject. The study focused on rainbow trout that were exposed to air after exhaustive exercise, such as doing combat with a fly-rod angler. While the study centered on a freshwater species, its findings are equally applicable to saltwater fish.

Jim Rizzuto fished his home waters of Hawaii to land this 22-pound bluefin trevally while using 16-pound-test line. It was a potential IGFA world-record catch, but Jim decided to tag and release it, a practice of many sportsmen throughout the world. Many anglers carry a portable scale, such as the Boga Grip, that allows for prompt weighing and quick release.

Upon landing, the trout is removed from the water and for a brief period is exposed to the air. During this brief period the gills' delicate lamellae will collapse and gas exchange may be inhibited.

The study showed that even fish exposed to the air for 60 seconds initially appeared to be returning to normal when released, but they died 4 to 12 hours later. This delayed mortality has been documented by several other studies. All of the studies conclusively proved that, just because a fish swims away, doesn't mean it necessarily survives.

The study showed that "only 28 percent of those fish which were exposed to air for 60 seconds after being fought and landed survived the next 12 hours as compared with 88 percent of those fish which were only fought and landed, but not exposed to air."

"Whether it be flounder, striped bass, or tuna in ocean waters, keeping fish in the water is the key to having them survive."

Lori Kelly Parker brings in a permit, being careful not to lift the fish from the water until it has stopped fighting long enough for her to unhook and release it.

The beak or claw barbless hooks have grown in popularity in recent years, as so many inshore species are now governed by size limit regulations that makes it necessary to return many fish to the water uninjured. The barbless hook helps in this regard, and surprisingly does not result in many lost fish, so long as an angler keeps a taut line. Other styles, such as the circle are also available barbless.

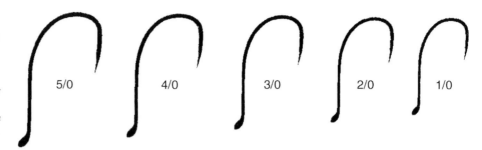

5/0   4/0   3/0   2/0   1/0

With the minimum size limits on many species, it's important to be able to quickly measure and release fish. Striped bass have no teeth and are best held by by the lower jaw. This immobilizes the fish and enables you to quickly remove the hook, as Johnny Creenan has done here. Walk the fish into the surf and hold it momentarily until it gets frisky, then release it.

The study clearly shows that "the brief period of air exposure which commonly occurs in many catch-and-release fisheries is an important additional stress in an exhausted fish and may ultimately have a significant impact on the number of released fish which survive."

The study's authors close their treatise with some very sound advice, "Keep your fish in the water!" If they must be removed, quickly return them to the water.

Easier said than done. But it does give one pause. This subject has been discussed with several fishery biologists. All agree that whether it be flounder, striped bass, or tuna in ocean waters, keeping fish in the water is the key to having them survive.

The easiest way to release a fish is to use a pair of pliers and bend down the barbs on your hooks, or use some of the fine-quality barbless hooks now on the market. Surprisingly, turning down the barbs doesn't result in lost fish, but it does

Moments after this photo Jack Noll, with gloved hand and holding the little tunny by the fork of the tail, promptly removed the hook and released it. Globe-trotting angler Ken Schultz, editor of "Ken Schultz's Fishing Encyclopedia," used a light spinning outfit and chromed jig to bring the tunny to boatside.

make releasing very easy. All you have to do is slide your hand down the leader and grasp the lure or hook between your thumb and forefinger, and in an instant the fish is free. You can release many species without removing them from the water.

Many anglers who fish with plugs for gamefish have turned to using plugs with only two sets of treble hooks instead of the customary three. They also bend down the barbs. Not only does this enable you to quickly release the fish, but saves you from jamming a barbed hook into your finger as you attempt to land or unhook the fish.

For surf fishermen, it's wise to make a conscious effort not to slide the fish onto the beach, where sand can remove the slime from its body and get into its gills. Instead, wade into the water, when the surf isn't too rough, and just release the fish much the same as you would a trout in a stream. If it's rough, just get as close as you can to the fish and lift it right up and swing it towards you. Then reach down and run your hand along the leader until you reach the lure or teaser and then quickly push it free. The fish is back in the water in a matter of seconds.

Even if you don't have the barbs bent down, the key in releasing toothless fish

Striped bass do not have teeth, and are best immobilized by holding their lower jaw with your thumb and forefinger, then promptly removing the hook. When held in this way, the fish is easily placed in the water, and held securely, with water flowing through its gills, and then promptly released.

such as striped bass is to hold them securely with thumb and forefinger in their lower jaw. This immobilizes the fish and lets you get the hook out quickly. Avoid getting your hand under the gill cover, as this often results in injury to the gills, especially with a thrashing fish.

For years many flounder fishermen used multi-hook rigs. The lead hook held the head section of a strip bait, with the primary hook well back in the bait. When inhaled by a flounder, the hook usually pierced the gills way back in the throat or into the stomach and was difficult to remove. It was an effective way to catch fish, but not with today's size and bag limits.

The wide-gap and circle hook are ideal, as the flounder or halibut are most often hooked in the corner of the mouth, making release easy. Always have a long-nosed dehooker with you for deeply hooked fish.

A half-inch-diameter piece of wooden dowel with 1/8-inch groove on one end can be helpful for fish that are deeply hooked. Slide the dowel down into the fish's mouth and place the groove in the bend of the hook. Push slightly and the barb should come out. Then, holding the dowel and the leader, simply remove the hook. Once you master this technique, hooks are easy to remove and the fish is back in the water quickly.

This same technique works very well with bluefish, king mackerel, barracuda, lingcod and weakfish, all of which have sharp teeth, where you can't risk putting your finger into their mouth

Another release device has been around for years and is unfortunately still in use aboard many party and charter boats. It is made from a 1/8-inch thick pick of heavy wire, with a loop in the end. The loop is placed over the leader and run as close to the hook as possible, while holding the leader, and the hook is twisted free. If at first the hook doesn't come free, the fish is literally shook or ripped free, often ripping away its jaw or gills. These release devices were great when all the fish went into the cooler, but they have no place in the scheme of things today.

The Boga Grip release device is extremely effective for handling fish. Its jaws are activated with minimal thumb pressure and firmly secure the fish by the lower jaw, enabling an angler to quickly and safely remove the hook. When the Boga Grip is used properly, the fish doesn't even have to be removed from the water.

Pelagic species caught on the troll are often difficult to release, partially because of their size, but more often because they just beat themselves to death if you bring them onto the deck. With albacore, school bluefin tuna and yellowfin tuna, many anglers swing the fish aboard, and quickly drape a wet Turkish towel over its eyes. This usually quiets the fish, enabling the angler to remove the hook and get the fish back into the water promptly.

Most of the pelagic species are caught with single-hooked lures. When the fish is alongside, with one person leadering the fish within reach, a second person can often grasp the hook with his hand. Most tuna and billfish that strike lures are hooked in the corner of the mouth and the hook can be quickly twisted free.

When tuna are hooked on a bait hook, many anglers don't even remove the fish from the water. They simply reach as close as possible and cut the leader, forfeiting the hook. The hook will quickly rust away or work itself free without harming the fish.

Species such as codfish, sea bass, rockfish, snapper and grouper, which are often caught around deep-water wrecks or rocks, often have their air bladder inflated as they're reeled to the surface. Fish that are released with these bladders inflated can have a hard time deflating and returning to the depths. Many anglers insert the point of an ice pick into the balloon-like bladder to deflate it, then return the fish to the water promptly. The theory is that the puncture heals quickly, and with the air gone the fish can easily return to the depths.

A short-handled release gaff with a wrist lanyard is a popular item among flats fishermen. The gaff is carefully placed in the lower jaw of a tarpon, with the fish remaining in the water. The hook is removed, and the fish is held until it regains its strength. The gaff is then slipped free and the fish swims off.

No matter how careful you are, not all released fish will survive. However, by practicing proper handling and prompt releasing, the fish you don't take home will have a much better chance to survive.

This permit is being held properly prior to release. The keys to keeping a fish alive are keeping it in the water as much as possible and releasing it quickly.

BRING THE CHILDREN AND FRIENDS ALONG

Among the most satisfying experiences a parent can enjoy is that of taking children and grandchildren saltwater fishing. Close behind is the satisfaction garnered by taking friends who have never experienced this wonderful pastime.

Each summer the New York Metropolitan Outdoor Press Association, a professional organization of thirty of America's most prominent outdoor writers, sponsors trips for youngsters to introduce them to fishing. The writers are on board and serve as mentors to the kids as they expand their interest in what can become a lifelong hobby. The smiles tell you they've enjoyed a pleasant day of catching summer flounder!

Unfortunately, many children, and even adults, are frightened by their first saltwater fishing experiences and often forego fishing forever. Included here are some thoughts and observations as to what may be the best approach to introducing children and adult newcomers to saltwater angling. Many well-intentioned fishermen use incorrect approaches that turn what could be a beautiful first experience into a disaster.

Planning is the key. You want to plan an excursion that is the least disruptive for family or friends, and one where the enthusiasm builds beforehand. Plan for the kind of fishing you feel will be appropriate and think about what you'll need for a day along the seacoast.

Problems can begin with the well-intentioned dad who wants to get the whole family up at 5 o'clock in the morning. The family never gets up at 5, and it's especially disruptive to hustle younger children out of bed too early. Plan to start the day as normal as possible, with everyone rising near their normal time, having a normal breakfast and then getting underway.

(Left) It's never too early to get youngsters used to fishing tackle. Kristine Rosko, the authors' granddaughter, began at an early age as is evidenced here. Eventually she had her very own closed-face spincast outfit and began a pastime she can continue to enjoy for a lifetime.

Also make plans for lunch. The easiest way to keep children occupied should the fishing be slow, or if they lose interest, is to have plenty of snacks and juice or soda along. Pretzels and potato chips are perfect, as is a lunch they're accustomed to. Make certain you all have plenty of clothes, for while at home the temperature may be comfortable, along the coast or on the water it's often much colder. Bring sunscreen, so the family doesn't come home with a bad burn. Sunglasses and hats are also very important.

Now, what kind of fishing to do? Better you know what not to do. Every dad would love to have his son or daughter catch a "big one" on their first fishing trip. Or have a friend on a charter fishing trip "catch a big one." Wrong approach.

Always start the youngsters with fish they can enjoy catching. Here, grandmother June unhooks a sea bass for Kelsey Rosko while fishing aboard the "Linda June" on a family excursion. Every youngster loves to bring home the catch and have it prepared for dinner. It's all part of the fishing experience.

"Most children want to be able to see land, and staying closer to shore can make the trip back quicker if you need to quit early."

Children or adults who haven't been there will probably not enjoy going off-shore on a canyon charter, nor will they enjoy wreck fishing in 200 feet of water. Youngsters will struggle, and often be brought to tears, if they are forced sit in a chair with a mate hollering at them that they should reel—which can be impossible even for an adult—when trolling 200 feet of wire line with an umbrella rig and a big bluefish on it.

Bob and Linda Rosko were just 11 and 13, respectively, when they visited the Gulf of Mexico for the first time. Here Bob unhooks a bluefish landed by his sister while drifting the placid Gulf waters from a small boat. Both landed their first fish at the tender age of 3.

Most children want to be able to see land, and staying closer to shore can make the trip back quicker if you need to quit early.

Children don't belong on jetties, either. Period. Coastal police will tell you that not a single week goes by that the first aid squad isn't called out to administer aid to someone who has been injured on a slippery rock jetty or promontory. The injuries can be extremely serious.

Children also don't belong surf fishing when the surf is rough. It's very easy to have a big wave overcome even a strong man, and tumble him about on the sand when he's not paying attention. Rough surf is dangerous!

Planning is critical. Start at the beginning of the season and take it from there. The first coastal fish to provide a great opportunity on all our coasts are flounder. They're caught for the most part in protected bays and rivers, where the sea is not apt to be rough. The weather begins to moderate at this time of the year, which makes it comfortable on the water on all three U.S. coasts. Perhaps most importantly, flounder are plentiful enough that there's usually enough action to keep everyone occupied.

When children begin fishing on board a boat they should always wear a personal floatation device, or life vest. Period. By wearing them at a young age, they automatically put them on when it comes time to go out on the dock or on a boat. Today's great PFD's are much more comfortable than the old, bulky life vests. The PFD's have animal inscriptions, bright colors and come in a variety of sizes. Aboard the "Linda June" there was every size, for 3-year-olds on up to teenagers and adults.

When it comes to fishing tackle, spin-cast reels and popping rods are best for children who haven't used conventional or spinning reels. They're simple to use. You just push the button to let the line out and turn the handle to reel line in. No mess, no backlashes, tangles or problems. They're economical, too.

The author unhooks a bluefish for granddaughter Kelsey Rosko as they drift the quiet waters of a coastal bay in the Northeast. Both Kelsey and Kristine, in the background, wear personal floatation devices when fishing on the "Baby Linda June."

"Mackerel fishing is perhaps the best kind of saltwater angling to get children started on."

Try to keep children away from crowds, especially if you're going on a party boat. Avoid the crowded weekends. If your schedule permits, take kids on a half-day boat during the week, with the afternoon trip ideal. Bait their hooks for them, but show them how it's done and explain the kind of bait you're using.

Children like company. If your son or daughter's best friend wants to come along, the day is usually more enjoyable for everyone, providing, of course, the young guest is well-behaved. Some children are terrors on board, and you quickly learn that an undisciplined child ashore is twice as bad on the water. Keep that in mind.

Mackerel fishing is perhaps the best kind of saltwater angling to get children started on. There are Atlantic mackerel, Pacific mackerel, Spanish mackerel and Cero mackerel. When the spring migration visits your section of the coast, it's the perfect time to take the youngsters along. A family group fishing from a small boat can make for great fun. If you don't have your own rig, give the party boats a try. Here again, the half-day boats are ideal, as the children are on the water for a limited period of time. When the fishing's good a couple of hours on the water is more than enough time to make a fine catch.

Once you hear the mackerel have arrived, watch the weather reports and look for calmer days. Remember, this is open-ocean fishing, and the boat can't return if it gets rough or your child becomes scared. Fifteen- to 20-mph winds create a nasty sea, and the whitecaps, spray and rocking boat can be frightening.

Rough seas can also make children and adults seasick. There's no better way to discourage a person from pursuing fishing than by taking them out and getting them seasick.

As the summer progresses, there are lots of great opportunities in the bays and rivers as populations of weakfish, spot, croaker and sand perch move in.

Crabbing and digging for hard-shell clams are two fishing-related activities that children just love.

Jimmy Krauszer is a friend of Kristine and Kelsey Rosko, and the girls often ask him to accompany them on fishing trips along the coast. Here Jimmy shows off a nice sea bass destined for dinner that evening.

Crabbing is easy to learn and you don't need a lot of equipment. Just grab a handline or wire trap with a piece of menhaden or mackerel bait and you're set to go. When children bring the blueclaws to the surface and quickly scoop them up with a long-handled net, there's excitement galore, not to mention the makings of a fine meal afterwards.

Clamming is lots of fun, too. You can use a clam rake to retrieve the clams in the sandy bottom in shallow water. Many people feel for them by burying their toes in the soft sand and working their toes as they move forward. Here again, you've got the makings of a fine chowder or clams-on-the-half-shell from the clean bay waters. It's great fun and a learning experience for young and old alike.

Still another fun pastime for youngsters, especially those in the 9-to-12 age group, is seining. You can't imagine what you'll collect in a seine net drawn through shallow waters adjoining marsh banks in bays and rivers. Let the children--even if it takes two of them--hold the seine being worked near shore, while you work in the deeper water and make the sweep. There'll be killies and spearing,

Bob Rosko was only a 13 when the author began taking him on jetty fishing junkets after sundown. He was soon catching striped bass, bluefish and weakfish like a veteran. Much like skiing, tennis and other partici-pant sports, when you master fishing skills at a young age you retain them for a lifetime.

grass shrimp, several different kinds of crabs, seahorses, even baby flounder, spot, tautog, weakfish and forage species. Some people even collect colorful tropical fish, especially during late summer, and keep them all together—shrimp, crabs and fish—in saltwater aquariums.

Summer surf fishing can also be enjoyable for the entire family. Everyone can don bathing suits and repair to a section of beach away from swimmers and surfers. Flounder, sea trout, surf perch, and redfish are regular residents that can easily be caught bottom fishing. My granddaughters often accompany me down to the beach after dinner and target stripers while using clams and chunks of mackerel as bait. Would you believe the most fun-filled evenings were when a variety of undesirable skates and dogfish were caught between dinner and dusk? All were promptly released. No formidable species, but plenty of action for girls who love to fish.

My dad took me aboard a make-up bottom fishing charter out of Shark River when I was just 7 years old. That day I caught my first weakfish, while those aboard cheered. I caught several others and also caught my first summer flounder. It was fun, the weather was nice, we fished just a few hours, and enjoyed a nice lunch and some cold soda. From those beginnings I've enjoyed a lifetime of this contemplative pastime. That pleasant initial experience made a lasting impact on me.

Your youngsters and friends can also enjoy our great outdoor heritage as they grow older. This book was written to tell you about many kinds of saltwater fishing in many places and to help you enjoy the total experience. For once you've been smitten, a lifelong passion may develop. It's something you'll cherish, as will your children, grandchildren and friends, and enjoy forever.

Bob Rosko unhooks a nice weakfish landed by daughter Kristine as they fished aboard the family's boat. Introducing youngsters to fishing at an early age enables them to enjoy the great outdoors for a lifetime. They learn to respect the water, about a variety of fish, ecology and the sea birds and waterfowl that are always present. Importantly, they enjoy doing things together as a family.

AMERICA'S FAVORITE 50 SPECIES

African pompano

The African pompano is really not a pompano at all, but a member of the threadfin family. It is found throughout the southern Atlantic and Gulf coast. Its Pacific coast counterpart is the Pacific threadfin, a distinct, yet very similar species.

Both species are most often caught by accident. They frequent reef areas for the most part, yet are often encountered by blue water trollers seeking pelagic species. They are included here because they're sterling fighters on light tackle and are a rare treat to catch. The African pompano has a very deep, thin body, with a head profile that is almost vertical. It has brilliant, silvery coloration, interspersed with traces of pale blue, red and yellow. Another distinct feature are the several long softrays of the dorsal fin that occasionally extend to the tail.

The African pompano can grow to 35 pounds or more. Their deep, powerful body makes them a tough challenge on 20-pound-class tackle on the offshore grounds, where they readily crash trolled baits such as mullet and balao. Once hooked, they bore to the bottom in powerful runs and with their broad profile are stubborn to bring to boat.

They particularly like the reef areas of Florida and the Bahamas that are also frequented by snapper and grouper. Many are caught with live goggleyes, pinfish, and blue runner baits. They'll respond to leadhead bucktail and plastic-tailed jigs worked just above the reef.

On the dinner table it has a rather heavy flavor, although many find its distinctive taste to their liking.

African pompano are powerful adversaries that test an angler and his tackle to the utmost.

(Left) All over America, anglers rise early to be on the water before sunrise. These anglers are setting forth on a typical morning, targeting any one of about 100 species caught by saltwater anglers fishing off the Atlantic, Pacific, and Gulf Coasts.

The long-finned albacore is found off all three coast. The tasty pelagic species is most often initially hooked via trolling, after which anglers switch over to chumming to hold the school near the boat. The fish are then baited with live anchovies or taken on chromed jigs.

Albacore

The albacore is the darling of the blue-water fisherman. Found on all three coasts, it readily responds to trolled lures and is particularly susceptible to chumming. Many refer to the albacore as a long-finned tuna, because of the long pectoral fin that often extends beyond its second dorsal fin. It is a very strong fish with a torpedo-shaped body and sharp tail propelling it through the water at great speed. It prefers water in the 60- to 66-degree range, cooler than that favored by most pelagic species. Often water temperature becomes the prime consideration when trying to locate schools of albacore that occasionally number in the thousands. Seldom are small albacore encountered by sport fishermen, with fish in the 20- to 40-pound-class being the norm. Schools containing fish up to 75 pounds are occasionally encountered.

Pacific Coast long-range party and private boats troll until fish are located. This often means long boat rides. Fish are usually encountered near a temperature break. It is not unusual for every trolled lure to be crashed simultaneously when a school is finally located.

When this happens the throttles are eased off, and as anglers bring to boat albacore hooked on the trolled lures, the deckhands begin chumming operations. Huge quantities of live bait, such as anchovies, are ladled from circulating live tanks, and tossed overboard to hold the fish close to the boat. Moments after the live chum is dispensed, you can often see the albacore boiling to the surface to take the baits. Then anglers bait up with anchovies and ease them back into the chum line. It's not unusual to have a dozen or more fish hooked simultaneously.

Atlantic anglers employ similar techniques, searching the offshore canyons of the northeast until they find the temperature breaks where the albacore are congregated. Trolling produces many fish, with trolling feathers, plastic-skirted lures and natural baits such as mullet, mackerel and balao accounting for many fish. Tackle in the 20- to 30-pound class is ideal for this fishing. Unfortunately, many of these fine gamefish are caught on heavier gear targeting bigger species.

Chumming for albacore on the Atlantic Coast differs from that of the Pacific, in that live baitfish for chum are not readily available. Instead, chunks of butterfish, menhaden or herring are used. Supplementing the chunks of chum is a soup made of ground menhaden mixed with sea water. The ground oily fish establishes a slick that excites the albacore and puts them in a feeding frenzy. Anglers then use whole butterfish, drifted in the chum slick, as bait.

Albacore is unquestionably the finest eating member of the tuna clan. Its meat is white and very mild and it is the only tuna that is permitted to be called "white meat tuna" when canned. On the Pacific Coast many anglers drop off their catch at coastal canneries and have it canned. Albacore is also delicious when steaked and marinated and prepared on an outdoor grill.

Amberjack are among the most stubborn fish in the sea. A fish this size often takes an hour or longer to boat. Amberjack are commonly found around coastal reefs, where they often respond to a chum line of chunks of fish.

Amberjack

Few anglers will dispute that the amberjack is among the most stubborn, tough fighters in the sea. It is a deep-water fighter, often taking a bait or lure near the surface, but then making a strong run into the depths.

Sport fishermen most often encounter fish in the 20- to 50-pound range while fishing the reefs and rocky bottom inshore from the Carolinas down to Florida and across the Gulf Coast. The amberjack can grow to about 175 pounds, making it one of the bigger species regularly encountered by small-boat anglers. The majority are caught within 20 miles of the beach.

Amberjack regularly strike small- and medium-sized trolled lures, such as spoons, feathers and jigs. They also take natural baits such as mullet and balao targeted for other species. They're also caught on chunk baits fished on the bottom where grouper and snapper are the targeted species.

Live bait is by far the most effective way to catch this powerhouse. On the fishing grounds, a live bait is hooked lightly through the back, just forward of the dorsal fin, and eased overboard and permitted to swim away as the boat drifts across the reef. The outfit is often placed in a rod holder, with the reel's clicker on and in free spool. Once the fish moves off with the bait—sometimes they toy with it—sit back, lock the reel in gear and hold on!

Some anglers set out live baits at intermediate levels while fishing at anchor over a reef for snapper and grouper.

Amberjack have a heavy flavor and most are released to fight another day. Some anglers fillet them and then cut small fingers, which are deep fried. Smoking is also a popular method of preparing amberjack.

Atlantic bonito is a favorite of small-boat anglers. It is often located just a few miles offshore. It responds to small, trolled lures, cast flies, fast-retrieved jigs and chum. The fish is often hook shy, and it's best to use a small bait and fluorocarbon leader.

Atlantic bonito

Scattered about the broad expanse of the Atlantic, the Atlantic bonito is a favorite of anglers fishing from small boats. It frequents primarily the open sea, and is most often encountered withing 20 miles of shore. A surface feeder, it travels in huge schools. Anglers in the Northeast encounter this tasty bonito during the summer months and it lingers in coastal waters until late fall, when falling temperatures cause it to seek more temperate climes. It is found year round along the southern Atlantic and Gulf coasts.

Anglers fishing from small boats frequently troll for the Atlantic bonito, which generally averages from 3 to 7 pounds and responds best to small lures. Three-inch spoons, cedar jigs and feathered jigs of the same size bring more strikes than larger lures. A favored technique is to troll these lures with the aid of a 3- or 4-ounce trolling sinker, which will keep the lures just beneath the surface. A pair of lines are generally fished up close on the first or second wake from the stern, while another pair of lines are streamed back 100 feet or so. Trolling speeds of 4 to 6 knots usually produce the most strikes as the bonito seem to prefer faster-moving lures.

Bonito also respond to a chum line. Often they'll stay near a ridge or high bottom. Ground menhaden or other forage fish is a favored chum. The most successful technique is to anchor on a piece of high bottom and chum sparingly with the ground fish mixed with sea water. A soupy chum is ladled overboard and supplemented by a handful of spearing, sand eels, or other baitfish. As the bonito swarm into the slick, they are often very hook shy, picking up the free-floating baitfish tossed as chum, but ignoring hook baits.

The advent of fluorocarbon leader material has helped. A size No. 1 or 2 hook carefully concealed within a sparing or sand eel will often coax strikes.

When chumming, the ideal tackle for the bonito is a light, one-handed spinning outfit or an equally light popping outfit.

Once a feeding pattern has been established off the coast, and especially when large schools are moving through an area, you can also enjoy fine results by simply shutting down and drifting. Use light outfits and tiny leadhead bucktail or plastic-tailed jigs, chromed or stainless steel jigs. Use a fast, erratic retrieve and explore every level of the water column. Bonito may be seen cruising just beneath the surface, but they will only respond to lures worked through the depths with a jigging action.

The Atlantic bonito is an excellent table fish. It has light-colored meat with a very delicate flavor that may be used with most any fish recipe. Most often it is filleted and the dark meat of the lateral line removed.

Atlantic mackerel are perfect when you take the youngsters fishing, as the action is often fast and furious. Joey Andelora used a light casting outfit and red tube teasers and jig combination to hook the pair of mackerel he's just swung aboard.

Atlantic mackerel

If ever there is a fish designed for youngsters, it has to be the Atlantic mackerel. Found from the Canadian Maritime Provinces, where it spends the summer, to its wintering grounds off the Virginia Capes, the Atlantic mackerel travels in huge schools along the coast, lingering for a week or two off most major sportfishing ports as it travels. Party, charter and private boatmen enjoy bonanza fishing when these fish are passing through. The small mackerel that average from but 1 to 3 pounds are fast and very strong for their size. They travel in large, tight schools. Schools are always composed of identical-size fish.

They're very easy to catch, which makes them an ideal species for the newcomer. Jigging is by far the most popular way to catch mackerel. A one-handed spinning outfit or a popping outfit works best. A 1- or 2-ounce diamond, Vike or Hopkins jig is tied directly to the end of the line.

Once a school of mackerel is located on the fishfinding gear, the engines are shut down and you drift through the schools. The jig is best worked by dropping it into the water and permitting it to settle a couple of feet at a time, stopping it momentarily and vigorously lifting the rod tip, causing the jig to dart toward the surface and falter, much like a wounded baitfish. If a strike isn't received by the time the jig reaches bottom, the reel is engaged and the jig is worked toward the surface using the same technique, reeling, jigging the rod tip, and then reeling again. When mackerel are plentiful the jig never gets to the bottom without a strike.

When the mackerel are finicky a mackerel teaser rig often brings results. Often called a "Christmas tree" rig, the mackerel teaser rig consists of three 2-inch plastic-tube tails, usually red, green and yellow (hence the nickname) with No. 2 or 3 hooks inside the tails. The plastic tails are tied to a leader via dropper loops at 1-foot intervals and a diamond jig is tied to the terminal end of the rig. When jigged, the teaser and jig combo gives the appearance of several frightened baitfish darting about and faltering. Mackerel just can't seem to resist it. It's not at all unusual to catch several mackerel at a time, and when hooked on a light outfit it's fast, exciting sport, guaranteed to keep everybody on board happy.

Mackerel is somewhat oily and has a very heavy flavor. When filleted, skinned and with the lateral-line removed, it's very tasty when steamed in aluminum foil on an outdoor grill. Mackerel may also be filleted and pickled in kosher salt brine, or lightly hickory smoked for a delicious hors d'oeuvre.

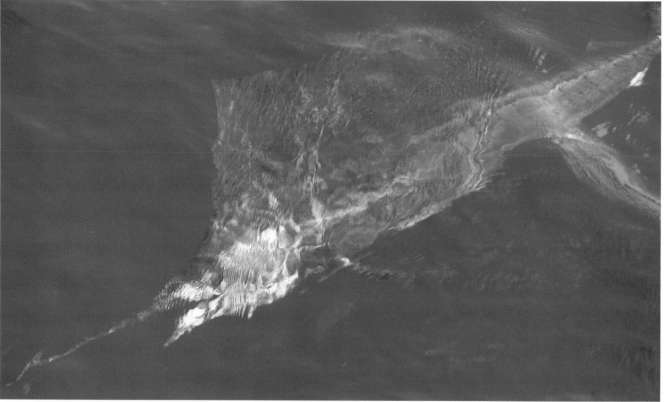

The Atlantic sailfish is an acrobat that often jumps clear of the water and tail walks across the surface in an exciting aerial display. Most sails are caught by trolling balao or mullet baits, although many anglers are very successful using live goggleyes as bait.

Atlantic sailfish

Found from the outer banks of the Carolinas south to Florida and across the Gulf Coast, the Atlantic sailfish is a spectacular light tackle gamefish available within range of the small boat angler. It is encountered along the inshore edges of the Gulf Stream, at times just a couple of miles off the Florida coast and less than 20 miles off Hatteras.

The majority are caught by trolling with light tackle. Balao are perhaps the most favored trolling bait, followed closely by boned and split-tail mullet and an ordinary strip bait cut from the belly of a bonito or little tuna. Success is almost assured during the winter months in Florida when northerly winds cause the sailfish to school up. When they locate schools of baitfish, they literally herd, or bail, the the fish before moving in to unmercifully feed until their appetites are satisfied. Trolling along the perimeter feeding schools often brings immediate strikes, as the fish peel off to inspect and attack skipping baits fished from spread outriggers.

Live baitfish is another popular choice for sailfish, particularly in Florida waters. Goggleyes, mackerel, blue runners, small jacks and pinfish are caught jigging inshore, or purchased from bait purveyors, and kept alive in baitwells until the fishing grounds are reached.

A loop of rigging thread is made that measures approximately 3 inches in diameter. A rigging needle is used to thread the bait through the eye sockets, and the thread is then looped and twisted and slipped onto the curve of a 5/0 live bait hook. Hooked in this matter, the baitfish can swim freely.

Some anglers fish the live goggleyes directly from the outriggers, usually fishing one bait from each outrigger, and trolling along slowly. Some anglers add a balloon to the line 6 or 8 feet from the bait so they can keep the bait near the surface. Then it's just a matter of power-trolling along, putting the engines in and out of gear periodically, so the bait isn't ripped apart.

This is especially exciting fishing, as often the bait will move about excitedly as a sailfish approaches. Often you can see the sailfish, its sail raised, moving in for an assault. Not only is the strike spectacular, but the aerial display that follows is truly awesome, with the sailfish, all 7 or 8 feet of it, in the air, tail walking and cartwheeling across the surface.

This same live-bait technique also works extremely well with a kite line.

Fly fishermen often employ hookless natural baits from outriggers to coax sailfish into a feeding frenzy. When the sailfish is lit up and attacking the hookless bait, the boat is eased out of gear, and the bait pulled in as the angler standing in a stern corner of the cockpit presents his fly. The sailfish, frustrated at not being able to eat the bait, will often turn and immediately charge the fly.

Almost all sailfish are promptly released at boatside.

Barracuda

The much maligned barracuda, properly called the "Great Barracuda," deserves a better reputation. Trollers targeting sailfish get irritated when big barracuda crash carefully prepared baits. Flats fishermen become frustrated when the fish charge in out of nowhere to snatch up a bait or lure intended for a permit, tarpon or bonefish.

But the barracuda presents a formidable challenge when caught on light tackle. Both on the offshore grounds and the shallow inshore flats, the toothy predator is often very cooperative, attacking most anything that looks like a meal.

Leadhead, bucktail and plastic-tailed jigs account for many barracuda, as do plugs, especially surface models such as darters and poppers. A lure that has grown in popularity in recent years is a 6- to 8-inch piece of red or green flexible plastic tubing. Slipped over a piece of leader material, a small treble hook is tied to the end of the leader, and the flexible plastic tubing is slipped down on the hook. When retrieved, the tubing swims in a spinning fashion on the surface, which drives most barracuda wild. The barracuda makes substantial runs against light tackle, often jumping repeatedly.

It's a fun fish to catch, but not very good table fare. Most are promptly released at boatside. Either cut the leader or remove the hook with a dehooker. The barracuda has menacing teeth and should be handled with care.

Blackfin tuna

The blackfin is among the smallest tunas, rarely growing to 30 pounds. Found in the warmer waters of the western Atlantic, it is plentiful and regularly makes a day's efforts on the offshore grounds worthwhile. Few anglers fish expressly for blackfins, but many catch them incidentally.

As a pelagic fish they feel most at home where their bigger cousins and the marlin roam. They're not adverse to moving inshore and taking up residence around reefs and ridges where there is a plentiful supply of food.

Most strike lures intended for billfish and big tuna. If, however, you include a selection of cedar jigs, small trolling feathers, plastic-tailed trolling skirts and spoons in your spread of

Blackfin tuna often move in under the lights of party boats to feed on the squid and other forage species that are attracted to the lights. They're a very strong fighter when taken on medium-weight tackle. They respond to live baitfish, chunks of balao or little tunny. Many are also taken by jigging, and once in the chum line they'll take saltwater flies.

lures, you'll find that you'll receive bonus strikes from the blackfin.

A favorite technique is to troll a pair of lines close in the wake, at the first or second wave, with the lines attached to outrigger clips secured to the transom of the boat. This keeps the lures in the water and prevents them from flipping about wildly. The fish often zero-in on the lures darting about in the wake and doubleheaders are not uncommon.

The blackfin readily responds to a chum slick. When anchored on a reef fishing for grouper or snapper, many boatmen fish a couple of outfits from the rod holders with chunks of balao or little tuna as bait. They place a mesh bag of frozen ground menhaden overboard.

Blackfin is among the tastiest of tunas. Filleted, and sliced into steaks, it may be broiled, sauteed or grilled.

Bluefin tuna are found in the Atlantic, Pacific and Gulf. This beauty was landed while on a long range trip off Southern California, where the tuna are generally smaller than the bluefins taken in the Atlantic and Gulf. Fish of this size are a great challenge on medium-weight tackle. They respond to small lures trolled tight to the stern. Many are also taken while chumming.

Bluefin tuna

Just a couple of decades ago bluefin tuna of every size roamed the waters of the northeast during the summer months in schools that numbered in the thousands. There were fish of all sizes, from "footballs" under 10 pounds to the popular 30- to 75-pound specimens that provided exciting sport on medium-weight tackle. Then there were the "giants," those Goliaths that occasionally weighed in at more than 1,000 pounds. Countless thousands of tuna topping 500 pounds passed through the Florida Straits each spring as they headed northward to the fertile, forage-filled waters of the northeast.

Today, all that has changed and the popular bluefin population is at near-endangered levels. Its plight is a classic example of extreme commercial overfishing and international and domestic bureaucratic incompetence in managing this fishery.

The bluefin tuna rightly deserves to be included in this selection of "America's Favorite 50 Species" because it continues to be a prize, although sport fishermen are severely restricted by limited seasons and size and catch limits. On those occasions when anglers are permitted to seek bluefin, they do so primarily for the sport, conscious of the fact that to kill this great gamefish would further reduce the population.

Historically, the giants of the clan were pursued by chumming from an anchored boat, or by trolling spreader bars rigged with either whole fresh mackerel or shell squids. That practice continues, but many who use these techniques are licensed commercial fishermen who ship their catch to the lucrative Japanese fish market.

Fishermen targeting the school bluefin tuna use time-proven techniques of trolling cedar jigs, spoons, trolling feathers and plastic-skirted jigs. The school tuna are readily attracted to a boat's churning wake and lures fished close in, on the first or second wave of the bait, bring the most strikes. Spreader bars also have proved effective in recent years, especially those made with a selection of small shell squids or feathered jigs.

School bluefin tuna also respond to a chum slick. Along many areas of the mid-Atlantic and Northeast, boatmen anchor at choice tuna grounds, often 5 to 20 miles from shore, and chum for the speedy adversaries. Most often a combination chum is used that consists of ground menhaden with chunks of butterfish, herring or mackerel.

Chunk baits are drifted back into the chum slick, with a moving chunk producing the best results. The tuna can be finicky in clear water, and anglers are best to employ fluorocarbon leaders.

When pressure-cooked in Mason jars, bluefin tuna is as tasty a fish as you'd ever want to eat. Freshly smoked tuna is also a great treat, as is raw tuna served as sushi. Unfortunately, few anglers ever get to experience this seafood treat as a result of the depleted stocks.

The time may well come when there is a complete moratorium—I have advocated such a ban for many years—on both sport and commercial landings of giant bluefin tuna. This might enable a great gamefish to return to its former population levels.

Bluefish

The bluefish is among one of the most popular saltwater gamefish sought by American anglers. Found in great numbers near Canada's Maritime Provinces during summer, its home range reaches the entire length of the Atlantic Coast and the Gulf of Mexico. Its popularity comes from the fact that it is basically an inshore species and lives within easy range of private, charter and party boats. It invades the surf, which makes it a natural for jetty, surf and pier casters. Bay and river waters also often teem with the tiny "snapper" blues 6 inches long. There are also schools of "alligator" blues weighing from 15 to 20 pounds, and just about every size in between.

It has been said a bluefish will eat anything that swims and that can't eat it first. Schools of bluefish are constantly on the prowl in coastal waters. When they find a school of forage species such as mullet, menhaden, sand eels, spearing or herring, there is a carnage beyond description. Often the blues gorge themselves to the point the water turns red as the animated chopping machines destroy a school of bait fish. Their sharp teeth cut through small fish in one bite. When filled to the bursting point, blues often disgorge what they've eaten and begin feeding again.

Bluefish range from Maine to Florida and along the entire Gulf Coast to Texas. Joe Basilio, the author's son-in-law, landed this beauty while trolling a bunker spoon with wire line from the "Linda June." Bluefish are inshore feeders that provide great sport for small boat anglers, surf and jetty casters.

Trolling with spoons, feathers, swimming plugs and leadhead jigs is perhaps the best technique. The key is employing a fishfinder to determine the depth at which the bait is located and the blues are feeding. If the blues are feeding near the surface there is no need to employ trolling sinkers, as lures trolled just beneath the surface prove effective. When the fish are located at intermediate levels, it's often wise to add 2- to 6-ounce trolling sinkers between line and leader to get lures to the desired depth. Still other times the blues are gorging on sand eels located right near the bottom and wire line that takes lures deep proves to be most effective. Multi-hooked umbrella rigs with trailing tube lures are especially effective when the bluefish are feeding in the depths.

Chumming for bluefish is very popular and may be done while anchored or drifting. The key is locating schools with fishfinders, or simply setting up at established locations such as lumps, ridges or offshore wrecks.

Ground menhaden is the most common chum. Popularly called "bunker" or "mossbunker," this oily forage species is ground and distributed overboard to form a heavily scented slick. Provide just enough ground chum to attract the fish, not feed them.

Many anglers employ a piece of menhaden as a hook bait. Baits measuring an inch in width by a couple of inches in length work just fine with a 5/0 through 7/0 hook. The key when working a bait in the chum line is to keep your reel in free spool, permitting the current to carry the bait. Because of their extremely sharp teeth, bluefish often bite right through a monofilament line or leader. It's wise to employ a long-shank hook, or a 6- to 8-inch piece of No. 8 or 9 stainless steel leader material.

Jigging with a diamond jig or leadhead jig is another fun technique that brings strikes from bluefish. It's particularly effective when the bluefish are in the depths, for the jigs may be worked to probe from the surface to the bottom and then back up again, encountering hungry bluefish anywhere along the way. Permit the jig to settle several feet at a time, stopping it and lifting the rod tip, causing the jig to dart towards the surface, then flutter back down.

It's exciting when bluefish are chasing forage on the surface. Whether you're fishing from boat or beach, this presents a great opportunity to catch these sterling fighters on surface plugs such as poppers, swimmers or darters. Casting a plug into a maelstrom of feeding bluefish invariably brings immediate surface strikes, with the fish jumping repeatedly.

Block tin squids, and chromed and stainless steel jigs may also be used when the fish are surface feeding, especially when very long casts are required.

Bluefish are fine table fish, but care must be taken when landing them. They should be bled and immediately placed on ice to maintain freshness. Most people prefer fillets with the skin and dark meat of the lateral line removed.

This big blue marlin was caught off the North Carolina Outer Banks and boated with a flying gaff. It was hoisted aboard via block and tackle attached to a gin pole. Some marlin are boated by tournament anglers or those wishing to have one mounted. The majority are released.

Blue marlin

The blue marlin is found in the offshore waters off all three U.S. coasts and reigns supreme as a prize target of blue-water trollers. The greatest majority are caught while trolling with heavy tackle and natural baits or big, high-speed trolling lures. Many innovative anglers have begun using slow-trolling techniques with live bonito or other fish and have had very good results. Baits are caught and kept alive in individual tubes through which water circulates, resulting in lively, big baits

213

when the fishing grounds are reached.

Most blue marlin are encountered beyond the 100-fathom line, in offshore canyons or along the edge of the continental shelf. They do not frequent inshore waters, but prefer the warm offshore waters, often congregating where there is an abundance of forage. They are found near temperature breaks and where schools of mackerel, squid, flying fish or other forage congregate.

Occasionally, small pods of marlin may be encountered, but for the most part they are loners, particularly the bigger fish. This forces trollers to cover miles of ocean. Blue marlin in the 300- to 1,000-pound range generally feed on very large bonito, tuna and dolphin. They occasionally take a small fish to satisfy their appetite. That old adage that big baits catch big fish certainly comes into play with the marlin. Don't hesitate to use the biggest artificials available, especially the Kona head and high-speed trolling lures that create a lot of surface disturbance. The same is true for live baits. Baits weighing up to 15 pounds are by no means too big when fished with 80- or 130-pound-class tackle.

Patience is a virtue for all serious blue marlin fishermen. They cover miles of ocean, probing weed lines, looking for temperature breaks and searching for concentrations of forage. It has been said the price of a marlin is eternal vigilance.

There is a very strong conservation ethic among blue marlin fishermen. The vast majority of marlin are released, although some big ones are kept for the taxidermist or by tournament fisherman.

Bonefish are an exciting challenge for anglers who enjoy fly fishing. General Norman Schwarzkopf employed his favorite long rod to present a shrimp fly to the Florida Keys bonefish boated by guide Craig Brewer. Most bonefish are spotted in water just one to 3 feet deep. Immediately after this photo was taken, the bonefish was released.

Bonefish

If ever there was a gamefish that could be called, lightning fast, it is the bonefish. It is found primarily in the warm waters of Florida, the Bahamas, Bermuda and Caribbean islands, Cuba, Mexico, Hawaii and many Pacific islands.

It is an inshore feeder, frequenting the shallow flats, which are easily waded, or fished from shallow draft flats boats. Almost without exception, bonefish are caught by sight casting, either while wading, or being poled along the flats from a boat. It is an extremely spooky fish that requires a cautious approach and perfect cast to hook.

The two most popular outfits used by bonefishermen are a one-handed spinning outfit and a 9- or 10-weight fly-casting outfit with a weight-forward floating fly line.

As the tide floods the bonefish moves in to the shallows to root along the bottom, where it feeds primarily on the crabs and shrimp. As it roots along the bottom, facing downward, its tail is often exposed. It's the tailing activity that gives them away and is usually an angler's first indication that bonefish are feeding on the flat.

When a bonefish is sighted, an angler must determine the general direction in which it is traveling. When it is within casting range a presentation with a live shrimp or tiny crab can be made. Bonefish will strike the bait resting on the bottom and the ensuing line-peeling run is something a newcomer never forgets and veterans always look forward to. It's not unusual for a 5- to 10-pounder to rip more than 100 yards of line from a spinning reel in less time than it takes to tell about it.

Once they become adept at catching bonefish on shrimp or crabs, some anglers move on to artificials. Small lead-head jigs are designed expressly for flats fishing. The delta-wing jigs are tied to resemble a small crab, and they're cast just ahead and to the side of a feeding fish. The delta-wing shape works better than bullet-head shapes on the shallow flats and results in the jig having a wiggling action when retrieved.

Fly casters employ much the same approach, moving within range of the feeding fish and presenting their offering as delicately as possible. The flies are small and tied to resemble the crabs and shrimp on which the bonefish feeds. Presentation is very critical, as the fish will spook wildly if the cast is sloppy.

The bonefish is considered a great gamefish wherever it is found. Anglers regularly release their catch, which ensures a healthy fishery will continue.

California halibut are bottom feeders that will readily strike a live anchovy bait drifted across sandy bottom. Many anglers forego heavy sinkers and live baits and employ light casting tackle and small leadhead jigs with plastic bait tails to entice strikes from the heavyweight flatfish. They're one of the tastiest fish in the Pacific.

California halibut

Found from central California south to the Baja Peninsula, the California halibut provides inshore fishermen with fine sport and delicious eating. Considerably smaller than the Pacific Halibut, the California Halibut grows to more than 60 pounds, although most caught by sports fishermen average in the 3- to 6-pound range.

It favors the sandy bottom typical of most inshore California waters. The majority are caught by drifting live baits such as anchovies or other small fish. A small dipsey or rubber-core sinker is used to take the bait to the bottom, with just enough weight to hold as you drift along. With a delicate bait, such as a live anchovy, the key is to employ a small, No. 1 or 2 beak or claw hook, hooked lightly through the lips. The key is keeping the bait on the bottom, as the halibut will seldom move more than a couple of feet off bottom to inhale a baitfish.

215

While most halibut are hooked with natural baits, they will strike artificials. A leadhead jig with either bucktail skirt or a plastic tail is very effective when lowered to the bottom and worked with the rod tip. Again, the key is keeping the jig on or near the sandy bottom.

The California halibut is judged by many as the finest-eating fish in the sea. Most anglers fillet their halibut, removing two fillets from the brown, top side of the fish, and two from the white underside. The fillets are then skinned, resulting in four pieces of white, delicious seafood that can be used for most any fish recipe.

You'll find the California yellowtail tight in among the kelp beds of Southern California and well offshore too. Many are taken on trolling spoons, feather jigs and plastic skirted trolling heads. The favorite technique is to chum with live anchovies and attract the fish within range and then cast a live anchovy bait.

California yellowtail

The California yellowtail has been called the amberjack of the Pacific. Even its profile is similar, although it is more streamlined than its cousin from the east.

They're a favorite of the inshore fishermen who work the kelp beds of Southern California and the Baja Peninsula. They have a fighting heart and, when taken on tackle balanced to their size, are an adversary that will test you and your equipment to the limit.

Most yellowtail are landed by anchoring off from the kelp and chumming with live anchovies or other small forage during the spring and summer months. Light- and medium-weight spinning or casting tackle is appropriate and terminal rigging amounts to simply tying a number 1 or 2 claw, beak or live-bait hook directly to the terminal end of the line. A single live baitfish is hooked through the lips and cast close to the kelp, but not in it. Avoid getting too close, for if you hook a big yellowtail, it'll often charge into the kelp and tangle or break the line.

The key is using an active, lively anchovy or sardine bait. When a bait is furiously swimming about it emits distress signals that are picked up by cruising yellowtail. The angler can sense the presence of a stalking yellowtail by the accelerated movement of the baitfish. There's no hesitation needed when you receive a strike, for the yellowtail will engulf the bait and speed off. It's best to fish with as firm a drag as your equipment will endure, for if you don't control the fish right from the start it will take out excessive line.

Another popular technique is to lightly hook a sardine just ahead of the dorsal fin and stream out 50 or 60 feet of line and permit the wind or current to carry you along. Dead-sticking the outfit in a rod holder, with the reel in free spool and the click set, can produces screaming strikes.

The majority of the yellowtail caught off the Coronado Islands and by the party boat fleet sailing from Los Angeles on down to Ensenada average 5 to 15 pounds. Fish of this size generally run in schools and it's not unusual to have several hooked simultaneously. There are plenty of heavyweights to test your skill, however, with occasional fish pulling the scale down to the 30 pounds or more.

While traditionalists stick with live bait, there's a sizable group of anglers who elect to troll small chromed jigs, spoons, feathers or plastic skirts, and strip baits along rocky promontories and ledges.

Fly casters often entice California yellowtail within range by chumming, although they usually have to cast to them blindly. Bright, predominately silver- and white-colored streamers, are the flies of choice.

As is the case with the entire amberjack family, the California yellowtail leaves a lot to be desired as table fare. Its meat is dark and has a heavy flavor, although there are some who feel it is the finest fish in the sea. Some anglers fillet the yellowtail and then cut the fillet into small "fingers" that are deep fried. Smoking is also a very popular alternative. If you're not going to use them for the table, take care to promptly release the game fighter.

World-renowned fly caster Lefty Kreh has caught practically every salt water species on this tackle. Originator of the the "Lefty's Deceiver" saltwater fly, he succeeded in landing this 22-pound channel bass on an 8-weight outfit while using a blue and white pattern of the fly. Often called redfish, they reside along the Gulf Coast and from the Carolina Outer Banks to Florida.

Channel bass

Found from southern New Jersey to Florida and across the Gulf Coast, the channel bass, also know as the red drum or redfish in Florida and the Gulf coast, is readily accessible to most anglers from the boat or beach.

It has a deep bronze coloration and a distinguishing black spot at the base of the tail. Occasionally, several black spots may be present. Channel bass grow to more than 70 pounds, but sport fishermen generally target those from 5 to 20 pounds.

The traditional method of catching channel bass along the Outer Banks is to employ a bottom rig, with a sinker of sufficient weight to hold bottom, with a 36-inch leader and 6/0 claw hook baited with either menhaden or mullet. This basic rig is fished from the surf, or from an anchored boat along the outer bars, sounds and bays. The channel bass feeds along the bottom and covers a lot of area as it searches for a meal. Both day and night fishing are popular, especially from the surf.

Channel bass are also caught by sight casting to schools that move along the outer bars. During the spring, schools of a dozen or more big channel bass can be observed as a dark shadow moving just beneath the surface. A large, hammered, stainless steel jig cast ahead of the school and worked slowly near the surface often brings quick strikes. Most of the large channel bass are released, as they're not as tasty as the smaller fish.

Throughout the southern part of their range and especially along the Gulf Coast, anglers often sight cast to feeding redfish along channel edges and mud banks where the fish tend to congregate on a flooding tide. They'll readily take crab or shrimp baits, or a piece of fish. A leadhead jig or small swimming plug cast to feeding fish readily brings strikes. Fly casters also use flies made to resemble small baitfish, shrimp or crabs. The key is a slow retrieve.

The popularity of blackened redfish in restaurants throughout the U.S. has caused a severe depletion of the population. Sound fishery management has helped the fish rebound in recent years. Anglers usually keep the smaller redfish, while keeping within local regulations, as they are by far the tastiest fish and can be prepared using a wide variety of recipes.

Cobia, also called ling along some sections of the Gulf, are very plentiful along the Atlantic Coast from Hatteras to the Keys. Many are taken as an incidental catch. Live baits drifted on float rigs are effective. Cobia have a habit of finning in the shadows of bridges and channel markers.

Cobia

The cobia is found from along the middle Atlantic Coast south to Florida and along the entire Gulf Coast. Basically an inshore feeder found in bays and rivers and especially along the surf and beaches, it will occasionally wander offshore several miles

A prize of both boatmen and beach casters, the cobia has a habit of cruising just beneath the surface as it searches for a meal. It also likes to wait near fixed objects, such as channel markers and buoys, and many are caught by small boat anglers who move about, searching out these haunts.

The cobia has a deep brown back, lighter brown sides and a very streamlined profile. It is a very powerful fish that grows to more than 100 pounds, although most range from 5 to 25 pounds. Ideally suited to medium and light tackle, it will readily take live baits such as crabs, shrimp, mullet, pinfish and other small forage species. Baits may be fished on the bottom, but when fish are sighted on the surface many anglers simply tie a size 5/0 through 7/0 beak hook directly to the end of a short length of 30-pound-test leader and cast live baitfish within range of the cobia. When a cobia is hungry it wastes little time in charging the bait. There are times, however, when you can place an attractive bait just a foot from its nose and it will simply ignore it.

The cobia is excellent table fare. Generally filleted and skinned, it may then be baked, broiled, or cut up and deep fried.

The codfish has for many years been a favorite of Northeast party boat anglers. Its once abundant numbers were depleted, but in recent years the species has begun a comeback due to reductions of commercial catches and closure of fishing grounds. Primarily a winter fishery, codfish are most often caught on clam baits on the bottom. On wrecks and ridges many are taken while using a diamond jig and tube teaser combination.

Codfish

While the codfish ranges from Hatteras to Greenland, it is most often targeted by anglers who sail from DelMarVa ports north to Maine. Occasionally, codfish move inshore, but for the most part they travel in waters from 20 to 100 fathoms, often to along the edge of the Continental Shelf. Found in some areas over open bottom, they prefer to congregate over irregular bottom, rocky bottom and ridges. It is at these locations that crabs, lobsters and forage species are plentiful. The codfish also hangs around the many shipwrecks found off our coast.

Primarily a bottom feeder, the codfish will move up to feed on shrimp, squid, herring, mackerel and other forage.

The traditional method of catching codfish, along with pollock, silver hake and red hake, is with natural baits fished on the bottom. Because of the depth in which they're found, medium-weight tackle is usually the best choice. A basic high-low rig is the most popular terminal tackle. A pair of 5/0 or 6/0 claw bait-holder hooks are snelled to 18- to 24-inch leaders. The lower hook is fished directly on the bottom, with a second hook 24 inches from the bottom. Sinker weights range from 8 to 20 ounces in order to hold in the depths, which can also have swift currents. Pieces of clam are the best bait, although squid, conch, snails and a fillet cut from herring, mackerel or a bergall all work well.

The majority of codfish are landed by anglers fishing from party and charter boats. Captains sail daily and can monitor the movements of the fish and they have an extensive file of Loran and GPS numbers of prime locations. When their fishfinding gear signals concentrations of codfish feeding up from the bottom, the skippers will often drift instead of anchoring, providing fine jigging opportunities for their anglers.

Heavy diamond and Vike jigs, weighing 8 to 16 ounces, are tied to the terminal end of a monofilament line. A dropper loop is tied into the line about 3 feet from the jib. A single red or green plastic-tube teaser with a 6/0 hook is slipped on the line.

The rig is lowered to intermediate depths, and then worked with a jigging motion. Codfish and the species that travel in their company, including pollock, hake, silver hake and red hake, all have very mild flavor and are among the finest-tasting fish in the sea.

The dolphin is one of the most colorful fish in the sea. It's also an excellent table fish. Male, "bull" dolphin like this one will strike trolled baits and lures. They'll also respond to a live baitfish fished from a kite. The most exciting fishing is to find a school of dolphin around a weed line, attract them with chum, and cast lures or flies.

Dolphin

The dolphin is among the prettiest fish in the sea. It has deep yellow sides and belly and hued blue and green back. Large male "bull" dolphin has a very distinct, almost vertical, shape to its head, while the female's head is more rounded. Dolphin are found worldwide in warm ocean waters and can grow to more than 70 pounds. The big dolphin are often taken quite by chance as anglers troll for marlin and tuna. The most exciting dolphin fishing comes from casting to the fish as it feeds along an offshore weed line.

Often a combination of wind against tide will collect huge amounts of floating weed. Seeking what little sanctuary the weed offers are myriad baitfish and the fry of major gamefish as well. The weed lines often stretch for miles and are sometimes several feet thick. As such, trollers often fish along the perimeter of the weed, using rigged mullet, balao, or the wide range of high-speed trolling lures, such as small Kona heads, strip baits or trolling feathers.

The weed lines present exciting casting opportunities. The key is easing up within casting distance of the weed and employing either light spinning, popping or fly-casting tackle to present lures to the edge of the weeds.

It's often possible to see the dolphin as they swim along in the shadow of the weeds in the clear, deep, blue water. Small leadhead jigs dressed with either bucktail skirts or plastic tails are cast to the weeds, permitted to sink a few feet, then retrieved with an irregular jigging action. This tactic can bring several dolphin streaking to the lure simultaneously.

Small swimming plugs, darters and poppers all excite dolphin into striking.

The fly rod devotee will find dolphin fishing among the most exciting offshore sports. Using a 9- or 10-weight outfit, and weight-forward floating fly line, it's relatively easy to probe the edge of the weeds with flies such as the Clouser, Deceiver, Half and Half, or Platinum Blond pattern. Favored hook sizes are 2/0 or 3/0. All of these flies closely resemble the myriad species of small fish found among the weed.

When hooked on light tackle, the dolphin provides an aerial display second to none. It is often in the air more than the water, but when it tires of its airborne antics it will settle down and make long runs just beneath the surface.

Dolphin will also eagerly respond to a chum line. Often they move in to feed on chum destined for tuna, but many anglers chum expressly for them, particularly around the weed lines and floating debris. Dolphin like to take up residence in the shadow of not only weeds, but floating debris such as a wooden pallet, piling, or tree limb.

Most any fish may be used as chum. Cut the fish, into small pieces and chum sparingly. For hook baits, use a piece of the same fish you're using as chum. A 2/0 or 3/0 claw or beak hook tied to the end of your monofilament line, or to a short leader, works just fine. You'll often see the dolphin darting about, picking up the small pieces of chum. Dolphin are sterling light-tackle fish, and perfect for one-handed spinning or popping outfits.

Dolphin are not only fun to catch, but are great on the dinner table, too. Most often filleted, they have a very distinctive flavor.

Grouper

There are more than 400 species of grouper in the world. They are all included in this single heading simply because as bottom feeders they generally congregate in much the same areas and are fished for using basically the same techniques. America's anglers target the Nassau grouper, black grouper, red grouper, red hind, coney, cag grouper, yellowfin grouper (not to be confused with the yellowfin snapper) and rock hind. There are hundreds of additional species encountered off our coasts, most of which have bright coloration and which vary little from species to species, making exact identification difficult.

Some species of grouper frequent inshore waters and are occasionally landed by anglers fishing from piers and bridges or rocky breakwaters. By far the greatest number are taken from offshore reefs, wrecks and ridges. It prefers this bottom to open bottom, for there is always an abundance of forage.

Because grouper are usually caught in deep water and around bottom that will cut a line in an instant, light tackle is usually out of the question. Most veteran grouper anglers use medium or even heavy tackle. This enables them to hook a fish and promptly pump it away from the reef. If the fish reaches the sanctuary of the coral or rock, it will quickly cut the line.

The time-proven bottom rig most often used for grouper consists of an egg-shaped sinker sufficiently heavy to hold bottom, a small barrel swivel and 36 inches of 30- or 40-pound test monofilament leader material. A 4/0 through 7/0 claw or beak hook is then snelled to the leader.

Live baits are favored, although small fish or pieces of fish work well, too. Many grouper fishermen fill their live wells with pinfish, grunts, goggleyes, or jacks. The baits are hooked through the fleshy part of the back, just forward of the dorsal fin. Lowered to the bottom, it's usually just a matter of time until a hungry grouper ingests the bait. The key is permitting the grouper sufficient time to take the bait. As soon as it begins moving away, strike the fish and use a firm drag to lift it off the bottom and away from obstructions.

Grouper will readily respond to artificials, particularly the leadhead jig. This is about the only lure that can effectively be used to probe the depths. Leadhead jigs ranging in weight from 1 to 3 ounces are most often employed. Either bucktail

There are many species of grouper found in the warm waters of the Atlantic, Pacific and Gulf Coast. Fish like the one just landed by George Poveromo test an angler and his tackle to the limit. Grouper readily respond to live baits fished on the bottom, as well as chunk baits. Anglers also employ leadhead jigs with either bucktail or plastic tails. Grouper are great table fish.

skirts or plastic tails may be used effectively, as they impart action to the jig as it is worked in the depths. Many anglers use 30-pound line on their jigging rods. They double the end of their line, then use a double surgeon's knot to tie in a 4-foot piece of 50-pound leader, to which their jig is tied. Either setup enables an angler to fish a very firm drag.

A popular technique is to approach the peak of a coral head and to use wind or tide to carry the boat and drift away from it. The jig is lowered to the bottom and as soon as it touches down the reel is engaged and the jig lifted smartly, causing it to dart towards the surface. Strikes usually come within a few feet of the bottom and are a real jolt, as the grouper are very powerful. The angler is often assisted during a fight by having the boat drift away from the reef.

Most grouper have mild-flavored white meat and are delicious. Most are filleted and skinned, and then prepared in a variety of ways. The fish is frequently cut into chunks called "grouper fingers" and then dipped in batter and deep fried, and served with a horseradish cocktail sauce.

King mackerel

The king mackerel is a common target of boatmen and occasionally comes within range of shore-based anglers, particularly pier casters. Called "kingfish" in many areas, it attains a weight of 100 pounds, although specimens half that weight are considered big. Most range from 5 to 35 pounds. It is an extremely strong swimmer and is noted for its cart-wheeling leaps.

By far the majority of king mackerel are taken trolling. Medium-weight tackle is the norm, while balao and mullet are the favorite natural baits, along with strip baits. Baits are usually rigged with a pair of hooks, one behind the other, as the king mackerel has a notorious habit of chopping a baitfish in half when it strikes. Kings will also respond to spoons, leadhead and feathered jigs trolled deep, often with the aid of downriggers or monel wire line.

King mackerel will respond to a chum line of finely ground menhaden supplemented with chunks of balao. This technique works particularly well when the fish are schooled up, and you can either anchor or drift in an area where you receive good readings. It's almost a necessity to employ a leader of No. 8 or 9 stainless steel wire, for the king mackerel has extremely sharp teeth. Depending on the size of the king in residence, preferred hook sizes range from 3/0 through 7/0, with either whole or chunks of balao or mullet a favored bait.

Many anglers use two treble hooks attached to a 6-inch piece of stainless steel leader material. One treble is inserted into the head of the bait while the trailing treble is inserted well back in the bait near the tail. Few strikes are missed when a king crashes a bait rigged in this manner.

Each morning shrimp draggers who work off the Carolinas, Florida and the Gulf Coast anchor up and proceed to sort their catch. King mackerel, little tuna, amberjack and other species often move up to the stern of the draggers and enjoy a free lunch. Many boatmen obtain a couple of pails of the "trash" and employ it as chum.

Pier casters have developed a unique and successful method of catching king mackerel. They employ a breeches-buoy technique to carry a live bait well away from the pier. Employing heavy surf tackle and 20-pound-test line, they tie a small snap swivel directly to the end of their line. They then snap a 4-ounce pyramid sinker to the end of the line with a combination barrel swivel and coastlock snap tied to a 30-inch piece of 40- or 50-pound leader. A pair of treble hooks is attached to the terminal end of the leader. A live baitfish, such as a pinfish, mullet, menhaden, grunt or blue runner, is carefully hooked so that it may swim freely. Some anglers even employ a pair of live baitfish, rigged one behind the other.

At this point an extremely long cast is made seaward from the end of the pier, casting out only the sinker. The coastlock snap on the leader is slipped over the line, with leader and hooks and baitfish attached, and permitted to slide down the line into the water. With a nominal amount of slack line, the baitfish will continue to swim seaward, working anywhere from the surface to the bottom, where the sinker is holding secure. The baitfish will often swim freely back and forth along all of the line in the water, sending distress signals as it does, and is often assaulted by a cruising king mackerel. While this technique is used primarily in Florida and along the Gulf Coast, it may also be used when it's necessary to present live baits to striped bass, bluefish, channel bass and tarpon from bridges, piers, jetties and the surf.

King mackerel is an oily fish with a rather heavy flavor. When prepared for the table most are filleted, skinned and the dark meat of the lateral line removed. Care should be taken not to overcook the meat, or it will become dry and the flavor strong. Smoking with hickory chips is a favored way of preparing this gamefish.

King mackerel, often called kingfish, are extremely fast and respond to a variety of lures and baits. They're taken by trolling, chumming and jigging. Nick Stanczyk landed this 28-pound beauty held by Marc Ellis while using medium-weight spinning tackle while fishing out of Islamorada, Florida.

The king salmon is king among anglers fishing the waters of Oregon, Washington and Alaska. It is the biggest salmon, occasionally weighing 100 pounds. Deep trolling in ocean waters with the aid of a cannonball sinker or downriggers and cut herring is a popular technique.

King salmon

California, Oregon, Washington and Alaska anglers rate the king salmon as the outstanding catch of the Northwest. Rightly so, for this great game fish, while averaging 10 to 25 pounds in weight, can grow to 100 pounds. An ocean traveler, the king salmon, popularly called Chinook salmon throughout most of its range, migrates into rivers at various times throughout the year to spawn. Often it travels hundreds of miles inland to deposit and fertilize eggs in swift-moving water.

Sport fishermen do most of their salmon angling in the open Pacific or the many sounds, bays and mouths of rivers. Trolling is by far the most popular approach. For years the accepted technique was to troll plug-cut herring with breakaway 2- to 3-pound cannonball sinkers at 35- to 50-foot depths. Others used planers or wire line and trolling sinkers to get the herring to the desired depth. Some anglers still employ this technique, but the advent of the downrigger has allowed anglers to use lighter-weight outfits. The heavy cable of the downrigger easily gets the offering, usually a cut herring, small sardine or anchovy, down to the desired depth. When a fish is hooked, the downrigger clip releases the line and enables the angler to fight the fish unencumbered by heavy weights

When the salmon move into the rivers they provide fine sport for both shore base casters and boatmen. In the shallow water the king salmon can often be observed chasing bait. Spoons, plugs and leadhead jigs this size prove very effective.

Fly casters also also get in on the action, particularly when the king salmon move into the many river systems emptying into the Pacific.

Few will dispute that king salmon is high on the list of tasty seafood. Its meat has a delicate orange color and is mild and flavorful. Big kings are usually steaked, while the smaller fish are filleted, and may be broiled, grilled or steamed. Many anglers also smoke their salmon fillets, which are delicious.

You'll catch lingcod from waters close to shore and well out into depths of several hundred feet. Many fishermen employ a multi-hooked ganion rig baited with herring and taken to the bottom with a heavy sinker.

Lingcod

The lingcod ranges from California north to Alaska and is caught from shallow inshore waters way out to depths that exceed 75 fathoms. Long and slender with an unusually large mouth, it doesn't win much praise for its looks. It is, however, sufficiently plentiful to provide anglers who good action and a fine meal as a bonus.

Although it grows to more than 75 pounds, most of the lingcod are in the 5- to 25-pound range and are fun to catch.

For many years anglers employed a string of five or six baited hooks fished as a ganion and sent to the bottom with heavy sinkers. Herring and chunks of other fish were used for bait, and while the lingcod was the target, many rockfish were caught as a bonus. This kind of fishing requires heavy tackle, heavy sinkers and a cumbersome rig that often results in several fish being hooked at one time.

The advent of fine-diameter fishing lines has enabled bottom fishermen to use lighter sinker weights, and this has improved lingcod fishing considerably.

Drift fishing for lingcod has gained in popularity along the California, Oregon and Washington coasts. A stiff-action casting rod rated for 15- to 20-pound line and any one of a wide variety of chromed jigs are often used. The jigs are available in a wide variety of shapes, sizes and colors and, when matched with a medium-weight casting rod, they let the angler probe the depths with his jigs, working them just off the bottom. When you hook a 20-pound lingcod on a jig several hundred feet down, you'll have your hands full.

Lingcod and rockfish are both welcome treats. Their firm, white meat is tasty and can be cooked many ways.

Lou Cappadonna swings a little tunny aboard for Randy Hawtin, who hooked it while trolling from the author's "Linda June." Little tunny are plentiful and provide inshore fishermen with exciting action.

Little tunny

Little tunny is actually a family composed of several species, and is known by a variety of names, depending on where you fish for them. Little tuna, bonito and false albacore are the most common monickers. It is easily distinguished from the bluefin tuna, yellowfin tuna and long-finned albacore by the series of distinct black spots on the side of its body below the pectoral fin. Caught off California, along the Gulf Coast and the Atlantic north to New England, little tunny is pound-for-pound one of the strongest fish in the sea.

Averaging 3 to 10 pounds, little tunny is usually caught by anglers trolling for other members of the tuna clan and their traveling companions, the Atlantic and Pacific bonito. It readily responds to cedar jigs, trolling feathers, plastic skirts, spoons and leadhead jigs with plastic tails. It prefers a lure trolled at high speed, with the lures worked in a churning white wake behind the boat. When little tunny is plentiful in an area, anglers usually fish with light tackle in the 12- to 20-pound range.

Ground menhaden is most often the chum of choice, but most any ground fish will bring the fish within range. Often small spearing, sand eels, sardines or other fry are added to the chum, exciting the tunny as they vie for the offering. A fluorocarbon leader is often best for this hook-shy fish.

Light tackle anglers often have an opportunity to cast to surface feeding fish, and when little tunny are chasing bait they're wild and will readily strike a small stainless steel or chromed jig, or a leadhead jig. Fly casters find the little tunny will readily strike most any small fly that resembles the baitfish they're feeding on, including the Clouser, Deceiver and Blonde patterns.

Occasionally little tunny will raid the surf, chasing schools of mullet, menhaden, spearing and other baitfish along the beach. This offers one of the few occasions when surf casters can catch a tuna from the sand. Here too a fast retrieve is essential. Cast into feeding fish with a metal squid, stainless steel jig or chromed jig, with a teaser fished a couple of feet ahead of it. Sometimes the little tunny will ignore the primary lure and wallop the tiny teaser swimming ahead of it.

Little tunny have very dark meat, with a very heavy, strong flavor. Most every serious saltwater angler has at one time or another tried to prepare this fish for the table. Unfortunately, its flavor just doesn't compare with other tunas or mackerel. As such, there isn't even any commercial fishing pressure on the species, and it thrives through its range. Most anglers bring the fish to boat or beach and promptly release it.

Pacific amberjack

The Pacific Amberjack draws the same respect from anglers as its Atlantic Coast counterpart. A powerful fish, it frequents inshore waters where it is widely sought by anglers who fish the kelp beds and rocky, irregular coastline.

The majority of those landed by sport fishermen range from 5 to 20 pounds, and when taken on light spinning or casting tackle they provide a good account of themselves.

You've got to know the capability of your gear and fish with a firm drag when pursuing Pacific amberjack. Should the fish make a sustained run and reach the sanctuary of the kelp or a rocky outcropping, a severed line is often the result.

Live bait is unquestionably the most effective choice. Anchovies, small sardines, perch fry or any other small forage fry may be used and cast to structure that holds the roving jacks. Live crabs and shrimp may also be used for this formidable adversary.

As with its Atlantic cousin, the Pacific amberjack has a strong flavor, making it among the least desirable table fish. Some are filleted and smoked. The majority of these sporting jacks are released.

Pacific amberjack are typical of most members of the jack family, in that they are extremely strong, using their powerful bodies to test an angler's tackle. Many are taken trolling with small feathers and jigs, strip baits and rigged natural baits. Chumming and baiting with live anchovies is also a popular technique around the many Pacific Coast kelp beds.

The Pacific barracuda is very popular with inshore fishermen along the California coast. It responds to a variety of small lures, including plugs, leadhead jigs with plastic bait tails, chromed jigs and spoons. The barracuda also likes to frequent kelp beds and many are taken by anglers anchoring just off from the kelp and chumming and baiting with live anchovies.

Pacific barracuda

About the only similarity between the Pacific barracuda and its Atlantic name-sake is the name. The Pacific barracuda is long and slim, has fewer, and less formi-dable, teeth than the Atlantic and is a lightweight, most often weighing from 3 to 10 pounds. It is one of California's most popular sport and food fish, with huge quanti-ties being taken each summer.

It's a perfect match for light tackle. Most anglers employ spinning gear, which makes it easier to cast live baits such as anchovies and sardines, especially to the kelp beds. The Pacific barracuda also readily responds to lures. A fast retrieve with a small spoon or leadhead jig, or trolling along the inshore rocky coastline, results in exciting sport.

Unquestionably one of the most popular table fish landed by party boat anglers and private boatmen, the Pacific barracuda has delicate meat that works well for almost any recipe.

Pacific bonito

The Pacific bonito is assuredly a different species than its close cousin the Atlantic bonito, but distinguishing between the two is difficult. They are very simi-lar, not only in looks, but habits.

The Pacific species is somewhat smaller, averaging less than 7 pounds. While bonito is found in far offshore waters, the major fishing effort occurs inshore, off the rocky California coastline, and especially along the kelp beds of southern California. A schooling fish, the bonito often attacks schools of forage species such as anchovies, sardines and other fry, with hundreds of bonito literally chasing the baitfish into the air as they feed.

The bonito responds well to chum of baitfish such as anchovies. This is espe-cially true when a chum line is established by boats anchoring just off from the kelp beds. The bonito often cruises along the kelp, sometimes invading the thick growth as it seeks out an unsuspecting baitfish. At such times it will zero in on fry selec-tively tossed into the water between the boat and kelp. Once you get several bonito milling about the boat, it often appears that dozens more join in.

Pacific bonito is a favorite of inshore fishermen. Many are landed through chumming along the kelp beds of the southern California coast, particularly by party boat anglers. A live anchovy cast towards the kelp will often bring a response.

Many bonito are also caught through trolling, and respond particularly well to small spoons, feathers and jigs. Although they sometimes feed on the surface, it's often best to add a 3- or 4-pound trolling sinker to your line to keep the lures several feet below the surface. Most trollers fish a pair of lines tight to the transom, out on the face of the first or second wave. They'll have another pair of lines back 100 to 125 feet. When a fish is hooked the boat is slowed but not stopped, allowing other excited bonito to wallop the remaining lures.

Small chrome or stainless steel jigs and spoons are effective when cast to schooling fish chasing bait. They're also effective when worked while chumming with live bait and also bring strikes when cast along the edges of rocky outcroppings and kelp beds.

The key with fishing for Pacific bonito is using small baits, small lures and light tackle.

Many people enjoy filleted bonito, although it tends to have a heavier flavor than tuna.

Pacific halibut

The Pacific Halibut is certainly the largest flatfish you're apt to encounter while fishing the waters off the United States. It grows to 500 pounds. The majority landed by rod and reel anglers range from 50 to 150 pounds, although off Alaska many bigger fish are brought to gaff. Size and bag limits on both commercial and sport fishermen have resulted in a very viable fishery for this species, which ranges from central California north to Alaska, and across the Pacific.

The big flatfish loves deep water and often is found in depths to over 3,000 feet. Sport fishermen fishing inshore waters most often probe the 50- to 200-foot depths and enjoy fine sport while using natural baits. Herring is the most widely available and popular bait,

Pacific halibut is the heavyweight of the flatfish clan. This beauty landed by Bruce Holt off Washington struck a leadhead jig with a plastic tail. Big halibut are usually fished for on medium-weight tackle with multi-hook ganion rigs baited with chunks of herring.

Drift fishing enables you to cover a lot of bottom. The rewards include many bottom feeders, such as this heavyweight Pacific halibut. Bottom fishermen may fish with natural baits, or use lures to coax strikes while propelled by wind or current.

and constitutes a major portion of the halibut's diet.

This is heavy-tackle fishing for the most part. A standard 7-foot boat rod rated for 30- to 50-pound-class line is favored, although some anglers go heavier. With its broad, flat body, it's difficult to pump a halibut up from the bottom.

The standard bottom rig consists of a three-way swivel tied directly to the end of the line, with a heavy sinker tied to one eye of the swivel. It may take 2- and 3-pound sinkers because you've got to get your bait to the bottom in very deep water and often heavy currents make it difficult to hold bottom.

A 3- to 4-foot long piece of 80-pound test monofilament leader material is tied to the other end of the swivel and a 6/0 or 7/0 claw hook is snelled to the terminal end. Some anglers snell a pair of hooks to the leaders, separated by about 5 inches, which enables them to place the head of the herring on one hook and insert the trailing hook into the back of the herring.

Many halibut fishermen currently employ the stand-up tackle popularized by Southern California long-range party-boat fishermen. Favored are rods rated for the 30- to 50-pound class. Pacific halibut also respond to heavy jigs lowered to the bottom and slowly jigged as you drift along. While effective, this is hard work.

With the increased popularity of fly casting in recent years, some long-rod devotees have actually developed techniques where they chum the halibut up off the bottom in shallow water, then use a sinking fly line and large streamer fly to get into the depths where the halibut are feeding on the chum. This, too, is a tough way to catch a halibut, but landing a big flatfish on a fly rod can be plenty rewarding.

The halibut is ranked as one of the Pacific's finest table fish. It has mild, delicate meat that is easily steaked. The key is cooking it for just a short period of time, until it flakes when tested with a fork.

Veteran angler Bob Stearns likes to fish with light tackle and he's shown here just having subdued a very big Pacific sailfish on a light casting outfit with 16-pound-test line off Golfito, Costa Rica. Most anglers employ 30-pound tackle and troll lures or skip baits for the sails, almost all of which are released.

Pacific sailfish

As with so many species, it's difficult to distinguish the Pacific sailfish from its Atlantic counterpart. There is, however, quite a difference in size. The Pacific sailfish grows to a huge 250 pounds and more, while its cousin to the east checks in at around half that weight.

Their habits are much the same. Pacific Sailfish prefer warm waters off Southern California and the Baja Peninsula and Sea of Cortez. Caught primarily by trolling rigged mackerel or flying fish baits, they're excellent light-tackle fish, with most anglers employing 20- or 30-pound outfits.

Trolling rigged baits streamed from outriggers is the most popular technique employed, although some anglers use live baits caught right on the grounds, especially small jacks, dolphin and bonito.

Predominately a surface feeder, the sailfish is attracted to trolled baits. Many anglers have taken to trolling with hookless natural baits to lure the sailfish, and then use fly-casting tackle to present a larger streamer fly to the excited fish. This technique requires practice and perfect precision and timing between the boat captain, cockpit crew and angler.

It is, unquestionably, one of the most exciting fish to take on the fly. When it strikes a hookless bait and suddenly has it pulled away, it excitedly charges about looking for its lost prey. The revved-up fish will often turn its attention to a fly and attack with vengeance, resulting in an exciting strike and sterling aerial display.

Most Pacific sailfish are released, which helps preserve this great species.

The author landed this permit, estimated to weigh 30 pounds, while fishing with Lori Kelly Parker, the first woman guide in the Florida Keys. The big fish was quickly returned to the water, as are most fish caught from Parker's "New Wave."

Permit

Of all the species included in this compilation of favorites, the permit, both Atlantic and Pacific species, is perhaps the least plentiful. Still, as a tough, wary adversary, they are ranked by all who have fished for them as a formidable target.

The Atlantic permit is the larger of the two species, growing to 50 pounds. The Pacific variety grows to about 20 pounds. On the Atlantic the permit is found in greatest numbers through south Florida and the Keys and throughout the Bahamas. Southern California anglers enjoy the greatest success as the permit is primarily a warm-water species.

The most exciting permit fishing is found throughout the Florida Keys, where it is stalked from shallow flats skiffs in water less than 3 feet deep. The permit frequents the flats on a flooding tide, rooting in the bottom for crabs and the shrimp found in the warm, clear waters. While it is more difficult, many anglers don a bathing suit and a pair of sneakers and wade the flats as they stalk the wily permit.

As permit root on the bottom its forked tail often breaks the surface. This presents a target to the angler poised in the bow of a flats boat. A careful presentation is essential in order to avoid spooking the fish.

Newcomers most often employ a shrimp or crab as bait on the flats. The crabs should be about 2 inches, point-to-point, with the pincer claws removed. A light- or medium-weight spinning outfit is used, with a 3-foot piece of 30-pound-test fluorocarbon leader tied in at the terminal end and finished with a 2/0 or 3/0 claw-style hook. The hook is pushed through the underside of the crab and brought out the top of the shell near the point. The angler must anticipate the direction in which the permit is moving, and casts to within 3 or 4 feet of the feeding fish. As the crab lands, it will still have mobility to swim about, but should be permitted to rest if it lands close to the permit.

When the permit finds the crab it may engulf it in a flash. The permit has a very tough mouth, so it's important to set the hook forcefully and to fish with a firm drag, maintaining maximum pressure on the fish. The initial run will test your tackle to the utmost. When the first run is over it's important to immediately pressure the fish to gain line, for if you don't it'll again peel line at unbelievable speed. The permit's broad body gives it awesome power for a fish its size.

Anglers who prefer artificials may present leadhead jigs with bucktail skirts tied to resemble a crab. Many of these jigs have a delta-wing design that enables an angler to "swim" them in the very shallow water.

Fly casters rate landing a permit on a long rod as a sterling accomplishment. Flies are tied to resemble the crabs and shrimp on which the permit feeds.

The permit is also found in deep water, such as the channels along the flats and offshore in the area of wrecks and reefs. In these locations the fish are often chummed within range using discards obtained from shrimp trawlers.

A favorite bait culled from the trash is the large mantua shrimp, which when drifted back with the chum regularly produce strikes from hungry permit.

The permit is so highly regarded as a gamefish that the great majority are brought to boat and quickly released.

The porgy, also called a scup, can be found in the middle and north Atlantic Coast. It is a fine table fish that is caught in great numbers by bottom fishermen with a light spinning or popping outfit, with a high-low rig baited with bits of clam, bloodworm or sandworm.

Porgy

Atlantic anglers from New England through Florida and the Bahamas enjoy fishing for the popular porgy. There are two primary species: The scup, found throughout the northern Atlantic Coast, and its close cousin, the jolthead porgy found further south. They are very similar in looks and habits, with the scup the smaller of the two, ranging from 1 to 3 pounds. The jolthead grows to 8 pounds or more.

Primarily a bottom feeder, it sets up residence on rocky, irregular bottom, where mussels and other food are plentiful. Their favorite haunts are reefs and ridges. Great numbers are also caught from the many man-made artificial reefs that have been constructed along the Atlantic coast. The construction debris, old ships, tanks and weighted tires attract a variety of marine growth, which attracts the scup and joltheads. Thousands may gather on just a tiny patch of bottom.

It's fun to fish for these scrappy bottom feeders with light tackle. A popping outfit is ideal. Terminal rigging consists of a high-low rig, with a pair of beak or claw-style snelled hooks attached to the rig, with one hook right on the bottom and the second, or high hook, 12 to 18 inches off the bottom. Hook size should be tailored to the size of the fish in residence, with a No. 6 or 8 ideal for palm-sized porgies and a No. 3 or 4 for big "shad porgies" or joltheads. Sinkers should be just heavy enough to hold bottom while you're anchored over choice bottom. A bank or dipsey-style sinker is often best.

You'll find that porgies aren't fussy when it comes to bait. They will strike pieces of clam, sandworms and bloodworms, squid, conch and snails. They're adept at stealing a bait from your hook. Many anglers soak their clams in a salt brine solution to harden the bait and make it more difficult to strip from the hook. Some fishermen use conch or snails instead, as both have very tough meat. The porgy has a small mouth, so use small pieces of bait.

As you lower the bait to the bottom keep a taut line and be prepared for a strike the instant it touches down. An angler who isn't prepared to strike can lose a bait without realizing it's happened.

When caught on a light outfit, porgies will give a good account of themselves and it's not unusual to catch doubleheaders.

Porgies have firm, delicious meat. They also have quite a few bones, so most anglers carefully fillet them. The meat freezes well, making the porgy a choice species for stocking the freezer late in the fall as the season begins to wane.

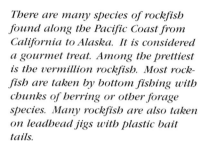

There are many species of rockfish found along the Pacific Coast from California to Alaska. It is considered a gourmet treat. Among the prettiest is the vermillion rockfish. Most rockfish are taken by bottom fishing with chunks of herring or other forage species. Many rockfish are also taken on leadhead jigs with plastic bait tails.

Rockfish

Worldwide there are reportedly more than 250 species of rockfish. Much like the grouper, the broad designation "rockfish" applies to all species for purposes of this discussion. They are all very similar in habit. Along the California, Oregon, Washington and Alaska coast there are perhaps 50 species landed by sport fishermen.

It is fair to say that the rockfish clan are the darlings of anglers who like their catch for the dinner table. Most rockfish have white, mild flavored meat that is truly delicious.

Rockfish frequent rocky bottom close to shore, but the greatest concentrations are located offshore, where they frequent depths from 100 to more than 5,000 feet. The depth at which they're found is the only negative in fishing for rockfish, as the angler must use heavy tackle out of necessity. To take a baited hook down several hundred feet, the depths at which most sport anglers fish, requires a very heavy bank or dipsey-style sinker.

Many rockfishermen employ stand-up style rods with 30- to 50-pound-class rods very popular. Some use throw-lever drag reels which, while designed for big-game fishing, are strong and have fast retrieve ratios. Dacron and monofilament lines may be used in this type of fishing. In recent years, however, the fine-diameter braided lines made of high-tech filaments have found favor. Lines made of microfilament and thermofused filament are often only 1/4 the diameter of monofilament or Dacron. They're extremely strong and have practically no stretch, which enables you to feel the strike of even a small rockfish in great depths. The new lines are excellent, but it requires a bit of patience to get used to them after changing over from heavier lines.

Terminal rigging most often consists of a ganion rig with 4 to 10 snelled hooks looped to the main line via dropper loops at intervals of 12 to 18 inches. This is rugged fishing and most anglers have their hooks snelled to 18 inches of 50-pound-test monofilament or fluorocarbon leader. Beak, claw-style and live-bait hooks work best. Seldom are hooks smaller than 1/0, with 4/0 through 6/0 the most common.

At the terminal end a large sinker loop is tied into the line with a sinker heavy enough to reach bottom. Depending on wind and tidal currents, it may be necessary to use anywhere from 16 to 32 ounces of weight, with bank, dipsey and cannonball style sinkers favored. The key is keeping your line as near perpendicular to the bottom as possible, hence the need for the heavy sinkers in very deep water. If you use too light a lead, the baits will tend to balloon off the bottom as you drift.

Herring and squid are among the favored baits. Use a fresh bait that is tough. Fishing at great depths, you don't want a soft bait that is easily ripped from the hook. Many anglers soak their herring and squid in a heavy brine solution made of kosher salt and fresh water. An overnight soaking is often sufficient, and really toughens the bait.

Rockfishing is fun fishing. In one day you're apt to catch a half dozen or more species, many of which are brilliantly colored and put up a good fight while being brought up from the depths. They're fine table fare and freeze very well.

Sand bass

The sand bass, and its close cousin the kelp bass, is found in substantial numbers among the kelp beds off California and Mexico's Baja Coast. It averages under 10 pounds, but gives a good account of itself considering its size.

Many party boats target both species, as do private boatmen, by anchoring just off from the kelp beds. The trick is to employ live anchovies, tiny sardine fry, perch or other small baitfish as chum. The live baits are tossed between the boat and the kelp and often will entice the bass to move out of the heavy growth to pick up an easy meal.

Spinning tackle is popular. Medium- and lightweight outfits work well because they can easily cast the anchovy a reasonable distance. The key is keeping the anchovy swimming near the surface, occasionally pulling it back as it seeks the sanctuary of the kelp. This excited activity of the bait and the distress signal it emits often attracts the kelp bass to investigate.

As both daytime and nocturnal feeders, many sand bass and kelp bass are taken on the night party packets that specialize in this type of fishing.

Sand bass and kelp bass will also strike artificials, especially small chromed spoons and leadhead jigs. Light tackle is the key, but a firm drag is essential to keep a hooked bass from reaching the kelp and entangling your line. As is typical of members of the bass family, these saltwater fish are both enjoyable to catch and a treat for dinner.

Sea bass

In recent years the population of sea bass along the middle and north Atlantic Coast has made a remarkable recovery. Many anglers feel there are more of these popular bottom feeders in the sea than ever before. While it prefers a habitat of rocky, broken, irregular bottom and ledges, it's the artificial reef programs of coastal states that have expanded the habitat, and the population, of the sea bass.

The sea bass, often called the black sea bass, is a rather small bottom feeder usually weighing 1 to 3 pounds. Smaller sea bass are occasionally found in bay and river waters, but the species is essentially an ocean dweller, summering inshore and moving offshore to the edge of the continental shelf during the winter months. They provide boatmen with fishing opportunities 12 months a year.

Conventional tackle is favored, with a light popping outfit and levelwind casting reel ideal in waters ranging from 10 to 50 feet deep. A light sinker is normally

Linda and Bob Rosko were just 11 and 7 years old when they visited California for the first time. Here they fished with their parents aboard a half-day party packet out of San Diego and enjoyed catching plentiful sand bass. Sand bass are especially popular among party boat fishermen as it's easy to put together a nice catch of fine table fish.

adequate. When the sea bass is located around deep water wrecks or ledges 100 to 250 feet down, a medium-weight party-boat rod is the tool of choice. Spectra filament line enables an angler to detect the strike of even a small sea bass, or the porgies that are often in residence on the same grounds.

The most popular terminal tackle for sea bass is a high-low rig. A pair of snelled hooks with 12- to 18-inch leaders are used. Beak or claw-style hooks 1/0 or 2/0 are most popular. A sinker loop is tied into the terminal end of the line ahead of a pair of dropper loops—one just a couple of inches from the sinker loop and another 18 inches above the first. One snelled hook is slipped onto the low or bottom loop, and the second is slipped onto the high, or upper loop. The sea bass isn't particular when it comes to choice of food. It normally feeds on mussels, clam spores, crabs, squid and the fry of other species found on rocky bottom and around wrecks. Strips of fresh squid are a popular bait, as are small pieces of clam, mussel, bloodworms, sandworms, conch, and snails. Many anglers harden their squid, clam or mussel baits in a kosher salt brine solution, letting the baits stand overnight while refrigerated.

You've got to be alert for often as you lower your rig to the bottom the sea bass will be after the bait in an instant. Be prepared to lift back smartly with your rod tip to set the hook. During a hot bite on a good patch of bottom it's not unusual to catch a sea bass on each of your baited hooks.

Sea bass will often strike artificials and many anglers employ a popping outfit and small leadhead jig with a plastic tail or a small chromed diamond or stainless steel jig. Jigging works particularly well when the sea bass is feeding on small bait-

The sea bass is the darling of bottom fishermen along the middle and north Atlantic Coast. Found in great numbers around the many artificial reefs along the seacoast and on rocky ridges and ledges, they provide lots of action to inshore fishermen during summer and on the offshore grounds during winter. A high-low rig baited with squid or clam is the favorite.

fish that are often found around wrecks.

Sea bass is considered one of the tastiest fish in the sea and has firm, white meat that keeps very well when frozen.

Sharks

There are more than 250 species of shark found in the waters of the world. The differences between species are often so subtle that only a trained marine biologist can distinguish one variety from another. Sharks differ from the other sportfish because they lack true skeletons. Their bodies are supported by cartilage rather than bones.

Sharks are quite properly called the most vicious fish in the sea. They are primitive creatures often intent on eating anything that doesn't eat them first. They can travel in schools, following other fish and culling the schools of sick or wounded fish that can't keep up. They serve a purpose in the scheme of things and certainly participate in the theory of "survival of the fittest." For if a fish can't keep up, it quickly becomes prey for one of the many sharks in the sea.

Many years ago, sharks were considered a nuisance by sport fishermen. Over time many anglers recognized the great enjoyment that could be achieved while stalking sharks, and in turn the fine dinner table qualities of some sharks.

The International Game Fish Association has recognized several species of shark as being among the most prominent sought by anglers. Included are the mako

Many species of shark are found on all three U.S. coasts and most provide fine offshore action. Moments after this photo was taken the wire leader was cut and this blue shark was set free. Most fishermen practice catch-and-release with sharks. Safety should always be a priority when handling sharks.

family, the blue, thresher, great white, porbeagle, hammerhead and tiger. These are the big sharks, ranging from 100 to over 2,000 pounds. The pelagic sharks usually stay in open water and often travel thousands of miles in their lifetimes.

There are, however, many other species of shark sought by fishermen, including the blacktip, bonito, bonnethead, lemon, leopard and dusky, to name a few. There are many other species, almost all of which provide exciting sport when hooked on tackle suited to their respective size.

On the offshore grounds it is customary to employ 50-pound-class tackle when challenging sharks often weighing over 200 pounds. Inshore and on the flats, where 20- to 50-pound specimens are encountered, light- and medium-weight spinning and conventional tackle is more appropriate.

All sharks are dangerous. You're dealing with a primitive fish that has vicious teeth and for the most part is impervious to pain. Even hours after being caught and resting on the dock, sharks are capable of inflicting serious injury. Treat all sharks with great care, even hours after they are caught, and absolutely never place any body parts, hands and feet especially, near their mouths.

Sharks are extremely smell-sensitive and are readily attracted to wounded or dead fish. Because of this, they're instinctively attracted to a chum spread of either ground or chunked fish, or a combination of both. Ground menhaden, herring, mackerel, sardines and other forage species are a favorite, as their oily meat establishes a distinctive slick that attracts many species of shark.

Chumming is done from party, charter and private boats, mostly in the open ocean. Because the sharks often travel with schools of mackerel, bluefish, tuna and other migratory species, it's wise to establish a chum slick in areas frequented by these species and to drift along, carried by wind or current and dispensing chum as you go. Eventually, the sharks are attracted to the chum and move within range. You may see them finning on the surface as they search for the source of food, and they'll occasionally come within a rod's length of the boat while searching for the source of the chum. They are most vulnerable to a properly presented bait when they are excited by the chum.

Terminal rigging begins with a ball-bearing swivel tied to the end of your line. The swivel is important, as sharks have a notorious habit of twisting up in the leader, and this violent twist can transfer to the line if you don't have a quality swivel.

Construction of the leader is important. Sharks can bite through monofilament or fluorocarbon, so it is essential to use either single-strand stainless steel or stainless steel cable leader material.

The length of the leader should always exceed the length of the sharks you anticipate catching. An average leader length for pelagic sharks is 10 feet. Leaders are usually built in two 5-foot sections, using a ball-bearing swivel to join the sections. This gives you two ball-bearing swivels -- one at the terminal end of the line and the other at the midpoint of the leader. The long leader also prevents the shark's sandpaper-like skin from fraying the line.

Wire and cable testing in the range of 200 to 300 pounds is adequate for leaders. Forged hooks such as the Sea Demon and Sea Mate in 8/0 through 10/0 are most often used. These hooks have a knife edge, long point and a brazed ring, all of which helps prevent hook failure when fighting a big shark.

Either whole fish or fillets may be used as bait, with many preferring the latter. While fresh bait is most effective for most species of fish, sharks are different. They generally react better to a smelly, decomposing bait.

Veteran shark fishermen use rigging thread or dental floss to tie the bait to their hook and prevent a shark from ripping the bait from the hook. Anglers often fish with three or four outfits while drifting along and chumming. The baits are set at intervals of 50, 100, 150 and 200 feet from the boat, at varying depths of the same distance. This usually puts a bait within a range of whatever water column the shark is cruising.

Inflated toy balloons are used to suspend the bait at the desired depth. Occasionally, when the current is swift, a sinker is attached to the leader to help keep the line as near perpendicular as possible.

It can be a lengthy wait before sharks arrive, so rods are usually placed in holders, with the reel's audible clicker engaged. When the shark takes off quickly with the bait, the drag is engaged and the shark struck repeatedly. Much the same technique is used for smaller sharks inshore and in protected bay and sound waters. Sharks also will strike trolled baits and artificials, although they are usually an accidental catch.

Sharks are particularly dangerous at boatside. Gaffing is the preferred landing method, and a tail rope is helpful in preventing the fish from thrashing about. The safest approach is to tie-off the shark in the water and avoid bringing it aboard.

Many sharks have a very strong flavor and an ammonia-like odor that makes them less than desirable for the dinner table. There are exceptions, however, as is the case with mako sharks, which are delicious. Unless a shark is destined for the table, it's best to use a pair of pliers to cut the leader and let it go. Never attempt to remove the hook. It eventually will rust out, and you don't risk severe injury.

The time may well come when a complete moratorium—as I have advocated for many years—on both sport and commercial landings of pelagic sharks will be imposed to enable these great gamefish to return to former population levels.

Silver salmon

The silver salmon is coveted by West Coast sport fishermen, ranking slightly behind the king salmon in popularity. It's smaller than the king, averaging 6 to 12 pounds. What it lacks in size the silver salmon, often called coho salmon, makes up for in fighting ability. It is an extremely active jumper that will take to the air repeatedly when hooked on light tackle.

Unlike the king salmon, which has a broad range, the silver salmon is a stay-at-home fish that seldom strays far from its birthplace in the coastal rivers of the Pacific Northwest. It feeds aggressively both in the open ocean and the rivers where it hatched. It does not feed on its spawning run, and as is typical of West Coast salmon, dies soon after spawning.

Trolling is the most popular method of catching silver salmon, and huge schools are often located deep in the water column in open ocean waters. Planers, downriggers, cannonball sinkers and wire line are just a few of the devices used to take lures and natural baits down to the depths at which the silvers are feeding.

Chromed spoons, deep-diving swimming plugs and leadhead jigs trolled behind wobbling spoons and spinners annually account for many silvers. Utilize deep-probing devices to get the lures to the depths where the fish are feeding. Fish-finding equipment can be very helpful when you're trying to discover where these fish might be feeding. Natural-bait anglers rig whole herring or plug-cut herring

Modern fishfinding electronics enable Northwest salmon anglers to cruise until they locate schools of fish. This angler used a conventional casting outfit to coax a strike from a big silver, which is caught both in the open ocean and in coastal river systems.

with the heads removed. Downriggers or cannonball quick-release sinkers help take the baits to the bottom.

When the fish are feeding 40 to 60 feet beneath the surface, they may also be coaxed into striking a chromed jig. This requires experimentation on the part of the angler, but on a good day you can experience a hit each time your lure reaches the strike zone. The key is slowly lowering your jig, while imparting action to it, and on the retrieve giving it action by smartly lifting your rod tip and then letting the jig fall.

Perhaps the most exciting silver salmon fishing of all occurs in coastal rivers. The swift-running rivers often swarm with feeding fish, accompanied by diving gulls that identify just where the schools are located. This is one of the few times that shore-based fly casters can regularly run up good scores. Some choose to fish from small boats and ease up to the surface-feeding fish and cast streamers. The silvers will respond to most any saltwater fly tied to resemble a small silvery baitfish. Size 1/0 through 3/0 hooks are favored.

Silver salmon are great on the dinner table. A special repast is to fillet the salmon and delicately smoke it in apple wood or hickory wood chips.

Snapper

The snapper family shares many traits with the grouper family. There are many different species and they thrive on many of the same reefs, wrecks and rocky or coral outcroppings. They're abundant from the Carolinas to Florida on the Atlantic, across the Gulf coast to Texas, and in the waters of the Bahamas, Bermuda and the Caribbean. On average they're smaller in size, although species such as the mutton snapper occasionally tip the scale at 25 pounds or more. The Cubera snapper at twice that weight.

For purposes of this discussion the snappers are grouped together, for anglers generally employ the same techniques and fish the same grounds. It is not unusual to land several different species of this popular bottom feeder during a day of fishing.

Among the more popular snappers are the yellowtail, silk, red, blackfin, mangrove, Lane, dog, gray and black. While some species of snapper are landed by pier and bridge-based anglers, by far the greatest numbers are landed by boatmen fishing over choice bottom. When drifting, avoid sand bottom, for if you're off the mark by just a short distance you'll draw a blank.

Killick, grapple or reef anchors made of construction rod help in anchoring on a reef. These devices snag the irregular reef and when it's time to leave the boat is backed down, and the soft iron rods are easily straightened and pulled free. Back at dockside they're bent back into shape for future use. Ordinary anchors can be virtually impossible to release from the coral or rock.

Anglers can bottom fish, chum the snapper to the surface, or employ artificials. Select light- or medium-weight spinning or conventional tackle rated for 10- to 20-pound line. The snapper is a formidable adversary that can provide lots of sport, but too often anglers use gear that is too heavy. Heavy gear is great if you hook a really big fish, but it detracts from the challenge when fighting average-size fish.

Chumming will bring snapper off the bottom in search of a meal. Chum works to the angler's advantage in several ways. It not only attracts the fish, but gets them away from the sharp coral and rock, where they can easily fray or entangle your line.

The easiest way to chum a reef is to first purchase a frozen block of ground menhaden. The frozen block is then inserted in a mesh bag and lowered over the side on a rope tied off to a cleat. You may supplement the ground chum with a nominal amount of diced pieces of fresh fish such as little tunny, mackerel or menhaden, or small pieces of shrimp. The key is to attract the snappers, not feed them, so chum sparingly.

A claw or beak-style hook with a baitholder shank is tied directly to the end of a monofilament line, or preferably to a length of fluorocarbon leader. Hook size is determined by the run of snappers in residence. You want to use a tough bait, as a snapper will strip a soft bait from your hook in an instant. A favorite bait of party and charter boat skippers is a small piece freshly cut from a little tunny (bonito).

Work the strip of bait through the hook twice and permit it to drift out with the current and chum. If the current is swift, add a small rubber-cored sinker to the line to take the bait to intermediate depths. Conversely, if there is very little current, a small float may be added to the line to keep the bait drifting along at a desired level.

For bottom fishing, as is most often practiced by the party boat and charter boat fleet, an egg-shaped sinker can be slipped onto the line. Then a small barrel swivel is tied to the terminal end of the line, followed by 24 to 36 inches of 20- or 30-pound test fluorocarbon leader and an appropriate hook. Lift back smartly to set the hook as quickly as a strike is telegraphed up the line. Any hesitation will result in a lost bait.

Small leadhead jigs with plastic bait tails or bucktail-skirted leadheads also bring strikes. Cast the jig out and permit it to settle to the bottom, and retrieve it with a whip retrieve. Keep repeating the procedure until the bait reaches the surface. Strikes will come anywhere from the bottom to the surface. It's not unusual to see several excited snapper chasing the jig until one finally decides to grab it. Then the fun begins!

There are few fish that can match the snapper as a gourmet treat. Firm, tasty white meat makes them a choice regardless of how you like your fish prepared. They also hold extremely well when frozen.

Most snapper, like this mutton snapper, feed around the clock. Many party boats, like the Yankee Capts. out of Key West, specialize in night fishing. Live pinfish and goggleyes are the favorite baits.

Charlie Waterman is one of America's foremost fly fishermen and he just loves to fish the Florida Everglades. Here he's just landed a fine snook that he coaxed from the overhanging mangroves. Fly fishing enables an angler to make a precise presentation, especially important when targeting species such as snook, tarpon, bonefish, redfish and permit.

Snook

The snook frequents the waters of Florida and some sections of the Gulf Coast and is popular because it is an inshore species and readily accessible to most anglers. It's most often found in the protected reaches of bays and rivers, although its frequents the inlets and open ocean and gulf, usually within a half mile of the beach. It is also found in the maze of waters of the Everglades and many river systems in Central America.

The snook is landed on the wide range of tackle employed by inshore fishermen who do their angling from boats, jetties, piers, bridges and the beach. Casting with either a popping or spinning outfit and surface swimming plugs, darters and poppers is popular. The snook frequents flats adjacent to river channels, weed beds and mangroves located in coastal estuaries. Often the snook lies motionless in the shadows, waiting for an unsuspecting baitfish to happen by.

Accurate casts are required to place the lure right up against the shoreline or mangroves. An erratic retrieve should be used to work in a manner that resembles a frightened baitfish scurrying away. A snook's strike at a surface lure is spectacular and usually accompanied by a series of jumps that take it clear of the water. It's essential to fish a firm drag and immediately pressure the fish away from the mangrove stumps or other obstacles. The snook has an uncanny ability to secure its freedom by entangling your line in the nearest obstacle.

Fly fisherman will find snook to their liking, too. It's often possible to sight cast to fish, or to simply blind cast into spots where overhanging mangroves leave a shadow on the water. Most of the saltwater streamer flies, sliders and poppers will bring strikes.

Pinfish, squirrel fish, shrimp and mullet are the most popular live baits.

A favorite method of rigging is to tie a 36- to 48-inch piece of 30-pound-test fluorocarbon leader to the end of your line. This is best accomplished by doubling the last 2 feet of a 12-to 15-pound-test line, and then employ a double surgeon's knot to attach the fluorocarbon.

Hook live shrimp lightly through the collar on their back. If the shrimp are dead, thread them onto the hook. With live bait fish there are several methods of hooking the bait: running the hook through the lower jaw and out the upper, in one eye socket and out the other, or placing the hook through the back just forward of the dorsal fin.

When fishing from a boat you can just cast out the bait and permit it to swim about as you drift over productive water. Bridge and pier fishermen lower their baits so they swim just beneath the surface.

If you're fishing along channel edges or where the water is deep, you can add a sinker between line and leader to keep the bait down near the bottom. When drifting or fishing in the shallows, some anglers employ a float and position it so that the baitfish swims just off the bottom.

Snook is fine table fare. It may be baked whole, steaked or filleted. Filleting is particularly popular, for when the skin is removed you can then easily remove the dark lateral line of red meat that runs the length of the fish.

Spotted weakfish is called trout or sea trout throughout much of its range. It is an inshore species found in bay and sound waters and especially where there is an abundance of weed beds.

Spotted weakfish

The spotted weakfish frequents much the same range as the channel bass and snook. It is also called the trout, speckled trout or sea trout, and is a close cousin of the weakfish or gray trout caught along the middle and north Atlantic Coast. As an inshore species, it finds favor among small boat anglers, pier and jetty fishermen, flats fishermen and beach casters.

Most spotted weakfish weigh from 1 to 6 pounds and are made to order for the light-tackle angler. There are occasions when you'll be fortunate enough to tangle with a 10- to 12-pound beauty, but this is the exception. A one-handed spinning outfit, popping outfit or a No. 8 or 9 fly-fishing outfit is ideal for most situations.

The spotted weakfish frequents shallow bays and rivers and the oceanside flats and shallows of the middle Atlantic and Gulf Coasts, seldom venturing more than a half mile from land. It has a very soft mouth, as does the weakfish, and must be handled with a light drag to prevent the hook from pulling free. When a big one is hooked, it's important to employ a landing net. Attempting to lift it from the water by the hook alone will often rip it free and the fish will be lost.

Drifting live shrimp across shallow grass beds in bays and rivers is a very popular technique. A 24- to 36-inch fluorocarbon leader is paired with a No. 1 or 1/0 claw or beak hook.

Often a splasher-float with a concave head is used to make a surface commotion as you pull back with your rod tip. This is used to suspend the bait at the desired level, usually just a foot or so off the bottom or above the grass. If the current is strong, many anglers add a small rubber-cored sinker to the leader, ensuring that it stays perpendicular to the bottom.

Live shrimp are hooked through the collar on their backs, although dead shrimp bring strikes, too. Dead shrimp are threaded on the hook, with just the hook point exposed. Big trout some anglers use live small pinfish, mullet or spot with good results.

Blind casting while drifting along and using leadhead jigs, small spoons or plugs also provides exciting sport. Although spotted weakfish will strike surface plugs, they usually feed near the bottom or in the middle of the water column. Leadhead jigs with plastic tails, bucktail jigs, and deep-diving plugs work best. The key is working your lure so it resembles a wounded baitfish or shrimp darting about.

Many anglers employ live grass shrimp as chum. While grass shrimp aren't always available, you can purchase small dead shrimp in your local fish market and use them as an effective chum. It's wise to cut the shrimp into small pieces, about the size of your pinky's nail, and to distribute them overboard sparingly, to be carried by the current from your anchored boat, or even from a bridge or pier.

Most anglers either tie their hook to the end of their monofilament line or to a short length of fluorocarbon leader material, bait up with a shrimp, and permit the current to carry it along with the chum. Occasionally a splasher-float is added if there is little current, or a rubber-cored sinker if the current is swift.

The spotted weakfish has a mild flavor. The meat tends to soften quickly, and special care should be taken to keep it on ice. It does not freeze well because of its soft texture.

The striped bass could well be America's favorite gamefish. It's found on all three U.S. coasts and has adapted to southern impoundments. It frequents bays, sounds and rivers, the surf and open ocean.

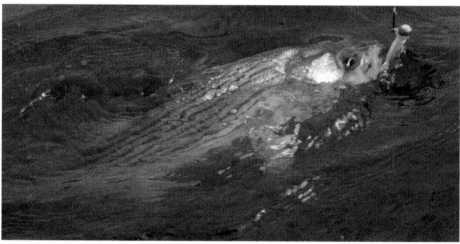

Striped Bass

The striped bass is unquestionably one of the most popular saltwater game fish in the U.S. It is found in large numbers from Maine to Florida's St. John's River, and sections of the Gulf Coast, from Florida to Louisiana. It was transplanted to the Pacific Coast in 1886 from juvenile stocks netted in New Jersey's Navesink River. The Pacific population has grown and the major fishery is located in the San Francisco Bay region, although stripers are caught from Los Angeles north to the Columbia River in Washington.

Stripers are also found in impoundments such as the Santee-Cooper Reservoir in South Carolina and the Kerr Reservoir in North Carolin. They breed successfully there and grow to large sizes in fresh water.

The striper is an inshore species that is caught using practically every technique found in this book. An angler may not only use the tackle of his choice, but use lures or natural baits, and catch this "prince of the unpredictables" from the surf, jetties, piers, bridges and boats. An angler with leisure time can repair to the coast and enjoy action at almost any time of the day or night from early spring until early winter.

While not a spectacular fighter, the striped bass will test the skills of an angler and his tackle. Many anglers choose tackle that is far too heavy. Fishermen catch stripers ranging anywhere from 3 to 50 pounds, and it can be a real challenge when a heavyweight is hooked on light gear.

Surf, pier, bridge and jetty casters employ natural baits fished on the bottom. Clams, squid, bloodworms, sandworms, crabs, shrimp, and chunks of herring or menhaden all produce well. Many casters also use live baits such as eels, mullet, herring, menhaden, mackerel, croakers, spot and scup. Many boat fishermen employ these same baits to score with stripers, and often use chunks of these baits as chum.

Drifting live baits from party, charter and private boats has gained in popularity in recent years. Trolling, too, is a very effective technique. In ocean waters, where the stripers are often found in 30- to 50-foot depths, wire-line trolling is often used to take lures to the depths at which the fish are feeding, especially where strong tidal currents form rips and eddies. Downriggers also probe the depths and are an alternative to wire line.

Fine trolling action is also enjoyed in the many tidal bays and rivers along the coast, where the fish are usually smaller in size and anglers may employ a popping outfit and a variety of plugs, spoons and leadhead jigs and bait tails.

Casting lures provides perhaps the most exciting striped bass fishing of all. The stripers often travel in sizable schools and will chase schools of menhaden, rainfish, herring and other forage species to the surface, where a feeding frenzy of stripers and sea gulls breaks out.

This exciting fishing is made to order for the fly caster, too. Flies tied to imitate small baitfish, like the Clouser, Half and Half, Deceiver, Popovic Slider and Poppers, can bring fast action.

Striped bass are great sporting and table fish. The striper's firm, white meat may be prepared in many ways. Larger fish are often steaked, while the smaller ones are filleted. In filleting, make certain to remove the dark meat along the lateral line after the fish has been skinned. Many cooks prepare a fine fish chowder from stripers and the tasty meat is often used as a crab substitute for deep-fried crab cakes.

The striped marlin is an exciting acrobat that provides Pacific Coast anglers with sterling sport on light tackle. A tag is about to be placed in the back of this marlin with the aid of a tagging stick. Tagging helps biologists track movements and growth patterns.

Striped marlin

To the Pacific Coast angler the striped marlin is the answer to the Atlantic Coast angler's white marlin, only bigger. Found relatively close to shore in the waters of Southern California, off the Baja Peninsula, and off Hawaii, the striped marlin is an acrobat second to none, providing exciting surface strikes and jumping repeatedly when hooked on light tackle.

The majority of striped marlin caught by sport fishermen range from 100 to 200 pounds, although they're known to grow up to 400 pounds. Most striped marlin are caught by trolled rigged baits, with experienced anglers employing 30-pound-class tackle.

The striped marlin feeds actively on the surface and is often sighted in schools of forage species. The boat is positioned to troll either rigged baits or live baits in close proximity to the feeding fish. The "stripers" feed on sauries, anchovies, frigate mackerel, oceanic bonito and many of the smaller mackerel and tuna.

Often a marlin will come up behind a trolled bait and stalk it, uncertain whether or not to strike, which can be nerve wracking for an angler. When a strike occurs, it is a wild, violent lunge. A drop-back is employed with the reel in free spool, enabling the marlin to take the bait, turn and swim away. As the fish accelerates, the reel is locked in gear and the rod lifted back firmly.

Many striped marlin are hooked on the long-range party boats that sail from San Diego. These boats most often drift and chum with live anchovies, and the billfish move up into the chum and are hooked on live anchovies, sardines or other forage species that may have been caught right on the grounds and kept in the boat's live well.

Most striped marlin are released to fight another day.

Summer flounder

Summer flounder are popularly called "fluke" throughout much of their range from Maine to the Carolinas. They are an extremely popular bottom feeder that winters along the edge of the Continental Shelf, moving inshore in late spring and staying until late autumn. During their long inshore visitation many invade rivers and bays, while a sizable population resides in the ocean from the surf line to several miles offshore. This makes them popular with both boatmen and shore based anglers, who catch them using a wide variety of techniques.

The summer flounder has several close relatives in the southern flounder and the gulf flounder, both of which are found in Florida and along the entire Gulf Coast. Their habits are all very similar, as are the techniques employed to catch them.

The summer flounder is the heavyweight, reaching 20 pounds, while the southern flounder tops out at about 15 pounds. The gulf flounder seldom reaches more than a foot in length. Most summer flounder average 1 1/2 to 4 pounds, with some reaching the 10-pound "doormat" status.

A light popping outfit is ideal for most bottom fishing in bays and rivers. Surf, pier and jetty casters often employ a one-handed spinning outfit with either a bottom rig or artificials. When fishing from boats in the deeper ocean waters, many anglers move up to a medium-weight boat rod and multiplying reel loaded with 20- or 30-pound test monofilament line. The fluke is often found 40 to 60 feet down, requiring a heavy sinker to hold bottom, hence the heavier outfit.

Many flounder fishermen employ a single-hook bottom rig that is easy to make up. Begin by tying a small three-way swivel to the end of your line. Then tie in a 6-inch piece of 15-pound-test monofilament line with a loop in its end onto which you can slip your sinker. Bank or dipsey sinkers are favored and may range from 1 to 16 ounces, depending on wind and current. Finally, tie in a 36-inch piece of 20-pound-test fluorocarbon leader snelled to a 1/0 through 4/0 wide-gap or claw hook.

You can use a strip of fresh squid or a freshly cut strip of bait from a dogfish, sea robin or other fish. Live killies, spearing, sand eels, mullet or other small forage species also work. Always make certain that the bait is hooked so it doesn't twist as it's drifted along. Use a tapered piece of squid or fresh cut bait, hooked lightly at the head of the taper. Live killies should be hooked lightly through the lips or eye sockets, while sand eels, spearing and other dead baitfish should be threaded on the hook so they don't twist.

Jennifer Basilio, the author's grand-daughter, loves to fish. This nice summer flounder responded to a strip of sea robin used as bait. Summer flounder and other flatfish are a great target species for young people. They're easy to catch and great to eat.

Some anglers favor using a pair of hooks. You can tie a dropper loop into your line approximately 24 inches above the swivel, onto which you slip a hook snelled to an 18-inch piece of fluorocarbon leader. Rigged in this manner, the high hook will not interfere with the bottom hook.

The key in fluke fishing is having a swift current or moderate wind to push the boat along so you cover a lot of sandy bottom. It's also important to use sufficient sinker weight so that the line is nearly perpendicular to the bottom as you drift. Flukes are aggressive, and even with a fast drift they'll strike your bait. There are times, however, when they'll mouth a bait and just hold on as they try to subdue it. Resist the tendency to lift back and set the hook. Instead, hesitate and even relinquish a little line before slowly beginning to reel.

When there is little wind or current to propel the boat, trolling becomes an excellent, though little-used, alternative to drifting. For trolling it's recommended that you use a single-hook rig to avoid tangles. The same basic rig described earlier is streamed behind the boat 50 to 75 feet, with sufficient sinker weight to drag or bounce along the bottom. The boat should be steered through known fluke haunts at near idle speed. Periodically work the rod tip as you troll to make the bait swiftly move forward and then settle.

Power-drifting is another alternative when there is little movement. The boat is driven forward for 50 or 75 feet with motor on, then allowed to drift for 100 feet or so with the motor off. Both trolling and power-drifting enable you to cover a lot of choice bottom, the key to scoring with summer flounder.

Casters fishing from the surf, jetties, piers and bridges should always keep their baits moving. Remember, the more area you cover with your rig, the better your chances of scoring.

Summer flounder will also readily strike lures. Small leadhead jigs with 3-, 4- or 5-inch plastic tails are very effective when cast out and retrieved irregularly along the bottom. Fishing a small Clouser saltwater fly as a teaser 24 to 36 inches ahead of the jig can also help.

Fly fishermen also catch many fluke, particularly when using a fast-sinking fly line and saltwater flies that imitate small, silvery baitfish. The long-rod devotees most often work the shallow back reaches of bays and rivers, working their flies in less than 5 feet of water as the summer flounder moves into the shallows to feed on the abundant forage.

Summer flounder, southern flounder and gulf flounder are considered by many seafood fans to be the finest eating fish the sea has to offer. They are easily filleted, with two fillets cut from the dark, upper side of the fish and two fillets cut from the white underside of the fish. The fillets are then skinned, resulting in four pieces of white meat. The flounder has firm white meat that freezes well, which makes it a popular target late in the season as anglers stock their freezers.

Surfperch

There are more than 20 species of surfperch found along the inshore reaches of the Pacific Coast from San Diego to Alaska. Unlike most fish, surfperch bear live young. They're also among the smallest species popular with surf casters, ranging from 5 to 18 inches in length.

What they lack in size they make up for in numbers. Most often they're found frequenting the open sand beaches, and around rocky promontories extending into the ocean. They also take up residence in the protected waters of bays and rivers.

There are many varieties of surfperch: silver, white, barred, calico, rainbow, kelp, redtail and spotfin, to name but a few. They're basically a bottom fisherman's delight, as where you find one you'll usually find many more. Surfperch are fun to catch on light spinning tackle, often just beyond the curl of the breakers or among the rocky outcroppings where a long cast isn't necessary.

A high-low rig works best, with a small dipsey-style sinker heavy enough to cast beyond the breakers. Most surf casters use a pair of hooks snelled to 12 inches of leader. No. 3 or 4 claw, circle or live-bait hooks are probably the most popular.

Sand bugs, that can be dug right from the sand near the surf line, clam necks, mussels, chunks of anchovy or herring, prawns, and any of the seaworms can be used as bait. The fish's mouth is small, so the bait should be, too.

While not game fighters, surfperch can provide lots of action and are an ideal species to target when you're taking youngsters along. Most of the catch is kept for the table. Because of their size, most are scaled and prepared whole. Larger surfperch are often filleted.

Swordfish

The swordfish, popularly called the broadbill swordfish, is a world traveler found in warm and temperate waters. To catch one on rod and reel will always be a sterling angling accomplishment.

Unfortunately, tremendous exploitation of swordfish by commercial longlining has diminished their numbers drastically, especially on the Atlantic Coast. Still, the swordfish continues to be a formidable adversary, worthy of the time and effort to cover miles of offshore waters in hopes of hooking one.

Found primarily along the edge of the continental shelf and in the many offshore canyons, the swordfish has unique feeding habits. It frequently feeds at depths of 300 feet or more, but can also be found cruising on the surface. It has the uncanny ability to move through the entire water column and its vast change of pressure without any apparent stress.

For many years sportfishermen cruised the offshore waters in search of swordfish on the surface. The fish could often be spotted "sunning" itself, with dorsal fin and tail fin exposed. The fish could be tempted to strike a bait such as a bonito, mackerel or large squid that was slowly trolled and maneuvered within their sight.

Frequently they would totally ignore the bait, but on rare occasion would charge the trolled bait and provide an exciting surface strike and line-consuming series of jumps. Fighting acrobatic fish weighing up to 400 pounds must have been awesome sport, indeed.

Some skippers developed a "pitch-bait" approach to presenting a bonito or squid to swordfish on the surface. The captain would maneuver the boat as close to the fish as possible, and a deckhand would pull 50 feet of line from the reel and have it laying loosely on deck. The bait would then be twirled, much like a cowboy swinging a lasso, and thrown out in front of the fish. Often this would startle a swordfish and it would simply sink beneath the surface, at the same time the bait was sinking and the loose line paid out.

If the swordfish picked up the bait, the angler in the fighting chair would continue to permit line to slip from the reel until the swordfish began to move off swiftly, at which time the reel would be locked in gear and the long fight was on.

It is rare to find swordfish on the surface today, simply because there are fewer fish. As a result, most anglers send their baited hooks into the depths during the night, which is when swordfish usually feed. Because the fish today are smaller on average, most anglers use 80-pound-class tackle. A ball-bearing swivel is tied to the end of a double monofilament or Dacron line, followed by a 10- to 14-foot leader made of 200- or 300-pound-test monofilament. Favored hooks include the circle-style in sizes 14/0 and 16/0 or the forged Sea Mate or Sea Demon in 8/0 through 10/0 size.

A cyalume chemical light stick is attached to the leader with dental floss about two-feet from the bait. A bank sinker of 8 to 16 ounces is tied to the swivel to help hold the line as near perpendicular to the bottom as possible. The dental floss is used to tie off the light stick and sinkers so that it can break away when a fish is hooked.

Finally, a whole 2- or 3-pound mackerel, bonito, herring, butterfish or silver hake is placed on the hook. The bait is usually sewn on with rigging twine, with the twine run through the eye sockets of the fish and tied to the curve of the hook. This forces the swordfish to inhale the bait and hook in one movement and keeps the bait from being ripped free at the time of the strike.

Whole squid 12 to 16 inches long is also an excellent bait choice. The hook is threaded into the center of the squid near the head. The head section of the squid is tied with dental floss to the eye of the hook in the squid's head. When rigged in this manner and drifted into the current, the squid's tentacles "swim" as if the bait were alive.

Usually three rods are fished from big sportfishing boats. The deep line is measured off to approximately 300 feet, at which point a toy balloon is inflated and attached to the line with an elastic band to suspend it at the desired level. The bait is placed in the water until it reaches the desired depth and then permitted to drift away from the boat another couple of hundred feet. The second bait is fished at a depth of 200 feet and permitted to drift 100 feet or so behind the boat. The final bait is fished at 100 feet and about 50 feet behind the boat. This setup results in few tangles and places baits at three different levels.

This swordfish being raised to the scales weighed in at 195 pounds and was caught aboard the author's "Linda June" while fishing the waters of the Hudson Canyon near the edge of the continental shelf. It was hooked at night on a whole butterfish sent deep with the aid of an 8-ounce breakaway sinker and a cyalume light stick.

249

The outfits are placed in rod holders, with the reels set in free spool with the clicker on. Temperature breaks can be prime areas to fish because the conflicting currents often cause a concentration of natural forage. It then becomes a matter of patiently putting in the time and drifting in the darkness across the slopes of the canyon walls or along the edge of the shelf.

When the clicker signals a swordfish is moving off at slow speed, the angler quickly positions himself in the fighting chair. As the line picks up speed, the rod tip is lowered, the reel drag engaged, and the fish struck with several sharp lifts.

It's important to keep firm drag pressure on the fish at all times. Don't try to boat a big broadbill that is still green and full of fight. Even after a battle of an hour or more it's not unusual for a swordfish to leap into the air close to the boat.

Many sportfishermen are conscious of the over-exploitation of swordfish and release any fish under 100 pounds. The swordfish is considered an excellent table fish, which unfortunately has contributed to its demise.

As is the case with sharks and bluefin tuna, there may come a time when the swordfish is protected by a fishing ban that will allow its dwindling population to recover.

Tarpon are very plentiful throughout Florida's Everglades. They're a challenge to casters, as they work in close among the mangrove-banked channels. They offer spectacular sport, leaping clear of the water repeatedly.

Tarpon

The tarpon is certainly one of the most exciting saltwater species caught by sportsmen from the Carolinas to Florida and along the entire Gulf Coast. Often called the "silver king" because of their chrome-plated body coloration, the tarpon is a jumper second to none. It's especially popular because it is an inshore feeder, usually found within a mile of shore. It frequents bays, rivers and sounds where it is targeted by anglers who fish from boats, beaches, piers and bridges.

It responds to natural baits and artificials, enabling an angler to choose his favorite tackle. When fishing headwaters of coastal rivers, and in sections of the Everglades, where tarpon range from 3 to 15 pounds, light tackle in the form of a No. 8 or 9 fly-fishing outfit, popping outfit or one-handed spinning outfit is ideal. In the open waters, such as Miami's Government Cut or the Boca Grande Pass, where the tarpon grows to 150 pounds, anglers must move up to heavier gear.

Newcomers to tarpon fishing often begin their quest with natural baits. There are two popular methods employed with natural baits. One is to anchor or stake out an area frequented by tarpon, and to wait as the tarpon, either individually or in small pods, move along, usually along the edge of a channel or flat. The other method is to move into open water, such as cuts, passes and inlets, and to look for tarpon rolling on the surface and cast a live bait to them.

A medium-weight multiplying or two-handed spinning outfit rated for 20-pound-test line is ideal, although some anglers opt for 30-pound gear. An 8-foot leader of 50- or 80-pound-test fluorocarbon leader is crucial, as the big tarpon have tough jaws that will fray and wear through lighter leaders. Most anglers double the terminal end of their line, and then tie in the fluorocarbon using a double surgeon's knot. An O'Shaughnessy, beak or claw-style hook works best with live bait. Many anglers have begun using circle hooks for tarpon as this style usually hooks the fish in the corner of the mouth and makes them easier to release. You'll be using big baits for big tarpon, so hook sizes from 7/0 through 9/0 are most popular, with 14/0 and 15/0 circle styles ideal.

Tarpon aren't fussy when they're on the prowl. Live baits such as mullet, pinfish, squirrel fish, menhaden and spot, along with live blue crabs, all bring a response from the silver king. Most often the live baits are hooked either through the lips, or through the fleshy part of the back just ahead of the dorsal fin. When anchored or staked out, you can use a large cork or plastic float to suspend the bait so it will be in the sight range of tarpon moving through. When a tarpon does move within range, the baitfish will signal its presence by moving about excitedly.

It's important to hesitate and permit the tarpon to take the bait. Many anglers excitedly strike the fish too soon, pulling the bait from its bony mouth. The tarpon is a spectacular fighter. When hooked it immediately becomes airborne, jumping repeatedly and making long runs between jumps. It's important to have a medium drag set to avoid break-offs.

If you're casting to rolling fish, you can dispense with the float. Just ease up to the rolling tarpon and cast your live baitfish or crab ahead of the fish or school and permit it to drift along. If the fish are in a feeding mood, they'll be after the bait in a flash.

Pier and bridge casters often use live baits, fished either with, or without a float, permitting the current to carry the bait into the rips and eddies where the tarpon take up station to feed. It's exciting shore-based fishing, where the angler must leave the structure to land the fish from adjacent beaches.

Big tarpon also respond to big spoons and plugs trolled along ocean beaches, and through cuts and passes. A 3- or 4-ounce trolling sinker is often used to take the lures to intermediate depths as the boat slowly trolls through known tarpon haunts. On the troll the strike is spectacular and the tarpon is immediately in the air.

Chumming also is popular, especially along the Gulf Coast, as is the case in Key West Harbor, where boatmen employ the discarded trash from shrimp trawlers. The favored technique is to anchor along the edge of a channel and use a nominal amount of chum to attract tarpon moving along in search of a meal.

Probably the most exciting method of tarpon fishing is sight-casting to tarpon on the shallow flats of south Florida and the Keys. Anglers may employ a popping outfit or one-handed spinning tackle to cast plugs or lightweight jigs to the feeding fish.

The ultimate sport is to use a 9- or 10-weight fly fishing outfit and large tarpon flies and sight-cast to cruising fish while being poled along the flats. Unlike bonefish or permit, which spook easily, tarpon often come within range and can be reached with casts of just 50 feet. The entire process—stalking, presentation and ultimate success as a tarpon bolts into the air—is truly exciting.

The tarpon is a great gamefish but not particularly desirable as food. As a result, most are brought to boatside, controlled by a hand gaff and released. If necessary, hold onto a tired fish so it can swim in the current at boatside and regain its strength.

Yellowfin tuna

Of all the species of tuna that frequent America's waters, the yellowfin tuna is the most popular. Sometimes attaining a weight of over 300 pounds, it provides exciting fishing to anglers sailing to offshore waters in the Atlantic, Gulf and Pacific.

The yellowfin grows very fast, weighing close to 150 pounds in just four years. Sportsmen most often encounter fish between 40 and 80 pounds, which are ideal for medium tackle. Yellowfin frequent tropical and subtropical waters and are particularly abundant in the canyons of the northeast, along the continental shelf and along the edge of the Gulf Stream. They seldom stray inshore, unless a temperature break pushes water to their liking and the accompanying baitfish towards the beach.

Yellowfin tuna are a popular target of offshore fishermen on all three U.S. coasts. Yellowfin are usually found well offshore, often several hundred miles from port. Most anglers start out trolling, then switch over to chumming when a school of yellowfin is located.

Trolling is perhaps the most popular approach to catching yellowfin tuna, and is used to locate the schools of fish. Once fish are hooked trolling, many anglers then switch over to chumming and jigging.

Yellowfin tuna are fun to catch with 30-pound-class tackle, although many anglers move up to 50-pound tackle to be on the safe side. The heavier gear is especially effective where fish in the 200- to 300-pound range are regularly encountered, as is the case of the long-range party-boat fleet sailing from San Diego.

Yellowfin respond to a wide variety of trolled lures. The important thing is to use medium or small lures rather than the many popular offshore trolling lures used for marlin. Lures measuring 5 to 8 inches generally prove most effective. Spoons, cedar jigs and their plastic counterparts, Japanese trolling feathers, plastic-skirted trolling heads and chromed jigs all bring strikes from the swift yellowfins.

It's wise to bring along a variety of colors. One day black brings the most strikes, the next day it may be a red-and-white combination, or solid yellow, that scores. Without a doubt the "green machine," with plastic head and trailing green plastic skirt, is the most popular yellowfin lure of all time and most certainly should be included in your offshore trolling kit. Reel Seat Spreader Bar rigs, with small plastic shell squid or feathers, are also a potent lure and should be included as well.

Party boats often troll a dozen or more lures astern, and charter and private boats also frequently troll 6 or 8 lines, for the large spread of lures will often bring an entire school of tuna to the surface. At times every line will be hooked up.

While many anglers continue to troll once the fish have been located, the normal pattern is to immediately begin chumming. On the West Coast live anchovies and sardines are used as chum, while along the Atlantic Coast's canyons chunks of butterfish and menhaden are favored. Along the Gulf Coast the boats frequently have a cooler full of shrimp-dragger trash for chum.

As trolled fish are brought aboard, anglers drift out hooks baited with whole squid, butterfish or anchovies. While at times the bite can be hectic, there are also many times when yellowfin tuna move into the chum line and are very selective, picking up the chum, but avoiding hook baits. Fluorocarbon leaders are almost a must when the tuna are finicky.

When chumming it's important to keep baits at a variety of depths because the fish are not always on the surface. A rubber-cored sinker helps take the bait deep. The key is keeping the bait moving so it drifts along naturally with the current. After you've let it drift along for 100 feet or more, reel in and repeat the drift procedure.

Occasionally you'll get tuna readings on the fishfinder indicating they're 75 feet down or more. This means the chum is drifting well above where the fish are feeding, and the only way to effectively present a bait to them is to use a 8- to 16-ounce bank-style sinker tied to the line with dental floss so it can break free when a tuna is hooked. Jigging is another option when the fish are feeding deep. Diamond, stainless steel and leadhead jigs with plastic tails all work effectively. Use a jig heavy enough so it can be worked perpendicular to the bottom and not be carried away by the current.

Veteran jiggers work the jig while it is being lowered into the depths, alternately letting line slip from the reel, and then lifting their rod tip, causing the jig to dart and flutter. After the desired depth is reached, many anglers work the jig, speed reeling the jig to the surface while working their rod tip. After it is worked through 40 or 50 feet of the water column, the jig is permitted to settle again. This is exciting jigging, for when a 50-pounder wallops it you know you're into something!

Yellowfin tuna is just great on the dinner table. Many anglers first fillet their fish, with two fillets off each side of the fish. Skin the fish and make certain to remove the dark meat of the lateral line. The fillets may then be cut into steaks and prepared many ways. Many anglers use fresh yellowfin as sushi, which is delicious when served with a hot sauce. The meat is excellent when pressure cooked in Mason jars, and just as tasty as the favorite brand you purchase at the grocery store. Yellowfin tuna may also be frozen and holds very well.

The wahoo is very powerful and fast. It is found off all three U.S. coasts and is often caught accidentally by anglers trolling for other big gamefish.

Wahoo

The wahoo is one of the fastest blue-water adversaries encountered by sportfishermen. Surprisingly, most are caught by accident by anglers seeking gamefish such as marlin, tuna and dolphin. Although most of its feeding is done at intermediate depths in tropical and subtropical waters, it frequently charges to the surface to strike a trolled bait or lure.

The wahoo grows to more 140 pounds and can measure close to 7 feet. It is unique because it has a fixed lower jaw and hinged upper jaw. Its mouth is filled with extremely sharp, small teeth, that will slice through a small fish as though it were cut with a knife. It is extremely important to handle the wahoo with care when it is landed.

More wahoo are probably caught by trolling surface skipping baits or lures than with any other technique. However, there are more effective techniques. Deep trolling consistently takes more wahoo than any other method. Using either wire line, deep-trolling lures or downriggers to take lures or baits into the depths puts your offering at the depth at which the wahoo are feeding and results in more strikes.

Many trollers employ solid 40- or 50-pound-test Monel wire with 30-pound-class trolling rods and reels. Unfortunately, the Monel is difficult to work with and prone to overrunning and kinking if not handled properly. As a result, many deep trollers have switched to stainless steel cable, which is much easier to handle but does have a nasty habit of having a strand break. The resulting burrs can injure fingers when you're letting line out or retrieving. The fact remains, however, that these lines get the lures down to the strike zone and are the most effective.

Downriggers also perform very well in getting the lures or baits to the desired level. One of the problems with downriggers is that they're bulky and often in the way when you're targeting surface species such as tuna and marlin, which is what most boats troll for in waters frequented by the wahoo.

Deep-diving plugs rigged with heavy-duty hooks are the most popular lures used by veteran wahoo anglers on all three U.S. coasts. The plugs have an erratic, deep-diving action that appeals to the wahoo. Natural rigged baits also take many wahoo from the depths, particularly mackerel, mullet and balao. Because wahoo have a notorious habit of biting a long bait in half when they strike, most anglers rig their baits with both head and tail hooks, with the hook that is placed well back in the bait accounting for most of the hookups.

Wahoo occasionally move into a chum line intended for tuna, but many are lost when they bite through leaders with their sharp teeth. When wahoo move in and begin biting through leaders, it's wise to rig a short length of stainless steel leader wire or cable.

Wahoo also respond to deep-jigging techniques, where the boat drifts with the current along the edge of a drop off, and anglers work bucktail jigs or leadhead jigs with plastic tails through the depths. With the fish usually weighing between 20 and 75 pounds, it's best to use medium-weight tackle. With lighter tackle it is almost impossible to control the line-consuming run of a big wahoo.

Wahoo are fine table fare. Small wahoo are either filleted or steaked whole. A favored cleaning method for fish over 25 pounds is to cut a fillet off each side of the fish, and then to cut the fillets into 1- or 1 1/2-inch-thick steaks. Almost all wahoo have ugly-looking parasites in their stomachs. These trematode parasites do not affect the table quality of the wahoo and are nothing to worry about.

Wahoo have delicious, mild-flavored white meat. The meat tends to dry out quickly, so take care not to cook it too long.

Weakfish

The weakfish ranges from the Carolinas north to New England, with the greatest concentrations found between the Chesapeake Bay and Montauk, Long Island. Basically an inshore feeder, its seldom encountered more than a mile offshore in the ocean, and spends most of the summer months along the surf and in the waters of coastal sounds, bays and rivers.

Called a "gray trout" in the southern portion of its range, the weakfish is an inshore feeder that is caught from late spring through autumn by small-boat anglers, surf and jetty fishermen, and pier and bridge casters. After years of population decrease due to commercial exploitation, the number of weakfish has increased dramatically thanks to better fishery management practices.

Weakfish grow to more than 15 pounds, but anglers most often register their best catches with fish in the 2- to 4-pound class. Any fish growing to more than about 10 pounds are classified as "tiderunners" and are considered trophies.

There's never a need to fish with anything heavier than a popping or one-handed spinning outfit when fishing the inshore waters from a boat. Off the surf, jetties, piers and bridge a light or medium outfit will serve you well.

Chumming is one of the most peaceful, relaxing approaches to weakfish angling in protected inshore waters. The favorite chum is the tiny grass shrimp, just an inch or two in length and practically transparent. They're found in coastal bays and rivers by the millions. They are easily netted with a seine or fine-meshed dip net worked around dock pilings and bulkheads. Two quarts of the macruran crustaceans is all you'll require for a half day's chumming.

Try to anchor in a waterway frequented by the weakfish with a nominal amount of tidal flow. The shrimp are tossed over the side a half dozen at a time and carried with the current.

Rigging is extremely simple. Just tie a No. 1 or 1/0 beak or claw-style hook with a bait-holder shank to the end of your monofilament line. If the water is clear, use a 3-foot fluorocarbon leader between line and hook.

Bait up with two or three of the tiny shrimp and ease them out in the current, to float along with the chum. If there is little current and your line tends to sink, add a small popping float with a concave head to the line, thus suspending your bait at a desired level, usually midway between the surface and bottom. Conversely, if the current is very swift and the bait is not settling, add a tiny rubber-cored sinker to take it deeper.

The trick in chumming is to keep the baited hook moving. Permit it to pay out 75 or even 100 feet, and if a strike isn't received, reel in and repeat the procedure. Once you get a school of weakfish feeding on the chum you can often hook fish each time you ease your bait back in the chum line.

The weakfish derives its name from its very delicate mouth structure, so exercise care and use a net when trying to boat a big one.

Weakfish also respond very favorably to a variety of artificials that resemble sand eels, killies, spearing, shrimp, crabs, squid and the fry of many species. Use small swimming plugs, darters, leadhead jigs with plastic tails, bucktail jigs and small-block tin squids or stainless steel jigs. A good technique is to drift along with the current, casting as you drift. Often you can drift for several miles on the open reaches of large bays and sounds, hooking weakfish that are cruising about searching for a meal.

These same lures may be trolled, especially when you've located a school of feeding fish in a tide rip caused by a breakwater, bridge pilings or bulkheads. Trolling the lures through these haunts quickly brings strikes once you find the

Weakfish are plentiful along the middle Atlantic and Northeast Coast, where they provide inshore fishermen with fine sport from late spring until late autumn. The author's unhooking a typical bay weakfish for Kelsey Rosko, his granddaughter, who hooked it on a sandworm bait drifted from the "Baby Linda June." Weakfish are a great table fish.

depth at which the fish are feeding. Here, experimentation is important. Use trolling sinkers to find the right depth.

Surf, jetty, pier and bridge casters also score with the same lures, especially at night when the weakfish tend to move close to the beach. They are often attracted to the shadow line of bridges and piers, where they often stem the tide in the shadow line, waiting for the current to carry food to them.

Bottom fishing can be very effective using a high-low with a pair of No. 1 or 1/0 claw or beak-style bait-holder hooks snelled to 12 inches of leader. Use just enough sinker weight, with a 1- to 3-ounce dipsey or bank usually ideal, to hold bottom if you're casting from the surf, jetty, pier or bridge, or drifting along with the current in a small boat.

A strip of fresh squid is a very effective weakfish bait, as are bloodworms and sandworms, fresh spearing, small live spot, or pieces of shedder or soft blue crab.

Fly casters score from small boats, especially when the weakfish are tight to the marsh grass or sod banks, feeding in shallow water. Many such spots also provide fine wading opportunities, where a fly caster may present a small Deceiver, Clouser, shrimp fly or streamer

Weakfish are good table fish, although their meat tends to be on the soft side, and it should be used shortly after the fish is caught. They're especially tasty when filleted and broiled but, again, don't freeze very well.

White marlin are darlings of Atlantic and Gulf Coast anglers. Although smaller than the blue marlin, they are aerial acrobats that are ideally suited to 30-pound-class tackle. Most white marlin are hooked while trolling natural baits such as balao, mullet and strip baits. They'll also strike high-speed trolling lures. Almost all white marlin are released by sportfishermen.

White marlin

It has often been said that the price of a white marlin is patience and eternal vigilance. It is simply one of the greatest offshore gamefish found along the Atlantic and Gulf Coasts. A middleweight as billfish go, it is selective in striking a trolled bait, occasionally moving into a spread of lures and following cautiously for up to a half hour.

Its strike is spectacular. When it decides it wants a bait there is no hesitation as it rushes in, mouth agape, to attack. The white marlin will jump repeatedly, making long, determined runs and taking out plenty of line. The majority of white marlin are taken while blue-water trolling in the Northeast's Atlantic canyons, where they'll gather to feed on forage that collects near temperature breaks.

Twenty- or 30-pound-class tackle provides maximum sport with this great gamefish. The traditional method is to fish a total of six lines from a private boat, with two lines dropped back 125 to 175 feet from outriggers, and two inboard lines dropped back 75 to 100 feet from the outriggers. The remaining two lines are fished from rod holders in the transom on the face of the first or second wave of the wake.

Balao and mullet are among the favorite rigged baits of offshore trollers targeting white marlin, with a whole squid or rigged eel also very effective. Often trollers slip a red or green plastic skirt over the head of the bait, adding to its tantalizing action. Trolled at 5 or 6 knots, the baits swim and skip actively, not only attracting strikes from white marlin, but the wahoo, dolphin and several species of tuna that frequent the same waters.

White marlin will also strike artificials and in recent years many have been landed on spreader-bar rigs consisting of 7 to 9 plastic-shell squid or soft plastic balao baits, with only a hook rigged in the trailing or chaser bait.

Plastic-headed green machines with green plastic skirts also bring strikes from white marlin, as do the wide variety of Kona-head high-speed trolling lures. When using lures you can usually push up the speed a couple of knots and cover a lot more water than with natural baits.

A rule of thumb is that when you find a concentration of mackerel, butterfish, squid or flying fish offshore, there are sure to be white marlin close at hand. The white marlin aren't always feeding, and it pays to concentrate on any area where the temperature breaks occur and where the bait is plentiful. By putting in the time you're enhancing your chances of scoring when the whites decide to feed.

White marlin are cherished as great adversaries by anglers and almost all are promptly released at boatside.

You don't have to go far offshore to catch big white sea bass like this beauty just landed off the California coast. Years of excessive fishing depleted much of the population, but a fisheries management and public participation in a stocking and recovery program have resulted in a fine improvement. White sea bass are hooked using a variety of techniques, including trolling, chumming, jigging and bottom fishing.

White sea bass

The white sea bass is found in abundance in the waters of Southern California, particularly around the many kelp beds. As far as scientists are concerned, it is really not a sea bass at all, but a member of the weakfish family. When you look at a line drawing of both species you can quickly notice the similarity.

Overfishing has diminished the quantity of fish available to sport fishermen, but an effective hatchery program has helped build up the stocks and fishing has improved greatly in recent years.

White sea bass grow to a top end of about 80 pounds, although fish that size are a rarity. Anglers fishing from party boats and private craft out of San Diego and Los Angeles and Long Beach usually tangle with fish from 5 to 20 pounds, which are great sport on light tackle.

The favorite technique is to employ live anchovies as chum and to anchor up just off from the kelp beds. Use light spinning or multiplying tackle and 15- to 20-pound-test monofilament line and a No. 1 or 1/0 beak, claw or live-bait-style hook. The anchovies are hooked lightly through the nose, lips or just ahead of the dorsal fin. They are cast toward, but not into, the kelp, where a lively anchovy will swim about actively, attempting to gain its freedom.

When the chummer tosses out live anchovies you can often see the white sea bass streak out to quickly catch the scurrying silvery baitfish. It's then that an anchovy on a hook stands a good chance of being targeted by the aggressive bass.

White sea bass are nocturnal feeders and the party boats often score well after dark. It's exciting as the big bass streak through the water, with anglers deftly attempting to keep them from reaching the sanctuary of the kelp.

Anglers who prefer to use artificials catch many white sea bass by casting jigs and small spoons towards the kelp, and by trolling along the perimeter of the kelp beds.

White sea bass are a valuable food fish, and anglers regularly land substantial numbers of this fine table fish. Many California anglers who are most appreciative of the resurgence of white sea bass now limit the quantity of fish they keep, which has helped with its recovery.

Plentiful from the DelMarVa Peninsula on north to the Maritime Provinces, the winter flounder spends its summer along the continental shelf, moving inshore in late fall, providing inshore anglers with a fall and spring fishery, and even biting all through a mild winter. Greg Hall bundled up to catch this average-size flatty, that was taken on a piece of bloodworm as bait.

Winter flounder

The winter flounder is one of the few species that is available to inshore winter anglers along the Northeast Coast, predominately from the Chesapeake Bay north to the Maritime Provinces. It spends the summer months out along the edge of the continental shelf, beyond reach of most small-boat anglers. During late fall it migrates inshore and winters in the protected reaches of bays, rivers and estuaries. It then returns late in the spring.

Called the "blackback flounder" in some locales, the winter flounder averages only 1 to 2 1/2-pounds. It's very active when it first arrives inshore, feeding aggressively after its long trip. By the time it arrives, many anglers have long since put their boats into drydock for the winter and often miss out on fine action, unless they decide to board the party boats that specialize in this fishery. During a mild winter the flounder feeds actively on grass shrimp, sandworms, bloodworms and clam spores.

A light popping outfit or one-handed spinning outfit is ideal for the winter flatfish. They respond quickly to a ground chum of clams, mussels, snails and conch, which may be mixed with whole kernel corn and boiled rice. This mixture is often frozen in disposable paper cups and inserted into a chum pot made of wire mesh when the fishing grounds are reached. When lowered to the bottom from an anchored skiff, the chum log begins to thaw and the trail is carried along the bottom, attracting any flounder feeding in the area.

A bottom rig is built around a three-way swivel. A two-hook bottom rig is attached to one eye of the swivel. The rig uses a pair of snelled hooks, with one hook snelled to the leader of the other, so that both hooks rest on the bottom. A bank- or dipsey-style sinker heavy enough to hold bottom is attached to the remaining eye of the swivel with a duo-lock snap, with 1- to 3-ounce models usually adequate in all but the swiftest current.

Winter flounder have very small mouths, so it's important to use a small piece of bait. Many anglers use sandworms or bloodworms and cut them into pieces 2 or 3 inches long. Strips of clam and mussel also bring strikes, as do several small grass shrimp placed on the hook.

During an extremely cold winter the winter flounder often stops feeding, becoming active again when the water warms in late winter or early spring. During early spring it receives the most extensive fishing pressure, for after a winter of inactivity most boat anglers are again eager to get on the water and catch some fresh fish.

The winter flounder is one of the favorite table fish of bottom fishermen because of its delicious white meat. Smaller flounder are often scaled and left hole, with the stomach cavity filled with a vegetable stuffing. Larger flounder are usually filleted and prepared in any number of ways.

Many other species available

In compiling a list of 50 favorites, it was admittedly difficult to exclude some fine game and food fish. The bigeye tuna is an example, as it is popular, but caught in limited numbers. Likewise with the croaker, a fun fish to catch, but with a limited following. Some of the species that didn't make the favorite 50 are mentioned throughout the book, and there are still more species found along the coast. Suffice it to say that most anglers agree that if it swims in saltwater, it's fun to catch. The fun, relaxation, enjoyment, and potential of a fine meal combine to create this contemplative pastime, irrespective of species.

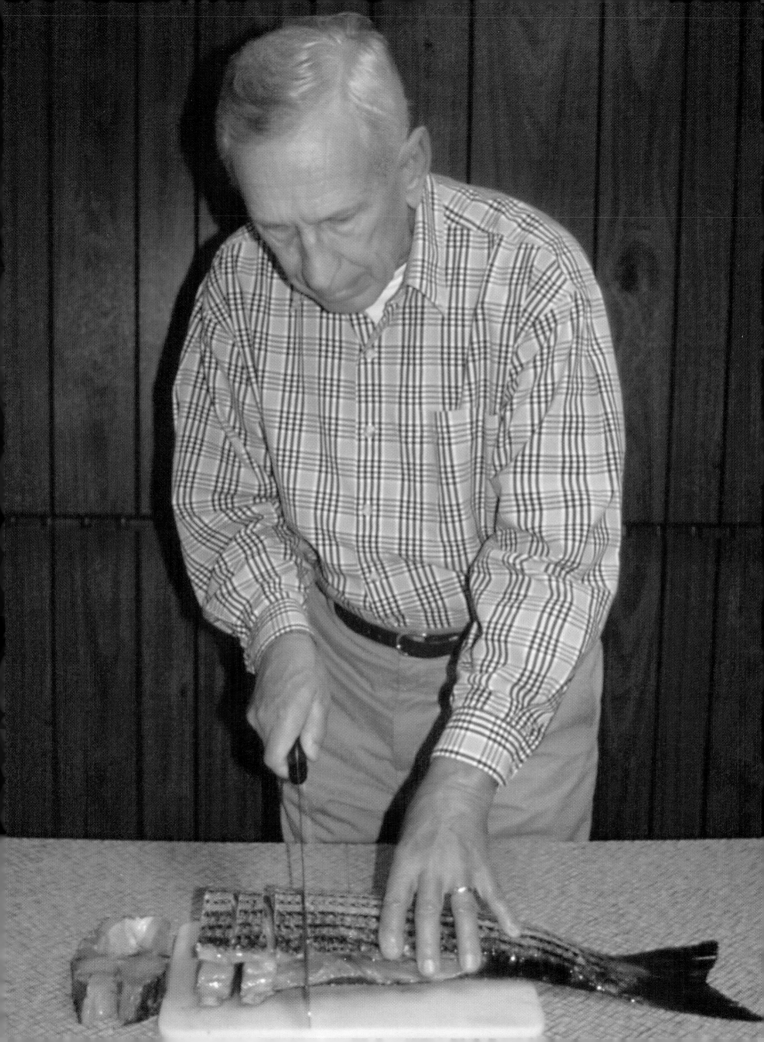

CARING FOR AND CLEANING YOUR CATCH

It's unfortunate that many wonderful table fish that would otherwise provide an excellent meal never arrive home in prime condition. Many people fail to realize that fresh fish seldom has a strong odor when being cooked. It's improperly cared for fish that often has a heavy, unpleasant odor. With a little effort, you can ensure that this doesn't happen and the fish arrives in prime condition for the chef to take over in the kitchen.

From the time a fish is landed, the quality of the meat will deteriorate unless it is properly cared for. It's probably not a stretch to say a majority of fishermen fail to properly care for their catch. All too often anglers, in their haste to enjoy exciting fishing, fail to follow a few basic steps that would preserve their catch. Fish are unceremoniously dumped into buckets of sea water, placed in burlap bags, piled in fish boxes lacking ice, or just left in the sun and wind to dry out. Little do anglers realize that from the moment it is caught the digestive juices and blood in a fish begin taking their toll. As this begins to occur, exterior forces such as sun and wind cause the fish to heat up and dry out from the outside. Just a couple of hours of this exposure and lack of care will result in a "fishy" taste and strong odor to the fish when it is prepared.

A fresh, properly-cared-for fish does not have a heavy smell, nor does the kitchen in which it is prepared.

Follow a few basic steps

There are a few basic steps that should be followed with all fish that you catch.

Fish that are bled within a few minutes of being caught always have a better flavor than those that are not. This is easily accomplished by inserting a sharp knife just behind the pectoral fin, on each side of the fish. The puncture will cause the blood to flow freely, with the fish's heart pumping it out.

The next step is to make an incision just forward of the anal vent at the bottom of the fish. Then insert your finger into the cavity made by the knife and grasp the round tube that feeds the anus, and make a clean cut. Make a cut along the bottom of the fish, just forward of the pectoral fin. This cut should be made crosswise, so that you can reach in and cut the tube that feeds from the mouth of the fish into the stomach. Then you can withdraw the entire stomach and entrails. This removes all digestive juices that would continue to function and cause the meat to deteriorate.

A final step would be to cut away the gills. The fish is now rid of its blood, entrails and gills, leaving only the prime-quality meat that you will later prepare for the table. At this point the fish should be placed on ice, in an ice chest or box that is well drained, so the fish does not rest in water.

Ice, ice, ice. There is no substitute, unless there's a refrigerator aboard the

(Left) Big fish are ideal for cutting into steaks. The author began by removing the scales from this striped bass, then removed the dorsal and anal fins and the entrails. Here he is using a serrated knife to slice steaks to a desired thickness. When the striped bass was caught it was immediately bled, which enhances the flavor and should be done with all fish.

261

boat. If you're on the beach, then bury your fish in the moist sand and cover it to keep it from being exposed to air, the sun and wind.

Cleaned in this manner, the fish will hold perfectly until you later decide whether to fillet or steak it, or to scale it for preparation whole.

There are a couple of tools that you should have available for the final cleaning of your catch. Make sure you have a sturdy, serrated knife that is capable of cutting through bone for those fish you wish to steak. Also essential is a long, thin-bladed filleting knife with which to fillet your catch and to then cut the fillets into thin pieces, chunks or fingers. Include a diamond knife sharpener to maintain a sharp edge. Finally, have a sturdy fish scaler handy to remove scales from fish that are to be cut into steaks or prepared whole.

Small fish are left whole

The general rule is that small, round fish in the 1- to 2-pound class are best left whole. This applies to species such as sea bass, sand bass, surf perch, kelp bass, porgies, and weakfish. The final cleaning is very simple, as all you need do is work your scaler from the tail to the head, removing all of the scales.

It's important to remove the first and second dorsal fins and the anal fin. This is easily accomplished by making a sharp cut just before the fin and working the knife alongside and back just beyond the fin on both sides. Make the cut deep enough so that you can firmly grasp the fin and pull it out. This removes the fin bones that could otherwise be an irritant when eating the fish.

The fish may now be fried whole, broiled, baked, or stuffed. Many people prepare the fish with the head intact, although if you wish you may use the serrated knife to cut it and the pectoral fins off.

Large fish may be cut into steaks

Many people prefer to cut large fish, say those over 6 pounds, into steaks. This is particularly true with species such as albacore, tuna, codfish, grouper, salmon, striped bass, snook and wahoo.

The fish should be scaled and the dorsal and anal fins removed. Then lay the fish flat on a cutting board and make your initial cut with a serrated knife just forward of the dorsal fin and cut the head off. Carefully cut the steaks to the desired thickness, sawing through the backbone and any pin bones of the rib cage. As you get to the tail section, the steaks will become smaller. You may want to leave the tail section whole, or fillet it rather than have tiny steaks.

Big flatfish, such as summer flounder, California halibut or Pacific halibut, may be steaked the same way.

Flatfish are perfect for filleting

Smaller flatfish are best suited for filleting. Lay the fish dark side up on a flat surface and work your fillet knife from the head to the tail along the somewhat depressed centerline of the fish. Cut to the backbone, but do not cut through it. Then work your thin filleting knife at an angle, cutting from the head to the tail and working the blade towards the fins on either the left side or right side of the centerline, cutting along the bony structure as closely as possible. In this way you will remove a single long fillet from the top of the fish. Then work from the head to the tail to remove another fillet from the dark side of the fish. You should wind up with two neat fillets and no meat remaining on the top of the flatfish.

Repeat the same procedure on the white side of the fish.

The final step in cleaning is to remove the skin. This is accomplished by placing a fillet skin side down and cutting from the tail towards the head, working the filleting knife between the skin and the meat. Exert downward pressure with the knife blade close to the skin and work the blade back and forth towards the head while grasping the skin with your hand. This technique removes the skin very easily and doesn't waste a shred of meat.

You now have four long fillets. The two from the top of the flatfish are thicker than those from the bottom, but all four are bone-free and ready for the kitchen.

Flatfish are very easy to fillet. The author prefers to cut two fillets off the top of the fish, such as the summer flounder he's filleted here, and two fillets from the bottom. Each fillet is then skinned.

Different technique required to fillet round fish

A different approach is used to fillet round fish such as striped bass, weakfish, bluefish, white sea bass, and cobia. Lay the fish on a flat surface and make a cut at a 45-degree angle from just before the dorsal fin to behind the pectoral fin, but do not cut through the backbone. Next, run your fillet knife from the cut you just made alongside the dorsal fin and as close to it as possible, cutting the entire length of the fish. Cut until you feel your knife point touching the backbone where it meets the rib cage. Continue cutting along he rib cage from front to back. After you've passed the anus you'll find there are no longer ribs, and you may push your knife all the way through the fish and continue cutting towards the tail.

As you cut along the rib cage of the stomach, there is very little meat between the ribs and the skin (with the exception of tuna) and you should just cut through the skin and work the knife to the anus, at which point you will have a whole fillet representing one half of the fish. Turn the fish over and repeat the same procedure on the remaining half.

With tuna, cut through the rib cage when you make your initial cut, as tuna have substantial meat between the ribs and the skin. After the fillet has been removed, you can carefully cut away the pin bones of the rib cage. Most anglers then make a cut the entire length of the fish, along its lateral line, resulting in two fillets from each side. They then carefully cut away the dark meat of the lateral line.

The next step is to remove the skin. Place a fillet, skin side down, on the cutting board. Carefully work the knife between the skin and the meat, beginning at the tail. With firm downward pressure along the skin, work the knife back and forth as you cut towards the front of the fillet. The remaining fillet should also be skinned.

Remove dark meat of lateral line

Many people use the fillets without making any further cuts. However, most round fish have a strip of dark meat running along the lateral line the entire length of the fish. This is easy to see once you've skinned the fish. This meat usually has a strong flavor and is often removed.

To remove this dark strip, place the meat dark side up and make a cut along the top edge of the lateral line at about a 45-degree angle, sufficiently deep to reach the approximate center of the dark meat and the length of the fish. Now make a similar cut at the same angle along the bottom edge of the lateral line. If you've used a very sharp knife and made the two cuts properly, you can lift the entire strip of the dark meat away from the fish and discard it. When cooked your fish will have a more delicate flavor without the dark meat.

Each person who cleans fish has a somewhat different approach, but these basic methods will help get your fish ready for the table.

Many people prefer to fillet round fish. This is done by removing one fillet from each side of the fish and then skinning it. Most fish have a dark strip of meat which is its lateral line and runs the length of the fish. This meat has a heavy flavor and is best removed and discarded.

Promptly freeze your excess

Most fish, when cleaned and cared for properly, can be kept in the refrigerator for several days. Beyond that it's best to freeze the meat for use at a later date. Fish that is simply wrapped in freezer paper or in plastic wrap or bags and frozen will often get freezer burn because it is exposed to the air.

The ideal way to freeze fish is to use a vacuum-bagging system, which removes all of the air and retains the freshness for months. Another approach is to place the the fish in a plastic bag, add enough tap water to cover the fish, and seal the bag tightly. When placed in the freezer, the fish will be frozen in a block of ice and will keep for months.

Quickly icing fish immediately after they've been caught, bled and cleaned, is the key to ensuring that the fish arrive home in mint condition. You just know that this catch will result in many delicious seafood dinners, thanks to the liberal use of crushed ice.

JUNE ROSKO'S FAVORITE SEAFOOD RECIPES

The seafood recipes included in this chapter have gone through a sort of evolutionary process.

Some recipes were tried and set aside. Some evolved through adding a personal touch, just a bit more seasoning, searing to seal in the juices, or smothering with vegetables and wrapping in aluminum foil to retain the fish's flavor. Ultimately ,the ones included here passed the final test at the dinner table. When the platters were returned to the kitchen with not a crumb left, the recipe had achieved its objective—to transform the catch of the day into a delightful dinner!

Most seafood recipes evolve

Using fish that has been properly cared for when initially caught, and then carefully cleaned, will help ensure that you end up with a delicious meal.

All too often, however, fish recipes are just that—a recipe on how to cook just the fish. This means the cook has to then plan the remainder of the meal. Fish alone is not a meal. To make it a more memorable experience, included here with most of the seafood recipes are the great vegetables and salads that make for an enjoyable meal.

Many of these recipes have been developed through years of trial and error, so don't be afraid to experiment and achieve the taste that suits you and your family.

Bon appetite!

These ingredients are waiting to be transformed into a fish chowder beyond words. Most any mild-flavored, white-meat fish may be used, including striped bass, codfish, rockfish, grouper and snapper. Many chefs use the meat from the head and rib cage to prepare their chowder, rather than wasting the small pieces of fish.

(Left) June Rosko prepares to serve a bowl of her favorite fish chowder, with just the right consistency and flavor. A rich fish chowder is a welcome dinnertime treat during the cold-weather months. Many seafood cooks rarely prepare recipes the same way twice. Seafood cooking is evolutionary, so by all means experiment until you achieve the right taste.

Fried

There are legions of fishermen who proclaim that fried is the only way to cook fresh fish. Few can take them to task, for a delicately fried fish is a gourmet treat. It can have lots of cholesterol, too, but this recipe is healthier than many.

While many chefs bread their fish using fresh eggs, Eggbeaters is a better choice for people concerned about cholesterol.

◆ **8 fillets of any flatfish, each measuring approximately 1/2 x 2 x 8 inches**

◆ **1 container Eggbeaters (equivalent of 2 whole eggs)**

◆ **1/2 cup enriched flour**

◆ **1 cup seasoned bread crumbs**

◆ **1/2 cup Canola oil**

Begin by dredging the fillets in flour.

Dip each fillet in Eggbeaters and then place the fillet in bread crumbs, thoroughly coating each fillet. You'll find that Eggbeaters have a stickier consistency than eggs, which makes for a nicer coating and ultimately a crunchier crust.

Complete all fillets before you begin to fry them.

Use an 8- or 10-inch frying pan and fill approximately 1/4-inch deep with Canola oil. This oil is low in unsaturated fats and is healthier than many other oils and fats.

The key in frying is to begin with hot oil. Many people make the mistake of pouring the oil in the frying pan and immediately placing the breaded fish in the cold oil. This results in the fish absorbing the oil, which is a no-no.

Heat the oil until it is piping hot over medium heat. When you add the breaded fillets, the oil should be sizzling and not quite cover the fillets. After a few minutes lift the end of a fillet to check its color. When they are a golden brown, use a turnover to carefully turn them. Be aware that the second side will fry faster than the first. Test the meat periodically and remove the fillets when the meat is light and flaky. If you fry the fillets too long they will tend to be dry and chewy.

(If you caught the flounder earlier in the day you may find that they curl up as you fry them. This is because rigor mortis hasn't yet set in. It just tells you how fresh the fish are!)

Remove the fillets from the pan and place them on paper toweling to remove excess oil.

Two fillets per person is usually adequate, and a main dish for four adults can be prepared in just a few minutes.

As the members of the flatfish clan are in their prime during the summer months, the perfect combination to go with the fish fry is corn on the cob and garden-fresh tomatoes.

Corn is in its prime when served the day it is picked. For four people you'll need perhaps eight small ears. Remove the husks and drop the cobs into boiling water. Tender, young corn takes but 8 or 10 minutes to cook.

While the corn is cooking, melt a small stick of margarine.

When the corn is ready, place it in a large plastic container and pour the melted margarine over the corn, which is a lot easier than trying to apply it with a knife. Salt and pepper to taste.

Slice several tomatoes and place them on a bed of lettuce, and serve with Thousand Island dressing (preferably fat free).

Fresh, fried flounder fillets, corn on the cob and a tomato and lettuce salad make for a summertime dinner that just can't be beat.

Stuffed

Most any fish discussed in this book may be stuffed. With small fish such as sea bass, weakfish, redfish, croaker, spot and flounder, the body cavity is filled with stuffing. Many people prefer to use fillets instead of the whole fish, and take a nominal size fillet, measuring about 1/2 x 3 x 8 inches, and join the ends with a toothpick, making a donut that is filled. Either way is delicious.

The key to stuffed fish is making a tasty stuffing and cooking it beforehand. Too often fish are stuffed with uncooked stuffing, which means that the fish has to be overcooked in order for the stuffing to be thoroughly cooked.

The ingredients you'll need include:

- ◆ **8 medium-size fillets of fish of your choice or 8 panfish**
- ◆ **1 whole red bell pepper**
- ◆ **1 whole green bell pepper**
- ◆ **6 small white button mushrooms**

- ◆ **1 3-inch-diameter Vidalia onion**
- ◆ **salt and pepper to taste**
- ◆ **2 tablespoons margarine**
- ◆ **1 cup seasoned bread crumbs**

Before preparing the ingredients, pre-heat the oven to 350 degrees.

Use a sharp knife and dice the peppers, mushrooms and onion into quarter-inch pieces.

Melt the margarine in a sauce pan and add the peppers, mushrooms and onion. Saute over medium heat until the onions take on that golden color indicating that they are caramelized. The peppers and mushrooms will have cooked through and softened as well. Much of their juices will be released and result in a light sauce. Take care to not let the sauce cook away.

Add the seasoned bread crumbs to the sauce pan along with just a touch of salt and pepper to taste. Stir together until you get a paste-like consistency.

Use a cookie tray that has been lightly sprayed with cooking spray. If you're stuffing whole fish, open the stomach cavity and, using a teaspoon, fill the cavity until it bulges. With fillets held together with toothpicks, place the donuts directly onto the cookie sheet, and use a teaspoon to fill them firmly to the top.

Add a tiny dab of margarine to the top of the stuffing or whole fish to keep it moist during baking.

Place the stuffed fish in the oven and set the timer for 8 minutes, but check it after 6 minutes. With the whole fish, use a fork to check the meat where you've removed the dorsal fins. It's done when it flakes or easily lifts away from the backbone. The fillets are done when they easily flake to the touch of a fork. Keep checking them every couple of minutes until they're done, but be especially careful not to cook them too long. There's really no set time. It all depends on the size of your catch.

While the stuffing is very tasty and filling, it's great to have a side dish of asparagus with a light Hollandaise sauce. A tasty salad includes a sliced fresh cucumber and Vidalia onion, with oil and vinegar dressing.

Grilled

It's very easy to dry out or overcook fish on the grill. To avoid this many anglers marinate their fish before grilling, and then baste the fish with the marinade as it is cooking. Some choose to wrap their fish in heavy aluminum foil, thus sealing in the juices. Both recipes are included here.

Steaks cut from albacore, yellowfin tuna, striped bass and cobia lend themselves to grilling. Cut the steaks from 1 to 1 1/2 inches thick.

> Ingredients include:
>
> ◆ **2 cups ginger-teriyaki or lemon-herb dressing marinade**
> ◆ **4 tuna steaks weighing about a half pound each**

Place the ginger-teriyaki or lemon-herb dressing in a Pyrex dish and marinate the steaks for an hour or two, as you don't want the marinade flavor to be overbearing.

Turn on your grill at least 15 minutes before you're ready to place the fish steaks on. You want the grill hot, so the sizzling heat seals the juices in the fish. Here again, timing is everything. Don't walk away and forget the fish. It normally takes but 3 or 4 minutes on each side, and you should baste with the marinade to keep the meat moist while you're grilling it.

If you like, include some vegetables with your fish while grilling. You can also prepare a delicious meal by utilizing fillets of bluefish, weakfish, striped bass, white sea bass or any other similar fish, instead of tuna on the grill.

Grilled in foil

If you want to prepare an easy dinner on the grill, you can simply make individual packets of fish and vegetables and seal them in foil and place them on the grill. Most and fish is delicious when prepared in this manner.

> You'll need the following for a meal for 4:
>
> ◆ **4 large fillets**   ◆ **2 3-inch red tomatoes**
> ◆ **2 3-inch Vidalia onions**   ◆ **1 cup mayonnaise**

Place the fillet on a large piece of foil and spread a nominal amount of mayonnaise over the fillet. Completely cover the fillet with thinly sliced onion, topped with thinly sliced tomatoes. Add just a touch of salt and pepper to taste.

Fold the aluminum foil tightly across the top of the fish, and turn up and fold each end, so the fish is sealed in an airtight packet. Do this with all four packets and place them on the grill. This recipe normally takes about 10 minutes at the most. You don't have to worry about the fish drying out, for the packet is completely sealed and the fish is in effect being steamed within the packet. To check its progress, unfold a corner of the packet, being careful not to get too near the steam that escapes, and test it with a fork. When it flakes easily, it's ready.

Both methods produce delicious fish that may be served over a bed of rice, with a touch of the marinade, or some of the sauce that forms in the aluminum packet. A side dish of creamed broccoli or cauliflower, with a Caesar salad, makes it a meal fit for a king.

June Rosko always plans the total meal, including lots of fresh salads and great vegetables as part of her dinner menu. She loves to include mixed vegetables roasted to a golden brown, to accompany fish dishes.

Baked

Baked fish is a delight when there's a chill in the air, but it's not the kind of dish you normally want to bother with on a hot summer day.

To feed four hungry anglers you'll need plenty of fish. This recipe has utilized more than a dozen different species of fish and has worked well with all of them, particularly flounder, halibut, striped bass, channel bass, weakfish, salmon, wahoo and snook. The secret is cutting fillets of moderate thickness, about a half inch is fine.

◆ **8 medium-size fillets**

◆ **4 3-inch fresh tomatoes, sliced**

◆ **1/2 cup skim milk**

◆ **2 tablespoons corn starch**

◆ **1/2 cup white zinfandel wine**

◆ **1/3 teaspoon fresh or dried basil**

◆ **3 tablespoons margarine**

Begin by spraying a Pyrex baking dish with a light coating of cooking spray. Place the fillets in the dish and cover with the tomatoes.

Use a 6-inch saucepan and melt 3 tablespoons of margarine over medium heat. Mix 2 tablespoons of corn starch (it doesn't get lumpy as does flour) with a half cup of water until it is smooth. Stir constantly while adding skim milk until the sauce is thick. Remove the pan from the heat and gradually stir in white zinfandel wine and basil.

Pour the sauce over the fish and tomatoes and place in an oven that has been preheated to 350 degrees. Bake for 25 to 30 minutes, until the fish flakes when tested with a fork.

A great potato dish can be prepared in the oven to compliment the baked fish. It does take a bit longer to prepare, however, and is best placed in the oven 10 to 15 minutes before the fish.

Slice 4 potatoes and 1 Vidalia onion. Place the slices into a Pyrex dish and add about 2 tablespoons of margarine, in small dabs, on top of the potatoes and onion. Salt and pepper to taste. Add just enough skim milk to not quite cover the potatoes. Lightly sprinkle with parmesan and place in the oven as you continue preparation of the fish.

Separately, steam some green or yellow squash with sliced mushrooms. You needn't prepare a separate sauce, as the sauce from the fish is delicious when spooned over the mushrooms and squash.

Serve with a fresh garden salad of a bed of spinach, halved cherry tomatoes, quartered white mushrooms and small pieces of green bell pepper. Just add your favorite dressing

Broiling is a quick and easy method of preparing fresh fish. June Rosko often uses disposable aluminum foil pans, as pictured here. She lightly coats the pan with Pam cooking spray and places several fillets in it. Slices of fresh tomatoes are placed on top of the fish. You may add sliced mushrooms, peppers or onions if you wish. Sliced lemons add that citrus tang.

Broiled

Broiling is definitely the easiest way to prepare fish and one of the healthiest. Small fish may be broiled whole, but fillets are often preferred. To keep from having a messy broiler you may want to use a disposable aluminum broiler pan big enough to hold all your fish. The pan also collects the sauce that is formed while broiling—an added bonus.

For a four-person meal you'll need:

- 1 disposable aluminum broiler pan
- 4 large fillets, measuring 1/2 x 3 x 10 inches
- salt and pepper to taste
- 1 tablespoon of ground paprika
- 1 teaspoon fresh or dried parsley flakes or basil
- 1/2 stick margarine

Pre-heat the broiler and lightly spray the broiler pan with cooking spray.

Place the fillets in the pan and lightly salt and pepper to taste. Sprinkle with paprika and parsley or basil. Finally, slice 1/16-inch pieces of stick margarine and place them evenly across the top of the fillets. As the margarine melts it will blend with the juices of the fish, the salt, pepper and paprika, and form a tasty sauce that will drain into the bottom of the pan.

Place the fish in the broiler and set the timer for 6 minutes. The timer will alert you to carefully watch the fish. Seldom will the fish take more than 10 minutes to broil, and this only in the case with thick fillets.

Use a turnover to remove the fish from the broiler pan and place it right onto the dinner plates. Then carefully pour a small amount of the sauce from the broiler pan over the fish.

A good, easy potato dish that goes well with broiled fish is made from red new potatoes, onion soup mix and a small quantity of Canola cooking oil:

- 6 small red new potatoes
- 1 package onion soup mix
- 1/2 cup Canola cooking oil

Thoroughly wash the potatoes and scrub the skins clean with a brush. Cut each potato into quarters. Use a plastic bag and empty the package of onion soup mix into the bag and add cooking oil. Mix thoroughly and then add the quartered potatoes and seal the bag. Shake the bag vigorously to coat the potatoes.

Empty the contents into a Pyrex baking dish and place in the oven at 350 degrees and bake for approximately 30 minutes, or until the potatoes appear done.

An easy vegetable dish to include is fresh steamed string beans served with just a dab of margarine.

It's good to regularly use up the odds and ends in the salad compartment and toss together lettuce, radishes, bell peppers, mushrooms and scallions with a fat-free honey dijon dressing.

Fish Cakes

Normally seafood lovers have an affinity for crab cakes, but it's not always possible to obtain the tasty crustaceans. It was noted striped bass angler Al Wutkowski who, through trial and error and a love of the kitchen, developed a recipe for fish cakes that so closely resembles crab cakes that even a gourmet could be fooled!

Although Al primarily uses striped bass as his fish of choice, the cakes may be made with any one of a number of species, such as codfish, sea bass, white sea bass, snapper, grouper or rockfish.

Al uses the following:

- **2 lbs. of striped bass fillets**
- **2 tablespoons mayonnaise**
- **1 tablespoon dijon mustard**
- **1 package Eggbeaters (equivalent of 2 eggs)**
- **2 cups Italian bread crumbs**
- **1 cup chopped Vidalia onions**
- **1 cup chopped green bell peppers**
- **1 cup whole kernel corn**
- **2 tablespoons virgin olive oil**

Al also includes these optional ingredients:

- **1 cup chopped celery**
- **1 cup chopped carrots**
- **1 teaspoon Old Bay Seasoning**
- **hot red pepper flakes to taste**

Begin by cutting the fish fillets into 4-inch cubes. Either poach or steam them until the meat is white and flakes easily. It shouldn't take more than 8 or 10 minutes. Remove the fish from heat and strain through a colander, pressing out as much water as possible.

Use a skillet to saute the olive oil, onions, green peppers, corn, celery, and carrots until the onions have caramelized and the vegetables are tender. Remove from heat and set aside.

Using a large mixing bowl, combine the mayonnaise, mustard, Eggbeaters and the previously sauteed vegetables. If you're including the Old Bay Seasoning and red pepper flakes, add them here, but do so sparingly to suit your taste.

Add the fish and mix until you have the consistency of crab meat.

Finally, mix in the Italian bread crumbs, just adding enough to hold the mixture together so it may be formed into fish cakes for cooking. Use a 1/4-cup measuring cup and pack the mixture tightly into it. While holding the cup's handle, slap the back of the cup firmly into the palm of your hand, which will release a nicely formed fish cake.

Fry the cakes in Canola oil, with just enough oil in the frying pan to not quite cover the cakes. Make certain the oil is sizzling hot before adding the fish cakes so you can seal in the taste and juices. Fry to a golden brown, and remember that when you turn them over it'll take less time to fry the second side.

For cooks who like to avoid frying, the fish cakes may be placed on a cookie sheet first sprayed with cooking spray and baked in an oven at 350 degrees. Baking time varies, but figure somewhere between 30 and 45 minutes until they take on a golden brown color.

After cooking, place the fish cakes on paper toweling and permit them to drain and cool. After just 5 minutes of cooling they have a more delicate flavor than when served too hot. Serve with either a hot horseradish cocktail sauce or tartar sauce.

A nice loaf of fresh French bread and a Caesar salad can round out the feast.

Fish chowder adds a new dimension to soup. You can experiment, adding ingredients of your choice to make a rich, flavorful chowder that can be eaten for several days.

Fish chowder

There are hundreds of chowder recipes using practically every fish that swims, and most of them are delicious. Here again, chowders take on the personality of their cook. Some cooks say they never make the same chowder twice. It's just a matter of using good ingredients and enjoying the results.

When going through the trouble of making a fish chowder, it pays to make a lot because it keeps well when refrigerated, and may even be frozen for later use.

Ingredients include:

- 3 lbs. white-meat fish fillets, such as striped bass, rock fish or grouper
- 3 qts. water
- 4 large Vidalia onions chopped
- 10 medium-size red new potatoes, peeled and cut in half-inch cubes

- 24 tiny carrots, peeled and cut in half-inch pieces
- 4 cups milk
- 2 12 oz. cans evaporated milk
- 1/2 cup margarine

This recipe makes enough for 15 or more servings, depending on your appetite.

Saute the chopped onions in a large soup pot until they are caramelized and golden. Add the water and potatoes and set stove to "simmer." Once the carrots and potatoes feel tender to the fork, add the fish and continue on simmer. When the fish begins to flake, add the 4 cups of milk and the 2 cans of evaporated milk. Salt and pepper to taste.

With everything mixed together, stir lightly and continue on simmer until it is piping hot, but do not boil the chowder.

Some cooks add whole kernel corn or diced bell peppers, both of which add to the flavor.

Serve the hot fish chowder with a generous portion of Oysterettes or a few slices of seeded bakery rye bread, and you'll leave the table content.

Blackened

Popularized in New Orleans, blackened redfish became the rage several years ago. If you're a fan of blackened seafood, most any fish tastes great. You may use either steaks or fillets, but not over 1-inch thick for maximum flavor.

A word of caution: This recipe will smoke up your kitchen, so turn the exhaust fan on high before you even begin cooking. An alternative, as recommended by Chef Paul, is to cook outdoors on the grill.

You'll need a cast-iron skillet for best results, although an ordinary frying pan may be pressed into service if necessary.

Begin by placing the skillet on the stove or grill with medium heat at least 10 minutes before you plan to cook.

Ingredients for a meal for four include:

♦ **4 large fillets or steaks, at least 1/2-inch thick, of your favorite fish**

♦ **1 shaker jar of Chef Paul Prudhomme's Blackened Redfish Magic Seasoning**

♦ **cooking spray**

Spray both sides of each fillet or steak with cooking spray. Then sprinkle both sides with a liberal coating of Chef Paul's Blackened Redfish Magic Seasoning. Raise the heat on the stove, and place the coated fish in the skillet. Be prepared to stand back, as it'll get smokey quick. Cook the underside until it forms a sweet crust, then turn and repeat, being careful not to burn or cook excessively. When it flakes easily, it's done.

Exercise care when using an iron skillet and use a pot holder at all times.

Sauteed vegetables prepared in a wok are a perfect side dish. Use sugar snap peas, string beans, yellow squash, zucchini, tiny potatoes and white onions for a tasty combination. Serve with a salad or finely chopped cole slaw.

Smoked

Every serious fisherman should have an electric smoker. It's just that simple. There are lots of times when you catch more fish than you can immediately use, and there's always the need for a tasty snack at cocktail time. What better snack than delicately smoked fish?

Just about any fish can be smoked. Small fish such as silver hake, mackerel, surf perch and flounder may be smoked whole. With larger fish such as salmon, striped bass, tuna, king mackerel, amberjack and bonito, it's best to fillet the meat, but leave the skin on the fillet.

Included below are the items you'll require for a starter. As with most fish recipes you can experiment and develop your own exotic brine.

♦ **1 electric smoker**

♦ **1 package hickory or apple wood smoking chips**

♦ **1/2 cup non-iodized salt**

♦ **1/2 cup white granulated sugar**

These silver hake, red hake and tuna fillets were smoked in a portable electric smoker. Smoking, like other seafood recipes, is an evolutionary thing. Experiment until you find just the right touch.

Most fish recipes can be prepared quickly, but smoking requires time and patience. As with good wine, it can't be rushed.

You'll require a brine solution. It is made by mixing 1/2 cup of non-iodized salt and 1/2 cup of white sugar. Add this to a quart jar half-filled with warm tap water. Place a cap on the jar and shake vigorously until the salt and sugar are dissolved, then fill the jar with water and again shake vigorously. Place the brine in the refrigerator to chill.

Place the fish in a Pyrex or glass baking dish (not metal) and pour in sufficient brine to cover the fish.

Brine small fish and chunks that are an inch or more thick for 8 to 12 hours in the refrigerator, turning several times. Through experimentation you'll find just the right amount of brine time to suit your taste.

After soaking remove the fish and pat each piece dry with paper toweling. Permit the pieces to air-dry for at least an hour, until the fish takes on a tacky glaze called a pellicle.

Place your smoker outdoors, in the driveway or on the patio, preferably on a day when there's no chance of rain. While the brined fish is air-drying turn on the electric smoker. Just plug it in and let it get piping hot, without any wood chips.

Place the fish to be smoked on the smoker racks and insert them into the smoker.

Fill the smoker pan with hickory or apple wood chips and insert it into the smoker. Within a few minutes the heating element will cause the wood chips to begin smoldering, giving off smoke which will rise through the smoker and exit.

It'll take a half hour or more for a pan of wood chips to completely smolder and stop producing smoke. Remove the spent chips and add another pan of chips. For average-size fillets two pans of chips are usually sufficient and give a delicate smoked flavor in an hour or two.

It is necessary to leave the fish in the smoker for a total of 6 to 10 hours to permit the heat of the smoker to dry the fish. Taste a small piece once it takes on that golden color, and adjust smoke time and dry time to get just the right flavor.

Some people make smoked fish their main course. It's especially nice when placed on a bed of lettuce on a dinner plate, encircled with cubed cucumbers, mushrooms, peppers, scallions and radishes. Just a touch of Russian or French dressing and you'll be glad you invested the time and effort to smoke your catch.

Smoked fish is also a welcome cocktail snack. Use a sharp filleting knife to slice the fillets into thin strips, and serve on wheat crackers.

People began smoking fish centuries ago, in part because it was an effective way of preserving fish. Today, thanks to portable electric smokers it is no longer a difficult task. A portable electric smoker has handy racks for the fish and pans for smoking chips.

Battered

For a change of pace, fish fried in batter is just great. It's easy to prepare, and tasty with a wide range of species. You can begin with fillets cut from porgies, sea bass, snapper, snook, grouper, rockfish or any other firm, white-meat fish. Cut the fillets into small, bite size pieces or fingers.

To prepare the batter you'll need:

- **1 package Eggbeaters (equivalent of 2 eggs)**
- **1/2 teaspoon sugar**
- **4 heaping tablespoons flour**

- **8 dashes Worcestershire sauce**
- **salt and pepper to taste**
- **Sufficient skim milk to make a heavy batter**

Mix all of the ingredients together and beat until creamy.

Place the batter mixture in the refrigerator for a couple of hours. This isn't absolutely necessary, but the batter takes on a better consistency when it sets for a while. Remove it from the refrigerator a half hour before using.

Place enough Canola oil in a pan to cover the fish and warm it until it is sizzling hot.

Lightly salt and pepper the fingers to suit your taste, then dip them in the creamy batter, thoroughly covering the pieces.

As you drop them into the frying pan they should sizzle. It only takes a few minutes on each side for the battered pieces to take on a golden brown color. This is one time a little extra frying time is permissible, as it'll get the batter covering nice and crunchy, while retaining the moistness and flavor of the fish.

Place the pieces on paper toweling as you remove them from the frying pan.

Battered grouper fingers, served with tartar sauce or horseradish sauce, with a side of french fries and a couple of ears of corn, and sliced fresh tomatoes is a meal that's tough to beat.

Pickled

Herring are caught by sport fishermen on all three U.S. coasts. Herring is actually a family of fishes that includes the skipjack herring of the Gulf Coast, the Atlantic herring, Pacific herring, and the blueback herring. They're considered a forage species for the most part, as are hickory shad, and many members of the mackerel family. All of these are fun to catch on light spinning gear, and readily strike Sabiki rigs, streamer flies and shad darts. What many anglers fail to realize is that all of these species are just great when pickled.

Stop by your local delicatessen and ask the proprietor to save you a glass 1-gallon mayonnaise jar to use for pickling. A crock works nicely, too.

First fillet the herring or mackerel and remove the skin.

Make a brine solution of coarse kosher salt and tap water (mostly salt and little water). Brine the fillets overnight, which removes the blood and firms up the fillets. Remove the fillets from the brine and lightly wash in cold water and pat dry with paper towel. Discard the brine.

Place a layer of fillets in the bottom of the mayo jar. Cover the fillets with thinly sliced Vidalia onions and a single bay leaf and a tablespoon of pickling spices. You may also add several thin slices of lemon if you wish. Add another layer of fish covered with onion slices and bay leaf. Repeat the process until you've used all of your fillets. Finally, fill the remaining space in the gallon jar with read wine vinegar, covering the fillets.

Place the gallon jar in the refrigerator. After a day the firm fillets will have begun to absorb the pickling spice and vinegar flavor. You can sample a piece, and if you like it lightly pickled it may just be right. Continued pickling will result in a heavier flavor.

The fillets may be cut into small pieces and served just as they come out of the pickling solution. Many people enjoy serving a small piece of herring on a Town House cracker with a dollop of sour cream on top.

Next time you catch a herring or any of the mackerel clan, or even those 2- or 3-pound hickory shad, don't think of them as fish bait. Fillet and pickle them for a cocktail treat second to none.

Steamed

With today's society being more health conscious than ever, steaming is the best way to serve a healthy, fat-free meal, while retaining the fish's delicate flavor. Surprisingly, steaming, or poaching, is one of the least popular methods of preparing a catch fresh from the sea. Perhaps it's because steamed fish alone is bland when compared to other methods of preparation. Hence it becomes important to prepare an equally healthy sauce that will enhance its flavor on the dinner table.

Practically every saltwater fish may be steamed, and for purposes of this recipe it is assumed a family of four would enjoy 2 to 2 1/2 pounds of fillets for dinner. Among the most popular species to use in the steamer are any members of the flatfish clan, summer, winter and southern flounder, California halibut and Pacific halibut. Weakfish, white sea bass, black sea bass, codfish and rockfish all steam nicely. Salmon is delicious when delicately steamed. Whole fish or steaks may be steamed, but most people prefer fillets. The secret again is cutting your fillets so they are not too thick. Once you've filleted your fish, if the fillets are over an inch thick, simply take your filleting knife and cut them lengthwise so you have uniform fillets of 1/2 to 3/4 inch thick.

Use the same steam platform you use to steam vegetables. Fill a large pot that will hold the steamer with about an inch of water. Bring the water to a boil and place the fillets on the steamer rack and cover the pot. As the steam rises, carefully check the fillets with a fork periodically. Depending on the size and quantity of the fish, it may only take four or five minutes.

Preparing a sauce of caramelized vegetables to accompany steamed fish takes more time than the steaming. Included below are the ingredients that make up a delicious sauce:

Use a vegetable peeler to remove the skin from the eggplant, squash, and peppers. Cut all of the vegetables into 1/2-inch squares.

Always plan your seafood dinner as a complete meal, including fresh vegetables and salads to accompany the fish. Using the basic ingredients pictured here June Rosko prepares a delicious steamed fish dinner, accompanied with vegetables roasted to a rich golden brown with garlic and olive oil. It's fun to experiment, so use the vegetables of your choice.

- ◆ 1 2- x 8-inch eggplant
- ◆ 1 2- x 8-inch yellow squash or green zucchini
- ◆ 4 3-inch diameter white mushrooms
- ◆ 1 large red bell pepper
- ◆ 1 large green bell pepper
- ◆ 2 3-inch diameter Vidalia onions
- ◆ 6 3-inch diameter ripe tomatoes
- ◆ 1 to 4 cloves of crushed garlic
- ◆ 2 tablespoons virgin olive oil
- ◆ salt and pepper to taste
- ◆ 1 handful of fresh basil or tablespoon of dry basil

You can easily steam fillets of most any fish on the grill. Place the fillets on a piece of aluminum foil, cover with a light coating of mayonnaise, a layer of sliced onions and garden fresh sliced tomatoes and salt and pepper to taste. Seal the package tightly and place on the pre-heated grill for 8 to 10 minutes and enjoy a seafood treat that's delicious.

Place the vegetables into an 8 x 16 x 2-inch Pyrex baking dish. Sprinkle with virgin olive oil and add salt and pepper to taste. Finally sprinkle with the basil and use a large, long-handled cooking spoon to thoroughly mix all ingredients.

Place the dish into an oven pre-heated to 525 degrees. It's important to check the baking vegetables at 5-minute intervals, carefully turning them frequently with the long-handled cooking spoon so they will cook thoroughly but not burn. In about 30 minutes the vegetables will cook down, with the dish appearing only half full and quite a bit of juice in the bottom.

To finish the sauce, set the oven from baking to broiling, and leave the oven door open. Continue stirring for a few minutes until the vegetables are thoroughly caramelized as the liquid slowly disappears. If the liquid completely cooks away, and you wish to have the sauce take on a deeper color, stir in a nominal amount of water to keep it from burning, turning all the time until it reaches the consistency you desire.

Place the fish on a serving platter using a small turnover. The steamed fish is very delicate and will fall apart easily. As it is quite bland, most people will lightly salt and pepper the fish before placing the hot sauce over it. A salad of fresh cucumber and onions with an oil and vinegar dressing compliments the meal nicely.

Don't hesitate to experiment

People who love to spend time in the kitchen preparing their favorite seafood will be among the first to tell you to experiment with your recipes. It's fun, and over time you'll be able to compile a list of your favorites.

When people come to visit they'll see that freshly caught, properly cleaned and cared for fish, that are enthusiastically prepared, can result in seafood dishes that are wonderful. Enjoy!

June Rosko often disposable aluminum foil broiler pans to broil the day's catch. Here she is prepares to serve golden brown fillets that required but eight minutes to broil. Served with a wedge of lemon, with the juice squeezed over fillet, and with a salad and fresh garden vegetable, is a most enjoyable seafood treat.

LET US CONTINUE THIS CONTEMPLATIVE PASTIME

O ften a book such as this has a conclusion. That just didn't sound like the right word to me. For after writing this treatise there was a feeling that it could well serve as a beginning for those who have read thus far.

It is, for June and me, a compilation of many fishing adventures, in many places. We've thoroughly enjoyed ourselves over half a century of fishing together, beginning from our days of courting, to just days before the day the final text for this book was delivered, when we walked those beautiful beaches of Mantoloking, casting for elusive stripers.

It is for you, the reader, to begin, or even resurrect, an opportunity to enjoy a lifetime enjoying this contemplative pastime of ours. In this era of rushing to do everything, saltwater fishing provides an escape. You can repair to a stretch of beach on a summer evening on any of our coasts and test your angling prowess. If the call of the horizon challenges you, head offshore and enjoy.

By now you may have found a chapter of particular appeal. While we've attempted to help you in the selection of tackle and related equipment, and discussed the various techniques to help you be successful in your pursuits, and even included our favorite recipes, there are a few parting thoughts we'd like to share.

Partner the fishing with everything that is important in your life. By all means include your spouse and children. Fishing is a family affair. It's something that you can enjoy for an entire lifetime. There's no best kind, or worst kind. It's what you find most relaxing. As you grow older you'll often find that your likes change, and so be it.

The things that won't change are those days on a wave-tossed jetty with salt spray stinging your face from an onshore wind. Or when you're beating your way toward shore in seas that give you white knuckles as you grip the helm. Or the peaceful quiet on a pitch-black night as you drift on a coastal bay with the call of a loon in the distance. The screaming gulls and terns, the leaping baitfish, and your pounding heartbeat.

This is all a part of saltwater fishing. It's more than just catching fish. It's a lifelong challenge that will give you many wonderful memories.

Saltwater fishermen enjoy a wonderful heritage. Combine preservation and conservation of this heritage to ensure that generations to come will enjoy the same rewards that we have been so fortunate to participate in.

It's that word contemplative. It has a certain ring to it. Once you understand it, you'll be a believer.

Milt Rosko had his first magazine article published by *Salt Water Sportsman* in 1954. Since then, he has authored more than 1,000 magazine articles that have appeared in many major outdoor publications. He has authored five books and numerous booklets on saltwater fishing, most of them dedicated to helping others enjoy fishing. He is the recipient of many national writing awards and is the dean of the New York Metropolitan Outdoor Press Association.

Now retired after a 45-year career in Anheuser-Busch management, he continues to travel and enjoy fishing along America's sea coasts with June. They reside in Mantoloking and Watchung, New Jersey.